Yoga-Nidrā

Other books by the same Author

1. **Bhagavad-Gītā**: A New Exposition in a Broader Spectrum; ISBN: 978-81-246-0525-7 (Hb), 978-81-246-0526-4 (Pb)
2. **Cyclic Universe**: Cycle of the Creation, Evolution, Involution and Dissolution of the Universe; **2 vols.**; Contents: **vol. 1**: The Unsolved Riddle: Eternal, Created or Evolved Universe; **vol. 2**: Integral Cosmology: Cosmic Creation, Evolution and Dissolution in Cycles; ISBN: 978-81-246-0190-7 (set)
3. **Japa Yoga (Mantra-Yoga)** — Theory, Practice and Applications; ISBN: 978-81-246-0388-8 (Hb), 978-81-246-0389-5 (Pb)
4. **Meditation**: Science and Practice; ISBN: 978-81-246-0211-9 (Hb), 978-81-246-0212-6 (Pb)
5. **Mind and Supermind**; **2 vols.**; Contents: **vol. 1**: Indian Perspective; **vol. 2**: Western Perspective; ISBN: 978-81-246-0053-5 (set)

Yoga-Nidrā
Yogic Trance
Theory, Practice and Applications

N.C. Panda

DK PRINTWORLD
Publishers of Indian Traditions

Cataloging in Publication Data — DK
[Courtesy: D.K. Agencies (P) Ltd. <docinfo@dkagencies.com>]

Paṇḍā, Nṛsiṃhacaraṇa, 1929- **author.**
Yoga-nidrā (yogic trance) : theory, practice and applications/N.C. Panda. — Fourth impression.
pages cm
"First published in India 2003"—Title page verso.
Includes bibliographical references and index.
ISBN 9788124602423 (HB)
ISBN 9788124602430 (PB)

1. Yoga — Therapeutic use. 2. Yoga. 3. Tantrism. I. Title.

LCC RM727.Y64P36 2022 | DDC 613.7046 23

First published in India 2003
Second Impression 2011
Third Impression 2018
Fourth Impression 2022

ISBN: 978-81-246-0242-3 (Hb)
ISBN: 978-81-246-0243-0 (Pb)

Printed and published by:
D.K. Printworld (P) Ltd.
Regd. Office: '*Vedaśrī*', F-395, Sudarshan Park
(Metro Station: ESI Hospital), New Delhi - 110015
Phones : (011) 2545 3975, 2546 6019
e-mail : indology@dkprintworld.com
Web : www.dkprintworld.com

In the memory of my dear mother,
late Kamala Devi,
the love incarnate,
ever in peace, tranquillity
and quietude;

One who was loving
for the sake of loving alone;

One who was enduring
all suffering inescapable,
without any trace of grouse;

One who forgave
even the bitterest foes;

One who smilingly
undertook all hardship
for the comforts of others;

One who endeared all
with love and compassion;

my mortal mother
who represented
the eternal, timeless
Divine Mother;

whose blessings showered
on her dear children

Key to Transliteration

अ *a* (but)	ङ *ṅa* (sing)[1]	न *na* (numb)[4]
आ *ā* (mom)	च *ca* (chunk)[2]	प *pa* (spin)[5]
इ *i* (it)	छ* *cha* (catch him)[2]	फ* *pha* (loophole)[5]
ई *ī* (beet)	ज *ja* (john)[2]	ब *ba* (bin)[5]
उ *u* (put)	झ *jha* (hedgehog)[2]	भ *bha* (abhor)[5]
ऊ *ū* (pool)	ञ *ña* (bunch)[2]	म *ma* (much)[5]
ऋ *ṛ* (rhythm)	ट *ṭa* (start)[3]	य *ya* (young)
ए *e* (play)	ठ* *ṭha* (anthill)[3]	र *ra* (drama)
ऐ *ai* (high)	ड *ḍa* (dart)[3]	ल *la* (luck)
ओ *o* (toe)	ढ* *ḍha* (godhead)[3]	व *va* (vile)
औ *au* (loud)	ण *ṇa* (under)[3]	श *śa* (shove)
क *ka* (skate)[1]	त *ta* (path)[4]	ष *ṣa* (bushel)
ख* *kha* (blokhead)[1]	थ *tha* (thunder)[4]	स *sa* (so)
ग *ga* (gate)[1]	द *da* (that)[4]	ह *ha* (hum)
घ *gha* (loghut)[1]	ध* *dha* (breathe)[4]	

ం *ṁ anusvāra* (nasalisation of preceding vowel)

: *ḥ visarga* (aspiration of preceding vowel)

* No exact English equivalents for these letters.

[1] guttural [2] palatal [3] lingual [4] dental

[5] labial

Prologue

When we think of good health, we very often refer to the body, and we rarely ascribe good or bad health to a healthy or unhealthy mind. The interaction of the body and the mind has been recognized by the Indian seers since time immemorial. Of course, this was not the case with René Descartes (1596-1650), the French rationalist and dualist who is regarded as the founder of modern Western philosophy and psychology. In the Cartesian psychology, the body and the mind could not directly interact. This concept of Descartes has already been discarded by modern Western psychology. It has already been recognized throughout the world that the practice of *yoga* makes the mind calm, tranquil and healthy. For an average person, it is often difficult to control the mind. For a *yogī*, however, it is practicable to restrain the mind. *Yoga-nidrā,* being a technique of Yoga and Tantra, is an effective means of controlling and regulating the mind.

A number of diseases are psychosomatic. They are rooted in the psyche (mind), but they blossom and bear fruits in the physique (body). Medical and surgical treatments of psychosomatic diseases do help the patients, but cannot uproot the original cause. Psychoanalysis and psychotherapy sometimes alleviate the symptoms, but not always. Psychoanalysis has its own limitations. The subjectivity of the analyst, the patient's cooperation and his limitations are some of the factors that act as constraints. Moreover, psychotherapy involves a psychology-specialist who is to diagnose the disease and treat the patient. On the other hand, *yoga-nidrā* is a self-therapy and it does not involve analysis.

There are many diseases which are due to physiological malfunction or dysfunction. Some are due to biochemical malfunction or dysfunction. Both the physiological and biochemical abnormalities can be corrected by resolves in *yoga-nidrā*. The resolve is retained by the deeper strata of the mind which, in turn, influences the appropriate portion of the brain that directs the relevant organ neurally through transmission of nerve-impulses and hormonally through the pituitary gland which influences the other endocrine glands.

A number of diseases are primarily caused by mental trauma and anxiety. Some of them are very serious and sometimes even fatal. Cardiac diseases and cancer are examples of this category. *Yoga-nidrā* may be practised to reduce or to get rid of tension and prevent and cure diseases caused by tension.

Yoga-nidrā is a potent tool to fortify the immune system of the body. Thereby many diseases can be prevented and cured.

In addition to the prevention and treatment of diseases, *yoga-nidrā* can be used to improve one's personality, to regulate one's habits and life-patterns, to get rid of some unwanted indulgence and addictions and to improve the quality of life.

Yoga-nidrā can be used for spiritual uplift too. Spiritual uplift can be graded and gradual, leading finally to liberation (*mokṣa*).

In this book, hypnosis and *yoga-nidrā* have been compared and contrasted. The resolve (*saṅkalpa*) is a suggestion and auto-suggestion. If considered on this point, both have a commonality. Except this, the two are different. The hypnotic state is an altered state of consciousness whereas the *yoga-nidrā* state is intermediate between the conscious state and the sleeping state. Hypnotic auto-suggestion being excluded, hypnosis involves a hypnotist who directs the subject. On the other hand, the resolve in *yoga-nidrā* is an auto-suggestion and auto-therapy which does not involve a second person. In the *yoga-nidrā* concept, the *yogī* induces a receptive state (half awake and half asleep, but still conscious) in which the Subconscious and the Unconscious receive and record the resolve for future action. They later influence the relevant organ through the brain favourably. They also influence the conscious mind.

The Indian concept of the separateness of the brain and the mind and the concept of the brain being the apparatus of the mind have been emphasized in this book. Freudian depth psychology and Indian depth psychology have been compared and contrasted. This is the first book of its kind to present a critical analysis of Freudian depth psychology and to elaborate the tenets of Indian depth psychology. This is also the first book to explain the benefits of *yoga-nidrā* in the context of Indian depth psychology and in the modern format of medical physiology, biochemistry and pathology.

Swāmī Satyānanda Sarasvatī of the Bihar School of Yoga has popularized *yoga-nidrā*. He and his associates have written some books on this topic. The present book is not a duplicate of what they have written. Academic depth psychology is elaborately treated in this book. The applications of *yoga-nidrā*, with special reference to medical science, have been scientifically presented. Furthermore, the techniques of *yoga-nidrā* have been well systematized and standardized. For the first time, *yoga-nidrā* has been assigned a scientific status in this book.

This book comprises four chapters. The first chapter presents a theoretical background of *yoga-nidrā* and a theoretical background of Indian depth psychology *vis-a-vis*

Freudian depth psychology. The Indian concept of mind has been presented lucidly for the first time. The second chapter gives the techniques of *yoga-nidrā* in a lucid, simplified manner. The third chapter deals with the applications of *yoga-nidrā*. Some of the applications, with special reference to diseases, have been somewhat technical. The discussions relate to medical science. Practising doctors, throughout the world, would perhaps consider the topic unbiasedly and objectively. It is expected that this book would serve as a standard reference work for the use of *yoga-nidrā* in medical practice.

The fourth chapter of this book is an addenda. A typical system of Tantric *nyāsa* has been given here. It would not be possible to induce the *yoga-nidrā* state without doing *nyāsa*. Hence it has a tremendous significance in the total process of *yoga-nidrā*.

Modern age, with technological civilization, over-ambition, rat-race for competition and alienation, is overburdened with tension, anxiety and frustration. It is hoped that the modern man would benefit much by practising *yoga-nidrā*. And this is expected to serve as a useful handbook.

It is a multi-disciplinary book dealing with Yoga, Tantra psychology and medical science. The attempt of the writer is introductory. If the introduction serves as a catalyst to accelerate further generation of higher thought, it would benefit humankind for the attainment of physical, mental and spiritual health.

March 31, 2002

N.C. Panda
(*Śaktipāda*)

Acknowledgements

I AM grateful to Dr. Pramod Chandra Samal and Dr. Bijoy Kumar Sahu (both of them were my students and are Professors now) for their help in the production of the book. Prof. Abhinna Chandra Sahu and his family members (Amitabh, Sujata, Amita, Smita, Kahnu and Shambhu — all of them are my disciples) have helped me in diverse ways in the production of the manuscript. I do appreciate their help with hearty thanks.

Mrs. Liliya Basu and Dr. Pradyot Kumar Basu of Nashville, TN, USA, were kind to donate some reference books that were very useful in writing this book. Dr. Rasikanand Tripathy of Lubbock, TX, USA, and Dr. Dwijesh Kumar Panda (my youngest brother) of Bhubaneswar donated books that helped me a lot as reference materials. My hearty thanks are due to all of them.

Sri Rabi Narayan Pradhan significantly contributed to the production of the manuscript and typescript of this book. I owe to him. I thankfully appreciate the secretarial assistance rendered by Sri Dhruba Charan Dehury.

My grateful acknowledgements are due to my publishers, D.K. Printworld, New Delhi, and especially to Mr. Susheel K. Mittal, the Director of this Publishing House of international repute.

I am not simply a writer of Yoga books. I am a *yogī* myself. A *yogī* who is also a householder does not get enough time to give to his family members. But I belong to the heritage of king and *ṛṣi* Janaka. Let me make up my lapses and deficiencies by expressing my sincere appreciation of the love and affection, for me, of my dear ones: Anwesha (Lisa), Siddhārth (Munu, Manu-Raja), Arpita (Soma), Lopamudra (Lopa), Madhusmita (Mita), Nibedita (Nita), Shephali (Prema), Bibhas (Tuna), Bikash, Prakash, Sudhir, Arati (Runi), Snigdha (Manu), Smita (Ilu) and Manorama (my wife).

March 31, 2002

Nursingh Charan Panda
(***Śaktipāda***)

Khanduali Mandir Road
Agastya Bhavan
712 Sahid Nagar
Bhubaneswar-751 007 (India)

Contents

List of Abbreviations

AU	:	*Aitareya Upaniṣad*
AV	:	*Atharvaveda*
BG	:	*Bhagavad Gītā*
BS	:	*Brahmasūtram*
BU	:	*Bṛhadāraṇyaka Upaniṣad*
CU	:	*Chāndogya Upaniṣad*
GMK	:	*Māṇḍūkya Kārikā* of Gauḍapāda
IU	:	*Īśopaniṣad*
KTU	:	*Kaṭhopaniṣad*
MAU	:	*Māṇḍūkyopaniṣad*
MS	:	*Manu-Smṛti*
MTNU	:	*Maitrāyaṇī Upaniṣad*
MTU	:	*Maitrī Upaniṣad*
MUU	:	*Muṇḍakopaniṣad*
PU	:	*Praśnopaniṣad*
PYD	:	*Pātañjala Yoga-Darśanam*
PYDVB	:	*Pātañjala Yoga-Darśanam Vyāsa-Bhāṣyam*
ṚV	:	*Ṛgveda*
ŚB	:	*Śāṅkara-Bhāṣyam*
ŚBrā	:	*Śatapatha Brāhmaṇa*
SK	:	*Sāṅkhya Kārikā*

SL	:	*Saundarya-Laharī*
SPS	:	*Sāṅkhya Pravacana-Sūtram*
ŚS	:	*Śiva-Saṁhitā*
ŚU	:	*Śvetāśvatara Upaniṣad*
TĀ	:	*Taittirīya Āraṇyaka*
TU	:	*Taittirīya Upaniṣad*
VāP	:	*Vāyu Purāṇa*
VC	:	*Vivekacūḍāmaṇi*
VPDA	:	*Vedānta Paribhāṣā* of Dharmarāja Adhvarīndra
VSS	:	*Vedāntasāra* of Sadānanda
YS	:	*Yājñavalkya-Smṛti*
YV	:	*Yajurveda*

List of Figures

1

Theory of Yoga-Nidrā

THE literal meaning of the Sanskrit word *nidrā* is 'sleep'. Thus, *yoga-nidrā* means 'yogic sleep'. But, in reality, the person who practises *yoga-nidrā* avoids sleep in the whole process. He is awake in the process, although his awareness is different from the normal state of wakefulness. His state of consciousness in *yoga-nidrā* occupies a stage which is in between the usual state of wakefulness and that of sleep. We will try to characterize this state later in this chapter.

THE ORIGINAL MYTH OF YOGA-NIDRĀ

Modern Science, in general, uses a language which does not contain symbols and myths. They do appear in literature, especially in the genre of poetry. Ancient Indian wisdom, in the field of philosophy, religion, art, literature and science, is a departure, however. Very often, the language used is symbolic and mythical even though the subject, dealt with, covers scientific fields. The modern practice of *yoga-nidrā* is traced back to a myth which is purely symbolic. Here, in this context, we render a classical Indian prayer into English:

ॐ शान्ताकारं भुजगशयनं पद्मनाभं सुरेशं
विश्वाधारं गगनसदृशं मेघवर्णं शुभाङ्गम् ।
लक्ष्मीकान्तं कमलनयनं योगिभिर्ध्यानगम्यं
वन्दे विष्णुं भवभयहरं सर्वलोकैकनाथम् ।।

om śāntākāraṁ bhujagaśayanaṁ padmanābhaṁ sureśaṁ
viśvādhāraṁ gaganasadṛśaṁ meghavarṇaṁ śubhāṅgam ।
lakṣmīkāntaṁ kamalanayanaṁ yogibhirdhyānagamyaṁ
vande viṣṇuṁ bhavabhayaharaṁ sarvalokaikanātham ॥

I make an obeisance
to God, Lord Viṣṇu,
the husband of Mother Lakṣmī,
the lotus-eyed,
the Lord meditated
upon by the *yogīs*,
the Lord who dispels
all the worldly fears,
the One and the only One
Lord of the many worlds.

I bow to Lord Viṣṇu,
serenely postured,
reclining on the Divine Serpent,
the Lord of all gods,
the one with a lotus-navel,
the foundation of the universe,
the cloud-hued one,
resembling the sky,
with all-auspicious body.

The expression *bhujagaśayanam* is the focal point here. The Sanskrit word *bhujaga* means 'serpent' and *śayanam* means 'sleep'. The classical picture of *ananta-śayanam* is presented in *fig* 1.1. The Lord of the universe reclines on the coiled body of the serpent named as 'Ananta' that spreads its hood over the Lord in the shape of an umbrella which protects a person from the scorching sun or the torrential rains.

The Sanskrit word *ananta* means 'that without finitude'.

Ananta Nāga (*nāga* means 'a snake') is the Divine Serpent with infinite strength. Who can support the Lord of the universe if it possesses a limited quantity of strength? The strength with reference to spring action in mechanics may be alluded to. And so is the coiled serpent on which the Lord reclines. A question is raised : Who other than the Lord himself can support the Omnipotent ? Ananta Nāga is not different from the Lord, the One and the only One Lord of the universe. He is the Rudra (fiercely roaring, terrifying) aspect of the Lord who engages himself in the continuing process of annihilation and the final process of dissolution.

One name of Lord Viṣṇu is Padmanābha (One with a lotus-navel). Brahmā emanates from the Lord through the umbilical cord. He is the same One Lord[1] who engages himself in the

***fig.* 1.1 The classical picture of *ananta-śayanam*.**

1. *ŚUŚB*, I.3; *ŚU*, VI.18; *BSŚB*, I.3.30; *MTU*, V.1: (*tvaṁ brahma tvaṁ ca vai viṣṇustvaṁ rudrastvaṁ prajāpatiḥ*); V.2; *MTNU*, IV.5; VI.5.

initial and the continuing processes of creation. Lord Viṣṇu stays in *yoga-nidrā*. His Power (*Śakti*) or Consort is Mother Lakṣmī who sustains the universe.[2]

Any picture is bound to be spatial. Nevertheless, Lord Viṣṇu does not reside in any special locality, either inside or outside the universe. He is non-local and non-temporal.[3] He is spaceless and timeless. He is immanent and transcendent. He is all-pervasive.[4] The Sanskrit word *viṣṇu* is derived from the verb-root *viś* which means 'to pervade'.

SEERS' IMITATION

Ancient Indian seers (*ṛṣis*) imitated the *ananta-śayana* of the Lord of the universe. They gave the name *yoga-nidrā* to the process. In the process, they came in communion with the Lord. They tried to get knowledge directly from the Lord himself. This is the revealed knowledge, directly perceived,[5] without the mediation of any of the sense-organs.

The seers could adjust the levels of their consciousness through yogic techniques for differing purposes. *Yoga-nidrā* is one such level. The final level is the *turīya*[6] in which the *yogī*'s self is identified with the Great Self.

The State of *yoga-nidrā* is intermediate between the waking (*jāgrata*) state and the dream (*svapna*) state. Hence, it is not correct to say that a person is in a sleeping state during *yoga-nidrā*. In the process, he has a tendency to go to sleep. But he avoids sleep through auto-suggestion done before the initiation of the *yoga-nidrā* technique.

---

2. *SL*, 1-2; *BS*, I.4.3; *BSŚB*, I.4.3; II.1.14; *BGŚB*, XIII.19; *ŚUŚB*, I.3.
3. *MTU*, VI.14; *BU*, III.8.8; IV.4.20.
4. *ŚU*, I.16; III.11; VI.11; *GMK*, I.1; I.28; *KTU*, I.2.22; II.1.4; *MTU*, VI.7; *MUU*, I.1.6; *BG*, V.15; X.12.
5. *BU*, III.4.1; III.5.1.
6. *MAU*, 7.

HYPNOTIC TRANCE

We would introduce the topic of hypnosis before we compare and contrast the mental state of *yoga-nidrā* and that of hypnotic trance. In the late 1700s, Franz Mesmer claimed that hypnosis worked by 'animal magnetism'. In 1842, a surgeon in Nottinghamshire, England, amputated a patient's leg while the patient was in a mesmeric trance. Notwithstanding this success and similar other ones, hypnotism was viewed with skepticism for more than two centuries. It was associated with the bizarre and occult. Hypnosis was successfully used in both World Wars by physicians, dentists and psychologists. Since then it has become a respected field of scientifc enquiry. Medical Associations and Psychological Associations in the advanced countries now support the teaching and judicious practice of hypnosis.

Hypnosis is associated with a state of altered consciousness. This concept has, however, been challenged. Sarbin and his associates[7] have proposed a *role-enactment theory* of hypnosis. They theorize that the subject becomes so deeply involved in a role that what is done takes place without conscious intent. Barber[8] is another theorist who believes that hypnotic behaviours can be accounted for by the usual principles of behavioural and cognitive psychology. Whatever may be the conceptualization of hypnosis, the phenomenon itself is no longer questioned.

Altered consciousness seems to be common in both hypnosis and *yoga-nidrā*. But the two states of altered consciousness in hypnotic trance and yogic trance are not identical. In spite of the provision of auto-hypnosis in *yoga-*

---

7. T.R. Sarbin, 1950.
   T.R. Sarbin, and W.C. Coe, 1972.
8. T.X. Barber, 1969.

nidrā, hypnosis, in general, involves two persons, namely, the hypnotist and the client or the subject. The former induces drowsiness or deep sleep by special techniques and suggestions in the latter and then suggests to do this or not to do that. The client becomes very suggestible in the deep trance-like state so produced. The heightened suggestibility is used to get clients to comply with the direct suggestions of the hypnotist. *Yoga-nidra,* however, is an auto-suggestive procedure in which the person brings himself to the altered state of consciousness or the yogic trance which is a transitional phase between wakefulness and sleep. In this state of yogic trance, the person repeats his resolve (*saṅkalpa*) which is short and definitive. This auto-suggestion is retained by the Subconscious or the Unconscious that subsequently translates it into action. Thus, the similarity between hypnosis and *yoga-nidrā* is apparent and not real.

THE HIDDEN OBSERVER

In the process of hypnosis, an intellectual task is carried on subconsciously or unconsciously. It is done without the surface awareness that it is being done. A subconscious process and a conscious experience go on simultaneously, without the former being available to the open consciousness. Hilgard uses the expression 'hidden observer' as a metaphor to describe this concealed entity that knows things that are not present in the person's open consciousness.[9]

We would refer to the 'self' (*ātmā*) in the context of *yoga-nidrā*. We have a strong conviction that the 'hidden observer' of Hilgard is not different from the 'self'.

---

9. E.R. Hilgard, 1973a.
   E.R. Hilgard, 1977.

FOUR STATES OF THE SELF

The *Māṇḍūkyopaniṣad* states that the universe is verily *Brahman*, that the self is *Brahman*, and that the self has four quarters (*catuṣpāt*).[10]

The first quarter is *Vaiśvānara*. Its sphere of activity is the waking state (*jāgrata*).[11] In this state, it cognizes external objects (*bahiṣprajña*) and experiences the gross (*sthūla-bhuk*) universe. *Vaiśvānara* has nineteen faces, namely, the five organs of perception, the five organs of action, the five *prāṇa*s, the mind (*manas*), the intellect (*buddhi*), the self-sense (*ahaṅkāra*) and the subtle organ of conception (*citta*).[12] Knowledge obtained in the waking state is always mediated through the senses.

The second quarter is *taijasa*.[13] Its sphere of activity is the dream (*svapna*) state. It cognizes internal objects (*antaḥ-prajña*). It experiences things stored in the subtle body (*pravivikta-bhuk*).[14]

In usual sleep, an individual experiences dreams, created by the mind out of imprinted materials in its memory store. The subtle body, in this state, is separated from the external world. It lives by itself in its internal world. Some of the dream-experiences are remembered on waking; but most dreams are forgotten.

The third quarter of the self is *prājña*.[15] It is a state of deep sleep (*suṣupti*). Dreams cease to be phenomenalized in this state of profound sleep. It is a desireless condition. The self is

10. *MAU*, 2.
11. *Ibid.*, 3.
12. *Ibid.*
13. *Ibid.*, 4.
14. *Ibid.*, 4.
15. *Ibid.*, 5.

completely unified and identified with the super-unified Consciousness (*ekībhūta prajñānaghana*). This is a blissful state in which the self experiences bliss (*ānanda-bhuk*) and identifies itself with true knowledge (*ceto-mukha*).

The self in the *prājña* state is *Īśvara* (God), the lord of all, the knower of all, the inner controller, the source of all, the beginning and the end of beings.[16]

Turīya is the fourth state of the self.[17] Whereas the third state is *Īśvara,* the fourth state is *Brahman,* the Absolute. It cognizes neither the internal impressions nor the external objects; it does not cognize both; it is not the super-unification of knowledge; it is neither cognitive nor non-cognitive. It is unseen, unempirical, ungraspable, devoid of distinctive marks, unthinkable and unnameable. It is the essence of the knowledge of the only one self, the one into which the cosmos is resolved (*prapañcopaśamam*). It is the peaceful, the benign, the non-dual.

NON-DISCRETE STATES

The four states that have been described in the foregoing paragraphs are continuous rather than discrete. They cannot be demarcated by initial points, terminal points and breaks in between. The *yogī* ascends the continuous column and reaches the summit which is the *turīya* or the fourth state. The *samādhi* state in *yoga* corresponds to the *turīya.*

In *yoga-nidrā,* the *yogī* stays somewhere between the waking (*Vaiśvānara, jāgrata*) and the sleeping (*taijasa, svapna*) states. Some *yogī*s prescribe a technique, the sequence of which is directed by the *yoga*-instructor or a tape-recorder. In this technique, the auditory sense is active. The concerned state refers to one which is in the lowest layer of the waking state,

16. *MAU*, 6.

17. *Ibid.*, 7.

but still above the border line between the waking and the dream states. We recommend a method in which a second person or any equipment is not involved and the gates of all external senses are closed. In our method, the *yogī* stays in a state which is shared partly by the waking and partly by the dream state. This state is self-induced.

In the dream state, the self experiences internal objects (*antaḥ-prajña*), that is, all impressions imprinted in the subtle body. It is a state very conducive to the Subconscious or the Unconscious to be sensitive or hyper-sensitive. In the waking state, the Unconscious is little affected by suggestions or auto-suggestions. In the semi-waking and semi-dream state, the Unconscious is rendered hyper-suggestible. In the condition of heightened suggestibility, the Subconscious or the Unconscious retains the auto-suggestions and directs the subtle as well as the gross body to function in accordance with the letter and spirit of the resolve.

THE WHIRLS OF THE *CITTA* AND THEIR RESTRAINT

As it has already been said, the *citta,* which is a component of the subtle body, is the thinking and conceptualizing subtle organ. Waves emanate from the brain, consequent upon the functioning of the *citta*. These waves have been charcterized as alpha, beta, delta and theta[18] and have been illustrated in *fig*. 1.2.

Alpha waves have a frequency somewhere between eight and thirteen cycles per second. They are slightly larger than the beta waves in amplitude. They are emitted during milder states of meditation. Relaxed awareness, passivity, anxiety-free and tension-free states and states of creativity are conducive to the emission of alpha waves.

18. Hans Burger, a German scientist, discovered brain waves (alpha and beta) shortly after the First World War.

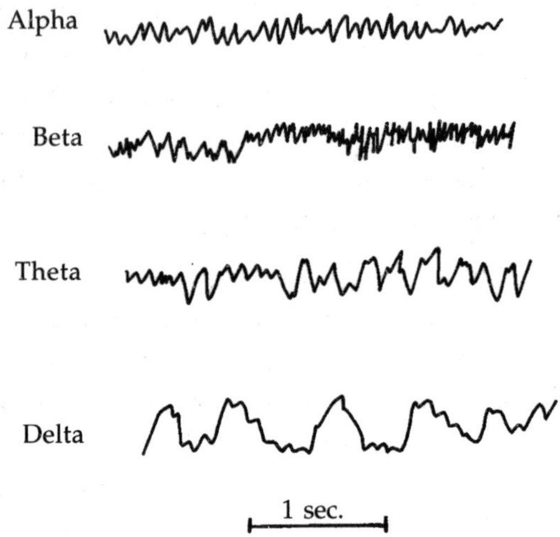

fig. **1.2 The four types of brain waves.**

Beta waves have a frequency, higher than thirteen cycles per second, with smaller amplitudes. They are the waves emitted in the waking state. They usually predominate on the EEG (electroencephalogram). The frequency becomes higher and the amplitude smaller with the rise in tension and anxiety and quantitative increase in rational thinking.

Theta waves have a frequency-range from four to seven cycles per second. They are emitted during dreaming. They are predominant in the deeper states of meditation. They are also emitted in states of intense creativity, ecstasy and moods of recepticity to ESP (extra-sensory perception). Theta waves are emitted in *yoga-nidrā*. They are associated with the subconscious and the unconscious mind. Children sometimes emit theta waves in their waking state. However, it rarely happens in wakeful adults.

Delta waves have a frequency less than four cycles per second. They have large amplitudes. They predominate in the state of dreamless sleep (*suṣupti*). They are also found in a very deep state of meditation.

Alpha, theta or delta waves are recorded in meditation, depending on the depth of the meditational state. When the level is less deep, alpha waves are emitted. This is a state intermediate between the waking (*jagrata*) and the dreaming (*svapna*) ones. When the level is deep, theta waves are emitted. This corresponds to the dream (*svapna*) state. When the level is still deeper, delta waves are emitted. This corresponds to the state of dreamless sleep (*suṣupti*).

When the *yogī* reaches the fourth state, the *turīya*, his *citta* becomes completely devoid of whirls. There is no emission of waves. It is a state free from mental pulsations (*niṣpanda*).

Patañjali defines *yoga* as the restraint of the whirls of the *citta*.[19] When these whirls are completely restrained, the seer (*ātmā*), at that time, stays in its own mode.[20] At other times, that is, when the whirls are emitted, the self acquires the modes of the whirls.[21]

WHAT IS MIND ?

Most physiologists, philosophers and psychologists of the modern world are in favour of the theory of brain-mind identity. They conceive of the brain as the anatomically structural and the physiologically functional unit and of the mind as the psychologically functional unit of one and the same entity. Starting from the Greek philosophers up to the time of René Descartes[22] and afterwards, the Western philosophy and religions equated the soul and the mind, and

---

19. *PYD*, I.2 (*yogaścittavṛttinirodhaḥ*).
20. *Ibid.*, I.3 (*tadā draṣṭā svarūpe'vasthānam*).
21. *Ibid.*, I.4 (*vṛttisārūpyamitaratra*).
22. For the philosophy and psychology or René Descartes (1596-1650), see Bertrand Russell's book, *History of Western Philosophy*, 1975 (2nd edn., 8th impression), London : George Allen & Unwin, pp. 542-51.

confined the soul or the mind to human beings only. Descartes is recognized as the father of Western psychology. His philosophy or psychology made a dichotomy of the body (matter) and the mind, each of which could not directly influence the other. The Cartesian psychology asserts that the body and the mind cannot directly interact. The human soul was the mind, as conceived by Descartes in his philosophy of dualism. Cartesian dualism was rejected by Western philosophers and psychologists in the twentieth century. They also rejected the existence of the soul.[23]

All Western thinkers, however, do not accept the theory of brain-mind (mind-matter) identity. Sir John C. Eccles of Australia, who shared the Nobel Prize for Physiology or Medicine in 1963 with Alan Lloyd Hodgkin and Andrew F. Huxley of England, does not accept the theory of body-mind identity. Sir Eccles is a distinguished neurophysiologist. He is of the view that mind exists apart from the brain.[24] Sir Karl Popper and Sir John Eccles argue that mind, as associated consciousness, has some control over the brain. They say that mind, and brain are separate, with weak, slow-acting interaction.[25]

Popper and Eccles state that mind and brain are separate. We accept this view. The brain is an organ with macro- and micro-anatomy. It is part of the physical body and grossly congnizable. If mind is a separate entity, what is its structural

23. For the rejection of the soul by modern Western philosophers, see N.C. Panda's *Cyclic Universe*, pp. 140-41. The relevant philosophies of Thomas Hobbes, La Mettrie, David Hume, Wilhelm Wundt, William James and Gilbert Ryle have been presented.

24. J.C. Eccles, 1953.
    Idem (ed.), 1966.
    Idem, 1973.

25. K.R. Popper, and J.C. Eccles, 1977.

nature ? What exactly is it ? We do not get the answer to our question in the book of Popper and Eccles.

Here we would present the Vedic and Vedāntic view of mind. The Vedānta has its own theory. In the evolution of this theory, some of the Sāṅkhya and the Yoga concepts have also been incorporated. One outstanding feature of the Vedāntic theory of mind is that mind is not spiritual, that it is not the self (*ātmā*) and that it is material, although its materiality is very subtle. The Vedic view of mind also emphasizes that mind can influence matter and vice versa.

CONSCIOUSNESS

Vedāntic consciousness is of two kinds, namely, Consciousness which is pure or fundamental and consciousness which is induced or empirical. Pure Consciousness is *Brahman*,[26] the absolute reality. The empirical universe and everything of the universe, including the human mind, are insentient. On the contrary, every created entity, micro- or macro- and non-living or living is conscious,[27] although the degree of consciousness is proportional to the height of the rung in the evolutionary ladder. The more evolved the apparatus of the created entity, the more the consciousness. The second type of consciousness is empirical rather than fundamental. As magnetism or hydroelectricity is induced, so is the induction of consciousness,

---

26. *BS*, III.2.16; *BSŚB*, I.1.4; I.3.19; III.2.16; III.2.18; *BU*, II.4.12; III.9.28; IV.5.13; *BUŚB*, IV.4.20; *AU*, III.3; *MAU*, 5; *TU*, II.1.1; *ŚU*, VI.11; VI. 13; *MTNU*, VI.17; MTU, VI.16.

27. On empirical consciousness, see N.C. Panda's *Mind and Supermind*, 1996, pp. 45-68; also see his *Cyclic Universe*, 2002, pp. 546; 555; 559; 561; 638; 766.

    Śaṅkara declares that all the non-living entities of the universe are conscious (*CUŚB*, VI.11.2: *cetanāvantaḥ sthāvarāḥ*) and that this type of consciousness is induced or empirical.

resulting from the proximity of *Brahman* which is all-pervasive.[28] Pure Consciousness, reflected on any insentient created entity, renders the latter empirically conscious.[29]

The Vedānta has a doctrine of limiting adjunct (*avaccheda-vāda*).[30] Space limited in a pot is *ghaṭākāśa*. Great Space, without any limiting adjunct (*upādhi*), is *Mahākāśa*. On breaking the pot (*ghaṭa*), the difference between *Mahākāśa* and *ghaṭākāśa* disappears. In the same analogy, *Brahman*, with *Māyā* as the *upādhi*, is *Īśvara* (God) and, with a created entity as the *upādhi*, is the self (*ātmā*).[31] In the latter case, when the *upādhi* is a non-living entity, the self is a *bhūtātmā*, and when the *upādhi* is a living entity, the self is a *jīvātmā*. *Brahman* and *Māyā* are coeternal, the former being the possessor of power (*Śaktimān*) and the latter the Power (*Śakti*), both being compared with fire and heat, respectively.[32] Thus, Reality is bipolar and at the same time non-dual, without involving contradiction. *Puruṣa* (the Supreme Person) is *Śaktimān*, the Father of the universe : *Prakṛti* or *Māyā* is the *Śakti*, the Mother of the

---

28. For the Vedāntic doctrine of induction (*pravartana-vāda*), reference may be made to *BS*, II.2.2-3 and *BSŚB*, II.2.2-3.

29. *Brahman* is the light of lights (*MUU*, II.2.10). It is the primary light (Consciousness) by the reflection of which everything of the universe is lighted (*BG*, XV.6 & 12; *KTU*, II.2.15; *MUU*, II.2.11; *ŚU*, VI.14). The *Brahma-sūtra* (*BS*, II.3.50) has a specific aphorism (*ābhāsa eva ca*) which speaks of the doctrine of reflection (*ābhāsa-vāda; pratibimba-vāda*). On this doctrine, Śaṅkara says (*BUŚB*, IV.4.18): *svataḥ kāṣṭhaloṣṭasamāni hi tāni caitanyātmajyotiśśūnyāni*: Divested of the light of the Self which is pure Intelligence, they are like wood or clods of earth.

30. *BSŚB*, I.1.11; I.2.22; II.1.14; III.8.12; *VC*, 245-6.; *VPDA*, Ch. VII; *YS*, III.144.

31. *BSŚB*, I.1.11; I.2.22; II.1.14; *VC*, 245 (*īśasya māyā mahadādikāraṇam, jīvasya kāryaṁ śṛṇu pañcakośāḥ*).

32. See the *Serpent Power* by Sir John Woodroffe, p. 31.

universe.[33] She is the Mother Creatrix who is the acting agent.[34] She is the womb and the Father is the seed-giver. The Father of the universe is the Chairperson (*Adhyakṣa*)[35] who is the inducer (*pravartaka*),[36] but not the doer (*akartā*).[37] The Mother of the universe is the creator, sustainer and destroyer of the universe. She herself is not illusion; but she produces illusion by her concealing (*āvaraṇa-śakti*),[38] projecting (*vikṣepa-śakti*)[39] and deluding (*mohinī-śakti*)[40] powers. *Māyā* herself is insentient, but in association with *Īśvara*, she is conscious and all-conscious.

VIRĀḌ OR MAHAT

The Vedic *Virāḍ* or the Sāṅkhya *Mahat* is the first evolute in the beginning of creation.[41] Its evolvent is *Prakṛti* or *Māyā*[42] which is never an evolute. According to the Sāṅkhya, *Prakṛti* or the primordial Nature is transformed into *Mahat*. The Vedānta, however, does not accept this doctrine of tranformation (*pariṇāma-vāda*).[43] *Virāḍ* is the Supermind, the

33. *BG*, XIV.3-4.
34. *BS*, I.4.3; *BSŚB*, I.4.2-3; II.1.14; II.1.24-5; *BG*, VIII.18-19; XIV.3-4; *BGŚB*, *Introduction*; IV.6; VII.6; VIII.18-19; IX.7-8; XIII.19; XIV.3-4; *XV*. 16; *ŚU*, I.3; *ŚUŚB*, I.3; I.4; *SL*, 1.
35. *ṚV*, X.129.7; *BG*, IX.10; *BU*, I.4.7; *CU*, VI.3.2; *ŚU*, VI.11.
36. *BS*, II.2.2-3; *BSŚB*, II.2.3-4.
37. *BG*, V.14; XIII.29.
38. *VC*, 115; *VSS*, 51-54; *BGŚB*, VII.25; *ŚU*, VI.10; *ŚUŚB*, VI.10.
39. *VC*, 113; 115; 117; *VSS*, 51; 54.
40. *BG*, VII.25; *BGŚB*, IV.6; VII.25.
41. *ṚV*, X.90.5; *SPS*, I.61; *SPS*, I.71: *mahadākhyamādyaṁ kāryaṁ tanmanaḥ*. In this aphorism, the Sāṅkhya clearly states that *Mahat* (*Buddhi*), the first evolute from *Prakṛti*, is the Cosmic Mind. The *Bṛhadāraṇyaka Upaniṣad* (I.2.1) also states that *Āpaḥ* evolved from the Cosmic Mind.
42. *SPS*, I.61.
43. For the rejection of the doctrine of transformation by the Vedānta, see Bhāmati's *Bhāṣya* of the *Brahma-Sūtra* (*BS*, I.4.27).

unified Great Mind in which all things of the previous creations are potentially present as cosmic impressions. At the termination of the immediately previous universe, *Virāḍ* was dissolved in *Māyā* in the analogy of salt (sodium chloride) in sea- water. Creation of the present universe is not *de novo;* it is the manifestation of what had been potentially latent in dormancy. It is the act of being patent from what had been latent. It obeys the laws of cause and effect (may not be strictly from *apparent* point of view; but chaos, chance and accident also obey statistical and mathematical laws). The repeating cycles[44] of the creation, maintenance and dissolution are not qualitatively and quantitatively identical, however. Mother Creatrix is a creative artist and, hence, evolution of the universe, starting from the appearance of the cosmic egg to the termination of the expanding phase (first *parārdha*) is creative, without being mechanically repetitive. Crudely speaking, manifestation of the universe from the unmanifest is analogous to the crystallization of the salt from sea-water, and dissolution of the universe to the process of salt being dissolved in water. The whole of the cosmic processes is an activity of the supermind of *Māyā*, the Divine Mother of the universe. According to the Vedānta, the universe is not a transformed product; neither *Brahman* nor *Māyā* is transformed into the universe. The Vedāntic term for the creation, sustenance and dissolution of the universe, with *Brahman* as the substratum (*adhiṣṭhāna*), *Īśvara* as the chairperson (*adhyakṣa*), *Mahāmāyā* as the executive agent (*kartrī*) and the cosmic phenomena as illusory (not hallucinatory) appearance, is *vivarta-vāda*. This term was coineu by the post-Śaṅkara Vedāntists. Śaṅkara's own term was *adhyāsa*.[45] *Adhyāsa* is brought about by *Mahāmāyā* through her concealing and

44. *ṚV*, X.190.3.

45. *BSŚB, Introduction.*

projecting power. The cosmos is a mental projection of the Mother Creatrix. And *Virāḍ* functions as the supermind of the Mother in the production of the cosmic phenomena. *Virāḍ* is the first manifested product from *Māyā*. It bifurcates in evolution. One pathway is material and the second one is mental. In the material pathway, *Āpaḥ* evolves from *Virāḍ*.[46] The *Āpaḥ* condenses into a super-dense singularity which is otherwise known as the cosmic egg. The cosmic egg stays for some time and then explodes.[47] Prior to the explosion of the

---

46. *Āpaḥ* is the Primeval Cosmic Fluid or Plasma. It is not the ordinary water (H_2O). The *Nāsadīya Sūkta* of the *Ṛgveda* names it as the *apraketaṁ salilam* or undifferentiated Cosmic Plasma (*ṚV*, X.129.3). The words *Nāra*, *Ka* and *Āpaḥ* are synonyms. Some of the other Vedic references to *Āpaḥ* are the following : *ṚV*, VI.50.7; X.17.10; X.82.5-6; *YV*, XIII.2-4; XXVII.25-26; XXXII.1-8; *AV*, I.4.1-4. The *Ṛgveda* (*ṚV*, I.22.6; II.35.1-15) describes *apāṁ napāt* which is the second generation offspring (f_2) of *Āpaḥ* (The word *napṛ* means 'grandson'). This is the first description of the plamsa state of modern physics in the super-heated cosmic soup of the nascent universe. The *Atharvaveda* (*AV*, I.33.1-4) states that *agni* is produced from *Āpaḥ*. The Upaniṣads and allied Vedic scriptures also echo the Vedic concept of *Āpaḥ*: *BU*, I.2.1-2; V.5.1; *CU*, IV.10.4; *KTU*, II.16; *TĀ*, X.22; *MS*, 1.8; *VāP*, VI.1-11. The *Bṛhadāraṇyaka Upaniṣad* (*BU*, I.2.1) categorically says that *Āpaḥ* was produced from the Cosmic Mind.
47. The idea of the formation of the cosmic egg is supported by the *Ṛgveda* (*ṚV*, X.81-2). Śaṅkara and Manu say that the cosmic egg was formed from *Māyā* or the *Mūla-Prakṛti*, the Power of of *Brahman* and *Īśvara* (*BGŚB*, *Introduction*; *MS*, I.9). The cosmic egg, subsequent to its formation, stayed for some time and then exploded (*CU*, III.19.1).

    Nothing can work and move without *Prāṇa*, the vitalizing, kinetic and dynamic principle. The explosion of the cosmic egg involves work and motion. This could be possible due to the *Prāṇa* which had evolved from *Āpaḥ* before the egg exploded. The unified force, the precursor of the four fundamental forces, namely gravitational, strong nuclear, weak nuclear, electromagnetic, was this *Prāṇa*. Even after the separation of the four forces, *Prāṇa* exists in a pervasive way in its own product,

cosmic egg, *Prāṇa* evolves from *Āpaḥ*. *Ākāśa* or space evolves from *Prāṇa*. The subsequent evolution of energy quanta, matter-particles, the four fundamental forces, hydrogen, other light elements, stars and galaxies took place from the source of *Ākāśa* in a superheated state.[48]

In the mental pathway of the initial evolution, *ahaṅkāra* evolves from the Vedic *Virāḍ* or the Sāṅkhya *Mahat* or *Buddhi*.

Ākāśa (Space). The word *agni* figuratively stands for energy, the precursor of all forms of energy. *Agni* was produced from *Āpaḥ* (*AV*, I.33.1-4). That *Āpaḥ* is the evolvent of *Prāṇa* has been mentioned in a number of Vedic and Vedāntic scriptures (*AV*, XI.4; *BS*, I.1.23; II.4.1; II.4.7-8; II.4.17; *BU*, I.2.6; II.1.20; III.9.9; *CU*, V.1.1; *MUU*, II.1.3; *PU*, VI.4).

48. *KTU*, II.1.7; *MUU*, II.1.3; *PU*, VI.4; *TU*, II.1. The *Taittirīya Upaniṣad* states that *Ākāśa* was generated from *Brahman*. Here the word *Brahman* has been used in a figurative sense.

Space, freshly generated in the nascent universe from *Prāṇa*, was superheated. The production of excessive quantity of heat (*tapaḥ*) has been mentioned in several scriptures (*ṚV*, X.129.3; *BU*, I.2.2; I.2.6-7; I.3.14; I.5.22; II.3. 2; III.8.9; *TU*, II.6.1; III.1.1; III.2.1; III.3.1; III.4.1; III.5.1; *PU*, I.4; *MTU*, VI.6). This superheated condition has been described as a Cosmic Sacrifice or *Aśvamedha Yajña*; *ṚV*, X.90.6-9; *ŚBrā*, XIII.1-5; *BU*, I.1.1-2.

The vigorous dancing of micro-particles in the superheated cosmic soup of the nascent universe has been described in the Vedas (*ṚV*, X.72.6: *atrā vo nṛtyatāmiva tīvro reṇurapāyata*). The whole of the freshly created Nature, with reference to the superheated nascent universe, has been personified by the Vedas (*ṚV*, I.89.10) as Mother Aditi. Micro-particles were produced from *Ākāśa* and they were reabsorbed into *Ākāśa*. This flux has been described in the Vedas (*ṚV*, I.89.9-10; X. 90.5).

Einstein identified Space (*Ākāśa*) with the dimensions (*dik*) of Space in his Special Theory of Relativity. This is, however, not correct. The dimensions are relative, but not Space itself. The Sāṅkhya (*SPS*, II. 12; *dik-kālāvākāśādibhyaḥ*) states that the (three) dimensions of *Ākāśa* and the (one) dimension of time (*kāla*) come from *Ākāśā* and the *upādhis*. They are mental constructs.

There is nothing like a cosmic *Ahaṅkāra*. Every created individual entity becomes the *upādhi* (limiting adjunct) for the *Virāḍ* or *Buddhi*. We name this embodied *Buddhi* as *buddhi*. From this *buddhi* evolves *ahaṅkāra* from which evolve the *manas* (mind), the five subtle sensory organs, the five subtle motor organs and the five *tanmātras*.[49]

For details of cosmology and cosmogony, reference may be made to the books *Cyclic Universe*,[50] *The Vibtating Universe*[51] and *Māyā in Physics*.[52]

THE EVOLUTION OF MIND

It may specially be noted here that Pure or Fundamental Consciousness (otherwise known as *Brahman*, the Absolute Reality) does not evolve. It is unchangeable, unmodifiable and constant.[53] Empirical consciousness also does not evolve. The apparatus through which Consciousness manifests as induced consciousness evolves. There are two sets of mental apparatus, namely, subtle and gross. The former belongs to the mind proper whereas the latter belongs to the physical body. The nervous system, including the brain, the spinal cord and the peripheral nerves, is the gross apparatus of the mind. The subtle structures of the mind constitute the proper mind. It is mind that controls the brain and not vice versa, although some feedback effect cannot be ruled out. This theory of mind rejects the theory of brain-mind identity.

Virāḍ or *Mahat* or *Buddhi* is the evolvent of egoity (*ahaṅkāra*)

49. *SPS*, I.61.
50. N.C. Panda, 2002.
51. N.C. Panda, 2000.
52. N.C. Panda, 1999.
53. *BG*, II.25; XII.3; *BGŚB*, II.18; II.20; II.25; *BSŚB*, I.1.4; I.2.22; II.1.14; II.1.27; II.3.7; *BUŚB*, IV.5.14; *BU*, IV.4.20; *KTU*, I.3.15; *ŚU*, II.15; *MTU*, I.4; VI.23.

that becomes an evolute.[54] It is the *ahaṅkāra* that gives the sense of 'I' and distinguishes 'not-I' from 'I'. *Manas*, five subtle organs of cognition, five subtle organs of action and five *tanmātras* evolve from *ahaṅkāra*.[55] From each *tanmātra* evolves one of the five gross states of matter (solid state, liquid state, energy state, gaseous state and ākāśic state). The *tanmātras* corresponding to these states of gross matter are *gandha* (odour), taste (*rasa*), form (*rūpa*), touch (*sparśa*) and sound (*śabda*), respectively.[56] This is the Sāṅkhya scheme of evolution. We do not accept this scheme *in toto*. This theory of evolution of the Sāṅkhya does not explain the evolution of the whole cosmos as we know today. Secondly, the Sāṅkhya asserts that the Primordial Nature (*Mūla-Prakṛti* or *Prakṛti* or *Māyā*) is transformed into *Mahat* which subsequently evolves into various evolutes, as it has been outlined already. We adhere to the Vedāntic doctrine of *adhyāsa* that rejects the doctrine of transformation. In the evolution of the cosmos, neither *Brahman* nor *Māyā* is transformed into the universe.

Āpaḥ (subtle Cosmic Fluid) evolved from *Virāḍ* or *Buddhi* (the Cosmic Mind). It super-condensed into a cosmic egg. The egg stayed for some time and later exploded. Before the explosion of the cosmic egg (rather prior to its explosion), *Prāṇa* was produced from *Āpaḥ*. This *Prāṇa* is also subtle and is the super-unified entity of all fundamental forces and all forms of energy. *Ākāśa* (Space) evolved from *Prāṇa*. The nascent universe, immediately after the Big Bang explosion, was a super-heated cosmic soup which was featureless.[57] *Ākāśa*, along

54. *SPS*, I. 71-72.

55. *Ibid.*, I.73; II.16-23.

56. *Ibid.*, II.10.

57. In the language of modern physics, the primeval, undifferentiated Space was perfectly symmetrical.

with the contents of the universe, expanded. For the subsequent steps of cosmic evolution, reference may be made to the book *Cyclic Universe*.[58]

What has been said in the previous paragraph refers to physical evolution. Mental evolution takes a parallel line. With the evolution of a physical entity, a mental apparatus evolves in it. *Virāḍ* or *Buddhi* which is all-pervasive becomes the *buddhi* (intellect) of the evolved physical entity. The physical entity serves as the limiting adjunct (*upādhi*) of its respective *buddhi*. Egoity (*ahaṅkāra*) evolves from *buddhi*. Every entity, non-living or living, has egoity. *Manas* (the knowing mental component) evolves from *ahaṅkāra*. *Prāṇa* which evolves from *Āpaḥ* is also all-pervasive. Every physical entity serves as an *upādhi* for *Prāṇa*. Thus, each non-living entity is in possession of three sheaths (*kośa*s), namely, the material sheath (*annamaya kośa*), the vital sheath (*prāṇamaya kośa*) and the mental sheath (*manomaya kośa*). Accordingly, each quantum, micro-particle, particle, atom, molecule, compound or crystal has both *prāṇa* and *manas*. By virtue of the possession of *manas*, each created entity, albeit non-living, is conscious.[59] Of course, the word 'conscious' does not connote, for this purpose at least, any highly evolved standard of consciousness in qualitative or quantitative terms.

In the course of the evolution of life-forms, advanced animals possess five organs of cognition and five organs of action. Again, each type of these organs has two varieties, subtle and gross. The five subtle organs of cognition and the five subtle organs of action evolve from *ahaṅkāra*. The ten corresponding gross organs belong to the gross body whereas the ten subtle organs are components of the mind. The

---

58. N.C. Panda, 2002, pp. 321-86; 457-740.

59. *CUŚB*, VI.11.2. Also see N.C. Panda, 1999, pp. 110-14; 315-16.

cognitive subtle organs are: visual, auditory, olfactory, gustatory and tactile. The subtle organs of action are : locomotive, prehensive, excretory, reproductive and vocal.

In addition to the three sheaths already mentioned, the human being (*Homo sapiens*) has two more sheaths, namely, the intellectual sheath (*vijñānamaya kośa*) and the blissful sheath (*ānandamaya kośa*).

Man has three types of body, namely, the gross body (*sthūla śarīra*), the subtle body (*sūkṣma śarīra* or *liṅga śarīra*), and the causal body (*kāraṇa śarīra*).[60] The gross body starts its existence at the time of conception in the mother's womb, grows by incorporation of nutrients from the mother's blood and, in post-parturient life from foods eaten. This body terminates at death and disintegrates. A group of structures of the subtle body and the causal body combinedly constitute the mind. The principal mental components are : *buddhi, ahaṅkāra, manas,* five subtle organs of cognition, five subtle organs of action, five *prāṇas* (*prāṇa, apāna, udāna, vyāna* and *samāna*) and *citta* (the subtle organ of conceptualization and mental creation).[61] The *citta* normally resides in the intellectual sheath (*vijñānamaya kośa*). With the death of the body, the five *prāṇas* merge in universal *Prāṇa*; the subtle organs merge in *ahaṅkāra* that, in turn, merges in *buddhi* and finally into the causal body. None of these subtle components lose their own identity. They hibernate and stay in a state of dormancy. The self resides in the causal body. While in association with the

60. *SPS*, III. 7.

61. *SPS*, III.9; *saptadaśaikaṁ liṅgam*; III.17; *MAU*, 3 : The *Māṇḍūkyopaniṣad* enumerates nineteen components of the subtle body. The five sub-*Prāṇas*, namely the *prāṇa, apāna, vyāna, udāna, samāna* are the common modifications of the three principal internal instruments (*antaḥkaraṇa*), namely *buddhi, ahaṅkāra* and *manas* (*SPS*, II.31). Here, we differ from the SPS and assert that the sub-*Prāṇas* are modifications of the *Prāṇa*.

causal body and the accumulated mass of karmic impressions (*saṁskāra-piṇḍa*), the self (*jīvātmā*) is bound (*baddha*) rather than free (*mukta*). It is this bound self, along with the causal body, the karmic impressions and involuted subtle body merged in the causal body, that transmigrates for rebirth.

As long as the *saṁskāra-piṇḍa* stays in the causal body as subtle traces, reincarnation repeats unavoidably. The fruition of a *karma* (*karma-vipāka*) erases the concerned *karma* from the mind's tape. There are yogic methods also to erase the *karma*s except the *prārabdha* (already initiated) ones. When all the karmic impressions are erased, the individual mind (*saṁskāra*s) disappears, the individual *buddhi* merges with the Cosmic *Buddhi* (*Virāḍ*) and the self, thus freed, re-establishes its identity with the universal Self in the analogy of *ghaṭākāśa* (space in a pot) becoming *mahākāśa* (Great Space) on the breaking of the pot. The karmic traces are the cause of rebirth. The bound self (empirically bound, of course) transmigrates from an old body to a new body. Since the causal body is the cause of rebirth, it is named so.

We have not yet exhausted the infrastructure of the mind. The Tantric anatomy describes seven *cakra*s that are subtle in nature. These are: *mūlādhāra, svādhiṣṭhāna, maṇipūra, anāhata, viśuddhi, ājñā* and *sahasrāra*. For more detailed knowledge on the *cakras*, reference may be made to the fifth chapter (*The Serpent Power*) of the book *Mind and Supermind.*[62]

Fig. 1.3 presents a gross view of the locations of the seven *cakra*s with reference to the gross body. It is to be stressed here that the *cakra*s are subtle rather than gross and they belong to the subtle body. However, for convenience in communication, reference points are made with relation to the gross body. Some schools of Yoga teach that these *cakra*s (at least the lower six) are vertical in plane and each one is twin in nature, both

62. N.C. Panda, 1996, pp. 215-91.

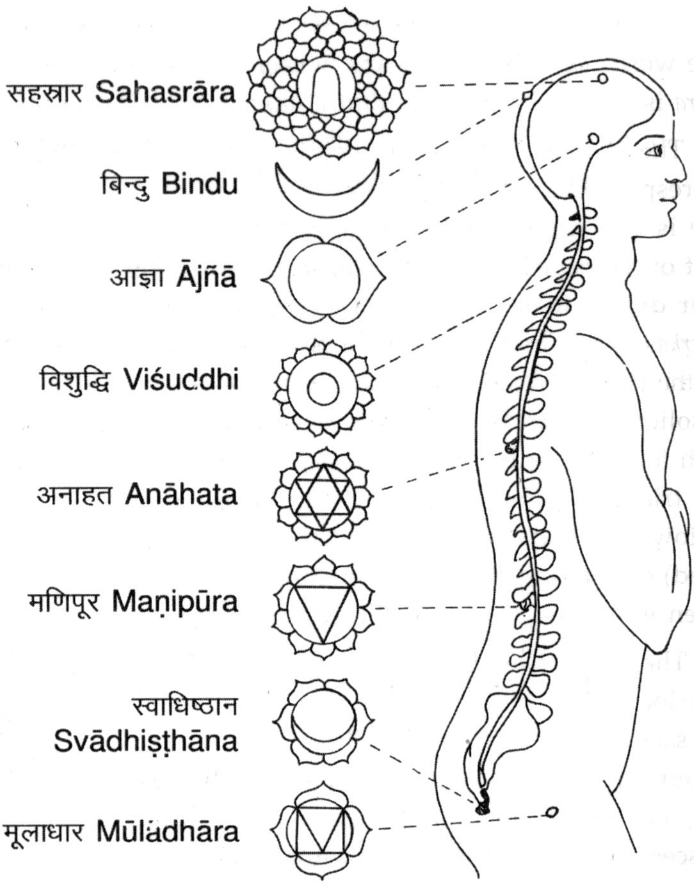

Location of the Cakras

(चक्रों की स्थिति)

fig. **1.3 A gross view of the locations of the seven *cakras*.**

on the front side and the back side. This is, however, not correct. If the spinal cord is imagined as a vertical line to serve as an axis, each *cakra* is located around this axis horizontally on a transverse plane. It may again be emphasized that the spinal cord, the vertebral column, the nerve plexuses, the body-organs, the pituitary, the pineal gland and such other structures are not *structurally* related to these *cakras*.

THE PSYCHIC CENTRES IN THE SUBTLE BODY

The word *cakra* literally means 'wheel', 'discus' or 'vortex'. A *cakra* is a psychic centre in *Tāntrik* language.

The *mūlādhāra cakra* is located in the pelvic floor at a level corresponding to that of the coccygeal plexus of nerves. Its site is two digits above the anus and two digits below the root of the penis. It is bulbous in shape, having a dimension of four digits. It has four petals, crimson-red in colour. The *mātṛkās* (letters representing the powers of the Divine Mother) on the petals are : *vaṁ, śaṁ, ṣaṁ, saṁ*. Its subtle element (*tattva*) is solidity (*pṛthvī* or earth). Its *maṇḍala* or *yantra* is a square, with four angles, eight spears on its four sides and an inverted red triangle within the square. The colour of the pericarp is yellow. The *tanmātra* of the *tattva* is *gandha* (smell). The *bīja* (seed) of the *tattva* is *laṁ*. The picture of the *mūlādhāra cakra* is given in *fig*. 1.4.

The *svādhiṣṭhāna cakra* is the second one from the bottom. It is located at the base of the penis. Its level corresponds to the sacral plexus of nerves. It has six petals, vermilion-red in colour. The *matṛkās* on the petals are : *baṁ, bhaṁ, maṁ, yaṁ, raṁ, laṁ*. Its *tattva* is liquidity (*āpaḥ*). Its *maṇḍala* or *yantra* is a crescent moon. Its pericarp is white in colour. Its *tanmātra* is *rasa* (taste). The *bīja* (seed) of its *tattva* is *vaṁ*. The picture of the *svādhiṣṭhāna cakra* is presented in *fig*. 1.5.

The third *cakra* from the bottom is the *maṇipūra*. It is located exactly at the level of the navel. This level corresponds to that of the solar plexus of nerves. It has ten petals, blue in colour, resembling heavy rain-clouds. The *mātṛkās* on the petals are: *ḍaṁ, ḍhaṁ, ṇaṁ, taṁ, thaṁ, daṁ, dhaṁ, naṁ, paṁ, phaṁ*. Its *tattva* is fire (*agni* or *tejaḥ*). Its *maṇḍala* or *yantra* is an inverted red triangle with three *svastika* marks. Its pericarp is red in colour. Its *tanmātra* is *rūpa* (sight). The *bīja* (seed) of its *tattva* is *raṁ*. *Fig*. 1.6 presents the picture of the *maṇipūra cakra*.

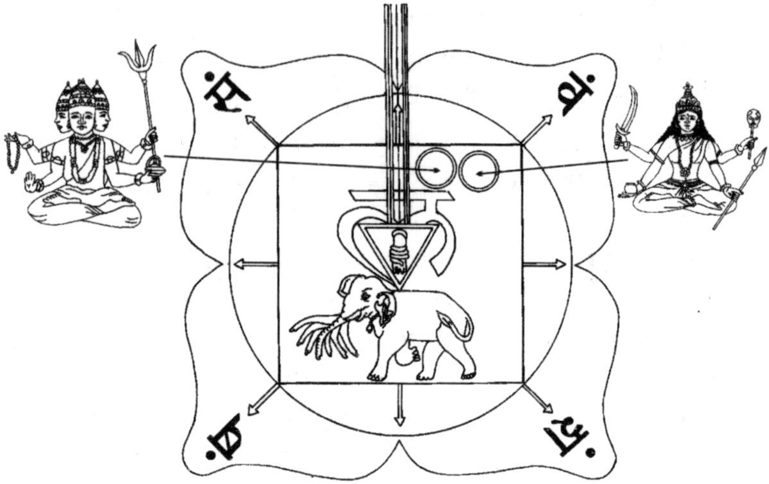

fig. **1.4 The *mūlādhāra cakra*.**

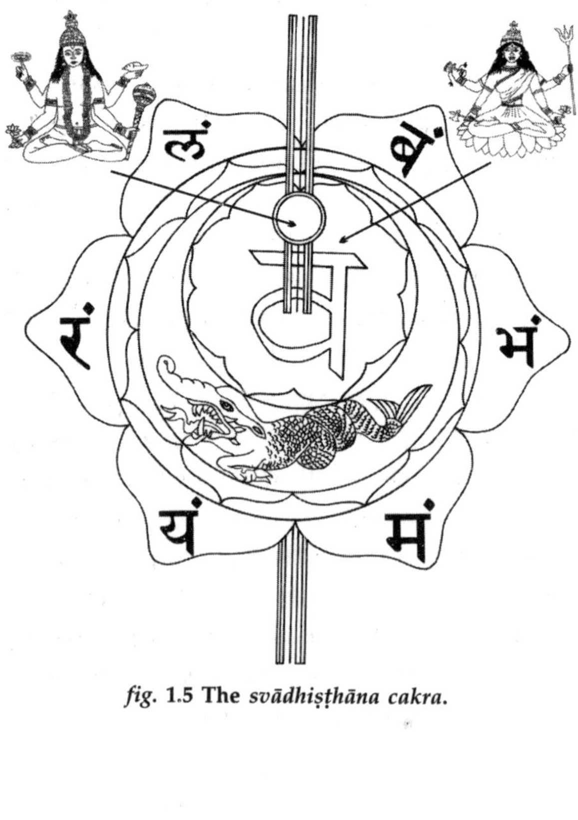

fig. **1.5 The *svādhiṣṭhāna cakra*.**

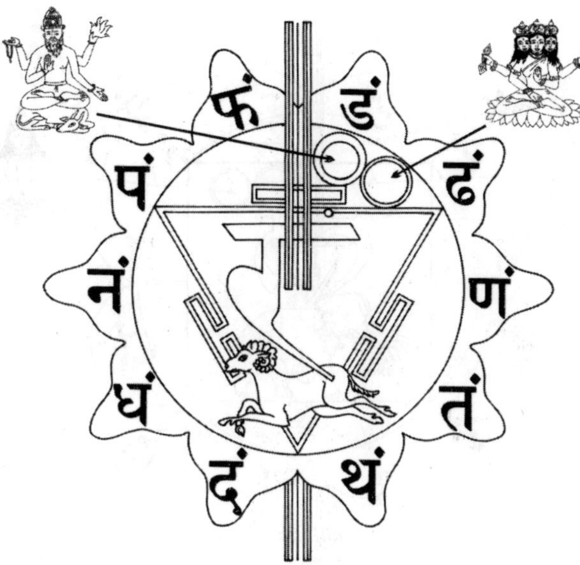

fig. **1.6 The *maṇipūra cakra***

The *anāhata cakra* is the fourth one from the bottom. It lies behind the base of the heart, at the level of the depression in the sternum. This level corresponds to that of the cardiac plexus of nerves. It has twelve petals, red in colour resembling that of the *bandhūka* flower. The *mātr̥kā*s on the petals are : *kaṁ, khaṁ, gaṁ, ghaṁ, ṅaṁ, caṁ, chaṁ, jaṁ, jhaṁ, ñaṁ, ṭaṁ, ṭhaṁ*. Its *tattva* is *vāyu* (air or gaseous matter). Its *maṇḍala* or *yantra* is a hexagon (two interlacing triangles), with an inverted triangle in the middle of the hexagon. The colour of the pericarp is smoky. The *tanmātra* of its *tattva* is *sparśa* (touch). The *bīja* (seed) of the *tattva* is *yaṁ*. The picture of the *anāhata cakra* is presented in *fig*. 1.7.

The *viśuddhi* is the fifth *cakra* from the bottom. It lies at the level of the throat-pit. This level corresponds to that of the cervical plexus of nerves. This *cakra* has sixteen petals, smoky-purple in colour. The *mātr̥kā*s on the petals are: *aṁ, āṁ, iṁ, īṁ,*

fig. **1.7 The** ***anāhata cakra***

uṁ, ūṁ, ṛṁ, ṝṁ, lṛṁ, lṝṁ, eṁ, aiṁ, oṁ, auṁ, ṁ, ḥ. Its *tattva* is *Ākāśa* (Space). Its *maṇḍala* or *yantra* is a circle, with a white inverted triangle within the circle and a round *candra* (moon) *maṇḍala* inside the triangle. Its pericarp is white in colour. The *tanmātra* of its *tattva* is *śabda* (sound). Its *bīja* (seed) is *haṁ*. The picture of this *cakra* is given in *fig*. 1.8.

The sixth *cakra* from the bottom is *ājñā*, located behind the spot between the two eyebrows. It lies in the brain directly above the spinal column at the level of the prefrontal area. It has two petals, white in colour. The *mātṛkās* on the petals are : *haṁ, kṣaṁ*. This *cakra* is the site of *buddhi, ahaṅkāra* and *manas*. Its *maṇḍala* or *yantra* is a circle with an inverted triangle within it. The colour of its pericarp is moon- or silver-white. The *bīja* (seed) of this *cakra* is *oṁ* (ॐ). *Fig*. 1.9 presents the picture of the *ājñā cakra*.

fig. **1.8 The *viśuddhi cakra***

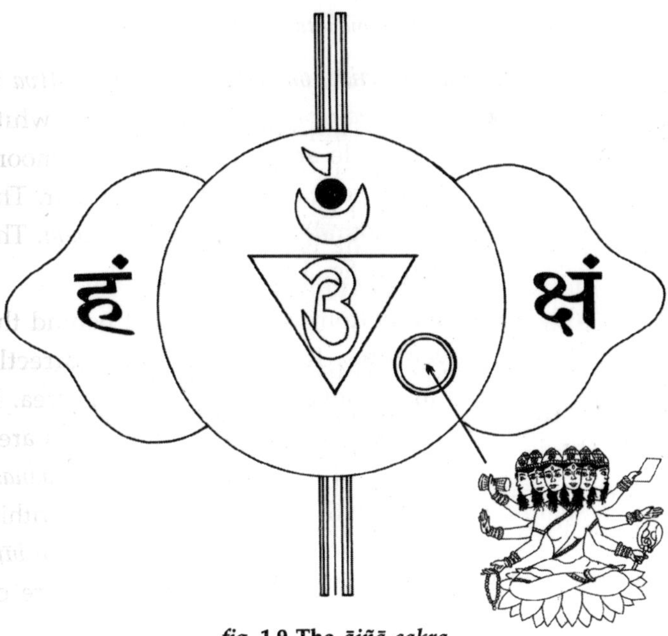

fig. **1.9 The *ājñā cakra***

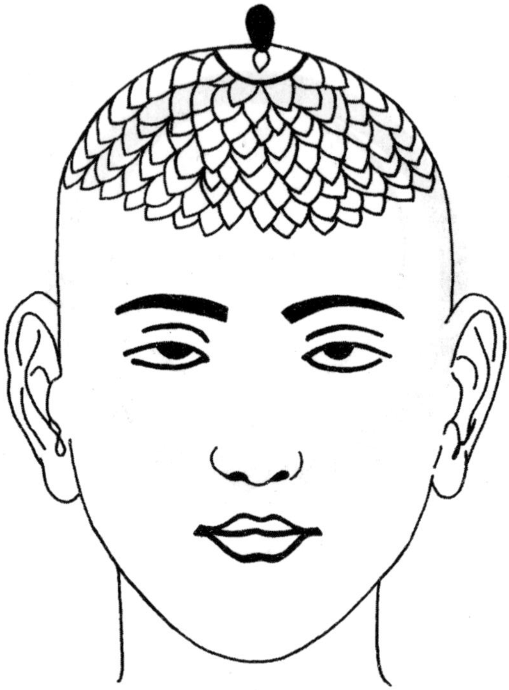

fig. **1.10 The *sahasrāra*.**

The *sahasrāra* or the thousand-petalled lotus occupies the peak position in the subtle body of a person. Some *yogī*s consider it as the seventh *cakra* whereas some others take it as the highest centre in the subtle body where Lord Śiva (God or the Auspicious Lord of the universe) resides. The *sahasrāra* is illustrated in *fig.* 1.10.

There is a centre known as the *bindu-visarga,* briefly known as the *bindu*. It is located at the top of the back of the head, where the Hindu brāhmaṇas (priests) leave a tuft of long hair. This centre is in between the *ājñā* and the *sahasrāra. Fig.* 1.11 presents the picture of the *bindu-visarga.*

What is called the *bindu-visarga* in the Tantra is the *dhruva* or the *prātibha* in the Yoga. The *maṇipūra* of the Tantra is the

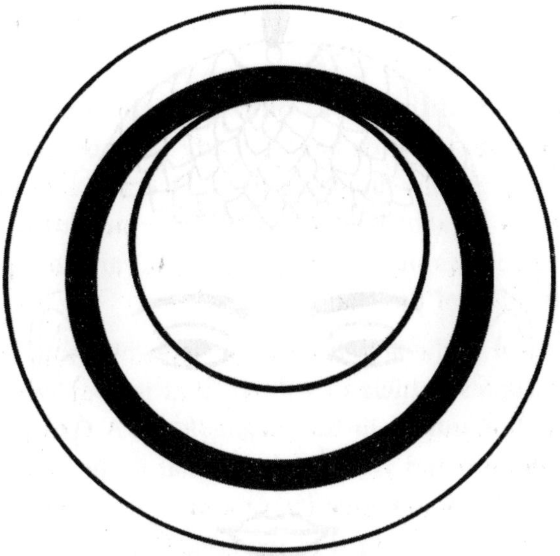

fig. **1.11 The *bindu-visarga*.**

nābhicakra (umbilical psychic centre) of the Yoga. The Yoga uses the word *kaṇṭhakūpa* (throat-pit) for the *viśuddhi* of the Tantra. Patañjali refers to the *kūrmanāḍī*, otherwise known as the *hr̥dayapuṇḍarīkam*. It is located inside the chest below the *viśuddhi* and above the *anāhata*. The yoga uses the term *hr̥daya* (heart-lotus) for the psychic centre *anāhata* of the Tantra. What is *sahasrāra* in the Tantra is the *mūrdhajyotis* in the Yoga. It is, however, to be noted that the Tantra is the only system that has made an elaborate probe into the anatomy of the subtle body.

THE SYMBOLOGY OF THE CAKRAS

With reference to the symbology of the *cakras*, we may focus our attention on the following features: (1) The number of petals, (2) the colour of petals, (3) the letters on the petals, (4) the colour of the pericarp (*karṇikā*), (5) the geometrical diagram (*yantra* or *maṇḍala*) inside the *cakra*, (6) the *bīja* (seed) *mantra* of the *cakra*, (7) the animal symbol in each *cakra* and (8) the presiding deity in each *cakra*.

All features of the *cakras* other than the animal symbols and the presiding deities have already been described along with the pictures. The animal is the vehicle (*vāhana*) of the *bīja* and, hence, is located below the *bīja*. The presiding goddess of the *cakra* resides in its pericarp (*karṇikā*) and the presiding god in the *bindu* of the *bīja*.

The animal in the *mūlādhāra* is an elephant (Indra's *airāvata*). *Makara* (Varuṇa's vehicle or *vāhana*) that is somewhat like an allegator is the animal in the *svādhiṣṭhāna*. A ram (*meṣa*), the vehicle of the fire god Agni, is the animal in the *maṇipūra*. The *anāhata* has a black antelope (*kṛṣṇasāra*) as its animal. A snow-white elephant is the animal of the *viśuddhi*. There is no animal in the *ājñā*.

Ḍākinī, Rākiṇi, Lākinī, Kākinī, Śākinī and Hākinī are the presiding goddesses of the *mīlādhāra, svādhiṣṭhāna, maṇipūra, anāhata, viśuddhi* and *ājñā cakras*, respectively. Their respective presiding gods are four-faced *bāla* (infant) Brahmā, four-handed Viṣṇu, three-eyed Rudra, three-eyed Īśa or Pinākī, Sadāśiva (*Ardhanārīśvara*, half male and half female, the famale half being Gaurī) and Śambhu (Parama-Śiva), respectively. The six female deities, serially from the *mūlādhāra* upwards, are illustrated in *figs*. 1.12 to 1.17. The six male deities, in the same order, are presented in *figs*. 1.18 to 1.23.

Three *cakras*, namely, the *mūlādhāra*, the *anāhata* and the *ājñā* have each an inverted triangle, representing a *yoni* (female sex-organ). There is a *liṅga* (male sex-organ) in each of these *yonis*. They are named *Svayambhū-liṅga, Bāṇa-liṅga* and *Itara-liṅga* in the *mūlādhāra, anāhata* and *ājñā*, respectively. The symolic *yoni* represents the mother of the universe and the symbolic phallus (*liṅga*) the father of the universe.

fig. **1.12 Ḍākinī, the presiding goddess of the *mūlādhāra*.**

fig. **1.13 Rākiṇī, the presiding goddess of the *svādhiṣṭhāna*.**

fig. **1.14 Lākinī, the presiding goddess of the *maṇipūra*.**

***fig.* 1.15 Kākinī, the presiding goddess of the *anāhata*.**

fig. **1.16 Śākinī, the presiding goddess of the *viśuddhi*.**

fig. **1.17 Hākinī, the presiding goddess of the *ājñā*.**

fig. **1.18 Bāla-Brahmā, the four-faced presiding god of the *mūlādhāra*.**

fig. **1.19 Viṣṇu, the four-handed presiding god of the *svādhiṣṭhāna*.**

fig. **1.20 Rudra, the three-eyed presiding god of the *maṇipūra*.**

fig. **1.21 Īśa (Pinākī), the three-eyed presiding god of the *anāhata*.**

fig. **1.22 Sadāśiva, the presiding god of the *viśuddhi*. (Ardha-nārīśvara — half female and half male, the female half being Gaurī.)**

fig. **1.23 Śambhu, the presiding god of the *ājñā*.**

There is a concept of *piṇḍa-brahmāṇḍa* in the *Tāntrika* philosophy. The Sanskrit word *piṇḍa* means 'body' and *brhmāṇḍa* means 'universe'. The body is a microcosm. Whatever is present in the universe is also present in the body, albeit in a miniature scale. Reality is bipolar. In the summit of the axis of the body is Parama Śiva (the Supreme Lord); at the bottom of the axis, the foundation of the *piṇḍa,* sleeps Mother Kuṇḍalinī who is the Power (*Śakti*) of the Lord and the Mother of the universe, the Father being Lord Śiva.

The Divine Father and the Divine Mother are never separated and for ever in union. In each of the six *cakra*s do the Father and the Mother preside. But their images seem to occupy an evolutionary ladder. Their colours also follow the same evolutionary pattern. Parama Śiva in the *sahasrāra* is formless, colourless, attributeless, functionless, constant and unmodifiable. Nevertheless, He is Pure Consciousness that, being reflected, renders every insentient thing conscious. That is the Great Magnet that induces electromagnetism of consciousness in everything, comparable to iron filings existing in the proximity of the former. The Mother aspect of Divinity is active, whereas the Father aspect is inactive, except being the Chairperson (*Adhyakṣa*) and the inducer.

There is a concept of *loka*s (worlds) in Indian cosmology. They are seven in number, namely, *bhūrloka, bhuvarloka, svarloka, maharloka, janarloka, tapoloka* and *satyaloka.* Each of the six *cakras,* serially from the bottom, corresponds to one *loka,* serially listed here. The *sahasrāra* corresponds to the *satyaloka* in the *piṇḍa-brahmāṇḍa.* In our opinion, these *lokas* in the total cosmos are not vertically situated one over the other in geometrical Space. The difference lies in grossness or fineness and in the number of dimensions. Spatially considered, every *loka* is present everywhere. An entity can jump from one *loka* into another provided its materiality (*dravya*) could be coarser or finer, as the case may be, and provided the transformed entity could acquire the changed dimensions. The *cakra*s, however, are vertically located in the *piṇḍa*, each one of them corresponding to a single *loka*.

In connection with the symbology of the *cakra*s, a pertinent question is raised here. The *cakra*s belong to the subtle body (*sūkṣma śarīra*). This body cannot be preceived by the five senses of cognitions. The seers (*yogī*s) claim to have seen the subtle body through their third eye (the occult sense of intuition). In spite of the sense-imperceptibility of the *cakra*s, we illustrate them by pictures and that too coloured pictures. Forms and colours have direct reference to the gross world (*sthūla jagat*). How can we explain this anomaly?

When the third eye perceives the subtle body, subtle structures are converted into gross structures. This conversion is analogous to the manifestation of electromagnetism into forms, colours and sounds in the television. This is perhaps the mechanism of manifestation of the subtle body for the third eye. If the perceivable anatomy and the inferable physiology of the *cakra*s are critically analysed, we have to consider the subtle *cakra*s as transducers, devices for converting non-electromagnetic signals into electromagnetic ones.

SYSTEMS CONTROLLED BY THE CAKRAS

The human subtle body has five supersensible sensory organs and five supersensible motor organs. The Sanskrit word *indriya* is applied for these organs. The former five are organs of cognition (*jñānendriya*) and the latter five are organs of action (*karmendriya*). Each of these subtle organs controls its respective gross organ of the gross body. Each of the lower five *cakra*s controls one sensory organ and one motor organ.

The *mūlādhāra cakra* controls the supersensible senory organ of olfaction (*ghrāṇendriya*) and the supersensible motor organ of excretion (*pāyvindriya*; the word *pāyu* means 'excretion'). The *apāna vāyu* functions in excretory activities; its main area of action is between the navel and the anal region; its source is the *mūlādhāra*. The large intestine (caecum, colon and rectum), the anal region including the anal sphincters — internal and external, the kidneys, the ureters, the urinary bladder, the urethra, the expiratory organs of the respiratory system and the sweat glands of the gross body are regulated by the *apāna vāyu*. The discharge of menstrual fluid and that of the vaginal secretion and semen ejaculation subsequent to sex-orgasm are also regulated by the *apāna vāyu*.

The *svādhiṣṭhāna cakra* controls the supersensible sensory organ of gustation (*rasanendriya*) and the supersensible motor organ for reproduction (*upasthendriya*). The two testes, the accessory glands of the male reproductive system (seminal vesicles, prostate), the penis, the two ovaries, the two oviducts, the uterus, the vagina, the vulva, the clitoris and the mammary glands are controlled by the *svādhiṣṭhāna* through the mediation of the subtle *upasthendriya*. The *vyāna vāyu* functions in pervasive activities; its area of action is the whole body; the circulation of blood and lymph and the electrical conduction through nerve-fibres are done through the *vyāna vāyu*; its source is the *svādhiṣṭhāna*.

The *maṇipūra cakra* controls the supersensible, sensory organ of vision (*darśanendriya*) and the supersensible, motor organ of locomotion (*pādendriya*). The *samāna vāyu* functions in digestion, oxidation of nutrients for the production of energy, and the utilization of nutrients in the synthesis of body tissues and in maintaining a balance in the metabolic activities. The stomach, the small intestine, the pancreas, the liver and all the upper abdominal digestive organs are regulated by the *maṇipūra*. Its main area of action is between the navel and the diaphragm, although it functions in all organs, tissues and cells for regulating the metabolic activities. The source of the *samāna vāyu* is the *maṇipūra cakra.* Both the legs function with the help of the *samāna vāyu.* Because of the relation between the legs and the *manipūra cakra* and the origin of the *vajrā nāḍī* inside the *suṣumṇā, vajrāsana* activates the digestive processes. The pressure points on the legs and feet exert feedback effects on the *maṇipūra cakra.* The bulb (*kanda*) at the *mūlādhāra* which is also the point of origin of the *vajrā nāḍī* is pressed while doing *vajrāsana.* This *āsana* activates all the three lower *cakras*, namely, the *mūlādhāra,* the *svādhiṣṭhāna* and the *maṇipūra.*

The *anāhata cakra* controls the supersensible, senory, cutaneous organ (*sparśanendriya*), containing tactile, thermal, pressure and pain receptors, including the receptors for the sensation of sexual pleasure. This *cakra* controls the supersensible, motor organ of prehension (*hastendriya*). The *prāṇa vāyu* functions in the beating of the heart, inspiratory activities of the lungs and the thoracic muscles and all types of absorptive activities in the small intestine, skin and other organs and tissues. Its main area of action is between the diaphragm and the collar bone, although it acts in the absorption of nutrients and other substances in the stomach, small intestine and skin. The source of the *prāṇa vāyu* is the *anāhata cakra.* The two hands are the motor organs that utilize the *prāṇa vāyu* in their functioning.

The *viśuddhi cakra* controls the supersensible, senory organ of audition (*śravaṇendriya*) and the supersensible, vocal motor organ (*vāgindriya*). The *udāna vāyu* functions in activities like vomition and hiccup. It also plays its role in pushing blood to the head against the gravity, in the functioning of the ears and in the overall functioning of the face and the head. Its area of action is above the clavicle (the collar bone).

The *ājñā cakra* is located in the *mūlādhāra-sahasrāra* axis behind the spot between the two eyebrows. Many writers unnecessarily connect it with the pituitary gland situated inside the cranium at the base of the brain. The frontal lobe and especially the prefrontal area of the brain lie in its proximity. Evolutionarily speaking, the prefrontal area is the most evolved one in the human species. It is the centre of wisdom, creativity and judgement. Nevertheless, both the pituitary and the prefrontal area are parts of the gross body whereas the *ājñā* is part of the subtle body. The whole of the brain, including the two endocrine glands, namely, pituitary and pineal, located inside the cranium, is controlled by the *ājñā*. The pituitary, being the master gland among the endocrine glands of the body, regulates all the others.

As it has already been described, mind is a composite subtle organ consisting of many subtle structures, out of which four are the most important ones. They are : *citta, buddhi, ahaṅkāra* and *manas*. The *ājñā* is the site for the last three. *Buddhi* is the subtle sub-structure for intellection and discrimination between good and bad, right and wrong, should and should-not. *Ahaṅkāra* is the subtle sub-structure for individuation. It imparts the I-sense, as distinguished from the non-I. It safeguards the interest of the 'I'. The *manas* is the subtle sub-structure for mentation. It is the thinking substance. It receives messages from the external world and also from different parts of the body through the input (afferent) pathway and sends order for action to different parts of the body through the output (efferent) pathway. It integrates and co-ordinates the actions of the sense-organs and the sensory and motor organs.

The literal meaning of the Sanskrit word *ājñā* is 'command'. The *ājñā cakra* is the command centre of all lower *cakra*s and the whole body, including the higher centres of the brain. It is a misgiving that the *sahasrāra* controls the cerebrum and the higher centres of the brain. It is, however, not a fact.

Parama Śiva (the Supreme Lord of the universe) sits in the *sahasrāra* (the thousand-petalled lotus). This is a lotus without colour and sound. Its deity (the Lord God) is devoid of forms, attributes and actions. He is the Presiding Chairperson, eternally and timelessly Silence, Absolute Quietude, the Benign and Serene. He is the light of lights, the Fundamental Consciousness that induces consciousness in every entity, otherwise insentient. He is *Saccidānanda* (Existence, Consciousness and Bliss). He is timelessly inseparable from His Power (*Śakti*), the feminine pole of the Bipolar Reality. This *Śakti* is Mother Kuṇḍalinī who resides in the *mūlādhāra cakra*.

Kuṇḍalinī is usually supine and dormant. This supine condition simulates a coiled, sleeping serpent. She sleeps in three and a half coils, with the tail-tip in the mouth. Her mouth closes the *brahmadvāra*, the opening gateway to the central *suṣumṇā nāḍī*. The central vertical hollow passage known as the *brahmanāḍī* which is the core channel inside the *citriṇī* is the pathway for the awakened Kuṇḍalinī for ascent (*ārohaṇa*) and descent (*avarohaṇa*). This *citriṇī* (*citrā*) is inside the *vajriṇī* (*vajrā*), and the latter is inside the *suṣumṇā*.

Some writers erroneously identify Kuṇḍalinī with energy (*ūrjā*). There is no difference between energy and matter, the latter being the packet form of energy. *Prāṇa* is the precursor of all forms of energy. *Āpaḥ* (the primordial Cosmic Fluid) is the evolvent and *Prāṇa* is its evolute. *Virāḍ* or *Mahat* evolves from the Primordial Nature (*Mūla-Prakṛti* or *Māyā* or Mother Kuṇḍalinī) and *Āpaḥ* evolves from *Virāḍ*. Thus, Mahā-Kuṇḍalinī is the Mother of the universe of matter and energy. There is no difference between Mahā-Kuṇḍalinī and Kuṇḍalinī, the former refers to the *brahmāṇḍa* (Cosmos) and the latter to the *piṇḍa* (an individual human body).

The *citta* resides in the intellectual sheath (*vijñānamaya kośa*) which is at a level in between the *ājñā* and the *sahasrāra* (at the *bindu-visarga*). The *citta* and the *ājñā* are in constant communion. It is also constantly lighted by the reflection of the consciousness of the self (*ātmā*). The *manas* cannot convert the input-data into concept; but the *citta* does it. Out of the stored data in the memory (*smṛti*), it can create new thoughts and ideas. If the *citta* is transparent, or at least translucent, rather than opaque, it can link up with the Supermind (the Superconscious) and can acquire intuitive knowledge (*aparokṣānubhūti*) or revealed knowledge.

Parama Śiva is not the individual self (*jīvātmā* or *ātmā*). He is the Supreme Self (*Paramātmā*). The *ātmā* sits in the *ānandamaya kośa* (blissful sheath). It is apparently and empirically associated with the causal body (*kāraṇa-śarīra*). The *karmāśaya* is located in the causal body. Reincarnation (rebirth) is a repeating process so long as the *karmāśaya* (repository of *karmas*) persists. When the *karmāśaya* ceases to exist, the causal body ceases simultaneously, ending in liberation (*mokṣa*). When this happens, the individual self merges with the Universal Self, the process being called *brahma-nirvāṇa*.

Where is the causal body located ? In which part of the causal body does the self (*ātmā*) reside ? The causal body is the innermost one inside the whole of the subtle body. The self resides in it at the level of the *bindu-visarga;* but its light of consciousness pervades each cell and sub-cellular structure of the body. The *karmāśaya* or the *saṁskārāśaya* (store house of *karmas* or *saṁskāras*) has a number of storing places that are located in the different *cakras*. All *vāsanās* are *saṁskāras*, although the reverse is not true. The *vāsanās* are thrown into the deepest layers of the *karmāśaya*. The word *vāsanāśaya* is used for the reservoir of *vāsanās*.

Here we may briefly describe the psycho-physiology of the *cakras* from the point of view of psycho-evolution. The *mūlādhāra* controls the excretory organs and the *svādhiṣṭhāna* the generative organs. It would not be wrong to say, however, that these two lowest *cakras* control the sexuality of a person. And, in this connection, the *mūlādhāra* plays a more important role in the sexual behaviour of a person. This basal *cakra* is concerned with solidity (*pṛthvī-tattva*) whereas the *svādhiṣṭhāna* is connected with fluidity (*jala-tattva*).

The *maṇipūra cakra* has to do with eating and digesting food and also the production of energy. Its *tattva* is fire (*agni*). Thus the three lowest *cakras* deal with sex, reproduction and food.

The *anāhata cakra* regulates our sentiments, emotions, love, compassion and such other humane qualities. It transcends animality and fosters human values. Its *tattva* is *vāyu* (air), subtler than earth and water.

The *viśuddhi* has *ākāśa* as its *tattva*. *Ākāsa* is the subtlest among the five states of matter. The *viśuddhi cakra* purifies the whole body. Between the *bindu* and the *viśuddhi*, there is a smaller psychic centre known as the *lalana cakra*, situated in the back of the nasopharynx, the inner cavity above and beyond the soft palate, into which the nasal passages open. The subtle nectar (ambrosia) that drips down from the *bindu* is stored in the *lalana*. In the ordinary situation, the nectar that dripples from the *lalana* reaches the *maṇipūra* where it is consumed in the fire of the *cakra*. By the practice of *khecarī mudrā* the *lalana* is stimulated and the *viśuddhi* is activated, and thereby the nectar drops to the *viśuddhi* which retains and utilizes it. The activation of the *viśuddhi* rejuvinates the body and delays the ageing process.

The body has its own immune system. It is likened to the defence department of a country. The immune system has many sites to produce soldiers and weapons. These sites are the thymus gland, the bone marrow, the spleen and the lymph nodes. All the white blood corpuscles are the soldiers of the body. The immune system produces antibodies, both cellular and humoral. It produces specific antibodies against spceific antigens. Animals and the human beings cannot live if the immune system fails. It is the *viśuddhi cakra* that controls the immune system. If this *cakra* is activated, the body develops resistance to diseases, especially infectious diseases. It also stimulates organs like the liver to detoxify toxins.

The *ājñā cakra* has no *tattva*. Its sphere of activity is more mental than physical. It transcends the five states of matter. Its *bīja mantra* is *O'Ṁ*.

THE PRĀṆA AND THE SUB-PRĀṆAS

The word *Prāṇa* has been used in almost all Yoga and Tantra scriptures. But its meaning has hardly been specified and clarified. *Prāṇa* is not life (*jīvana*). *Virāḍ* (the Cosmic Mind) or *Mahat* was the first evolute from the *Mūla-Prakṛti* (Primordial Nature), the Power (*Śakti*) of *Īśvara* (God). *Āpaḥ* (the Primordial Cosmic Fluid; not water or H_2O) evolved from *Virāḍ*. *Āpaḥ* super-condensed into a Cosmic Egg that stayed as the Egg for some duration. The Egg exploded. Prior to the explosion of the Cosmic Egg, *Prāṇa* evolved from *Āpaḥ* and, with the explosion, *Ākāśa* (Space) evolved from *Prāṇa*. All types of energy quanta and matter particles evolved from *Prāṇa*, pervasive in *Ākāsa*, in the superheated state of the nascent universe. Space expanded and is still expanding although the present rate of expansion is decelerated. All the four fundamental forces, namely, gravitational, nuclear (strong), weak and electromagnetic, separated in sequence from *Prāṇa*.

The super-unified force and the super-unified energy is the *Prāṇa*, the third evolute in the primary stage of cosmic evolution. *Virāḍ*, *Āpaḥ*, *Prāṇa* and *Ākāśa* are all-pervasive. According to the scheme of evolution, an evolute can undergo dissolution, in the involutionary phase, only into its immediately previous evolvent (its immediate precursor material).

The Sanskrit word *Prāṇa* means 'filling potency', 'vitalising' or 'breathing strength into an entity'. The Sanskrit word *vāyu* has been derived from the verb root *vā*, meaning 'to blow'. Its popular meaning is 'wind'. Many writers have translated *prāṇa-vāyu* as 'vital breath'. Such a translation may not be wrong in its proper context. But, in the context of Vedic cosmology, *prāṇāyāma* and *cakra-nāḍī* physiology, *vāyu* is not air or wind and *prāṇa* is not life or breath or vital air. *Prāṇa* is the primordial energizing subtle fluid that pervades all Space and energizes everything. It is the super-unified force-*cum*-energy. No particle, atom, molecule, micro- or macro-body, living or non-living entity can work without *Prāṇa*. Being a subtle fluid, it blows in open space and flows in tubular structures such as *nāḍī*s.

The concentration or density of *Prāṇa* is not uniform in every spot of Space in the total Cosmos. The vital strength of a body is more with the higher accumulation of *Prāṇa* and less in the reverse condition. A body is vitally debilitated if it absorbs and stores less quantity of *Prāṇa*.

Prāṇa generally enters into the bodies of animals and human beings with respiratory systems through the inhaling air. The more air one can inhale and the longer time one can retain the inhaled air in the lungs, the more *Prāṇa* one can accumulate. *Prāṇa* flows through the blood vessels to each cell of the body. The transport of oxygen from the lungs in the form of oxyhaemoglobin is a separate phenomenon and may not be confused with the flow of *Prāṇa*. This circulating *Prāṇa* is stored in batteries of the body. And the *cakras* are these batteries. The *yogī* can collect and store *Prāṇa* in the *cakras* directly from the cosmic source, even without the mediation of the inhaled air.

It has already been stated that each *cakra* is a transducer. The same *Prāṇa* is collected and stored by all the *cakras*. But each of the lower five *cakras* converts the same *Prāṇa* into a different sub-*Prāṇa*. These sub-*Prāṇas* are : *apāna* (in the *mūlādhāra*), *vyāna* (in the *svādhiṣṭhāna*), *samāna* (in the *maṇipūra*), *prāṇa* (in the *anāhata*) and *udāna* (in the *viśuddhi*). The functions of these sub-*Prāṇas* have already been described.

NETWORK OF RIVERS AND RIVULETS

Blood carrying nutrients and oxygen reaches all cells of the body through arteries, arterioles and capillaries. In the same analogy, *Prāṇa* flows inside the body through *nāḍīs* and branches and sub-branches thereof to reach each nook and corner of the body-system. The *nāḍīs* are not blood vessels; neither are they nerves. Whereas blood vessels and nerves are structures of the gross body, *nāḍīs* are tubular structures of the subtle body. They cannot be recognized by dissecting the gross body. They cannot be detected by the microscope. They are not discernible to the two eyes by which we see. They are visible to the third eye of the *yogī*. Their existence and functioning can also be inferable by virtue of the gross effects they produce. The gross effects are detectable and measurable.

The *Ṣaṭcakranirūpaṇa*[63] states that the total number of *nāḍīs* in the human body is 72,000. The *Śiva-Saṁhitā*[64] numbers them as 3,50,000. Some *nāḍīs* are wider and longer and some others are narrower and shorter. The discrepancy in the numbering of *nāḍīs* is perhaps due to the subjectivity in deciding the counting of minor sub-branches or alternatively in ignoring them. The network of the *nāḍīs* in the subtle body of a human being is illustrated in *fig.* 1.24.

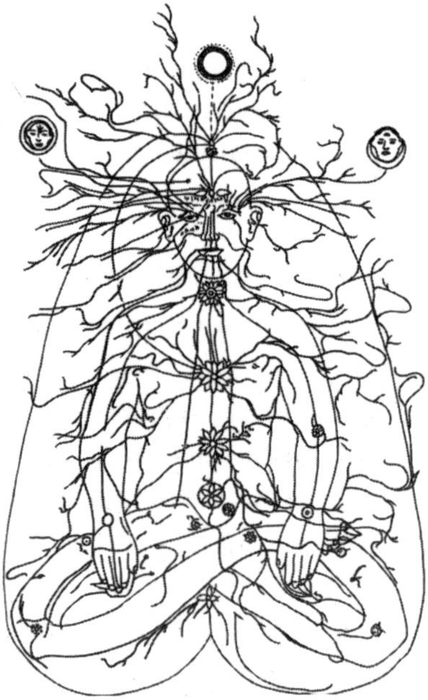

***fig.* 1.24 The network of the *nāḍīs* in the subtle body of a human being.**

63. T. Vidyaratna, (ed.), 1987, p. 79: The *Gorakṣa-Saṁhitā* has been quoted as follows :

ūrdhvaṁ meḍhrādadho nābheḥ
kandayoniḥ khagāṇḍavat ।

tatra nāḍyaḥ samutpannāḥ
sahasrāṇāṁ dvisaptatiḥ ॥

The *Ṣaṭcakra-Nirūpaṇa* forms the sixth chapter of the book *Śrītattva-Cintāmaṇi* written by Pūrṇānanda Svāmī.

64. *ŚS*, II.31, edited by R.B.S.C. Vasu, 1990.

Suṣumṇā, iḍā and *piṅgalā* are the three principal *nāḍīs* in the subtle body. Out of these three, the *suṣumṇā* is the main one. It flows vertically in the middle of the spine. What we call *suṣumṇā* is really a complex of four psychic channels, arranged cylindrically one inside the other. This is possible because of their unequal diameters. The outermost tube, the *suṣumṇā* proper, contains three *nāḍīs* inside it. The second internal tube, the *vajrā* or the *vajriṇī,* contains two *nāḍīs* inside it. The third internal tube, the *citrā* or *citriṇī,* contains the innermost channel, the *brahmanāḍī,* that is a hollow channel, albeit without a solid cylindrical wall. Really speaking, the *brahmanāḍī* is a hollow channel inside the *citriṇī* and is not tubular in structure. The starting orifice of the *brahmanāḍī* at the bulb (*kanda*) of the *mūlādhāra* is known as the *brahmadvāra.* Its terminal orifice at the *sahasrāra* in the head is called the *brahmarandhra.* The *citriṇī* is white in colour like the moon. The *vajriṇī* has the colour of the sun, or that of the filament (*keśara*) of the pomegranate (*dāḍima*) flower. The *suṣumṇā* possesses the colour of the redness of fire. The *citriṇī,* the *vajriṇī* and the *suṣumṇā* are of the nature of *sattva, rajas* and *tamas,* respectively. The *suṣumṇā nāḍī* complex pierces all the lotuses (*cakras*) of the subtle body.

The *iḍā* (the *candra nāḍī* or the lunar channel) traverses its course on the left side of the *suṣumṇā.* The *piṅgalā* (the *sūrya nāḍī* or the solar channel) runs on the right side of the *suṣumṇā.* Whereas the *suṣumṇā* is a subtle tubular structure running vertically inside the spinal column, the *iḍā* and the *piṅgalā* run outside the spine. The *iḍā* is white in colour and is of the nature of *sattva.* The *prāṇa* flowing in the *iḍā* has a cooling effect. The *piṅgalā* takes the colour of the sun and is of the nature of *rajas.* The *prāṇa* flowing in the *piṅgalā* has a heating effect.

The courses of the *iḍā* and the *piṅgalā* along the left and the right side of the *suṣumṇā,* respectively, are not fully parallel, however. According to one view, the two side *nāḍīs* intertwine at each *cakra* (*fig.* 1.25). They start at the *mūlādhāra* and spiral about the *suṣumṇā* up to the *ājñā,* intersecting at each *cakra* along the way. They intertwine, like the braids of hair, and thus change their left and right paths alternately while meeting at each *cakra.* We do not agree to this view. According to a second view, the *iḍā* originates from the left side of the *mūlādhāra* and passes through the left nostril on its way to the *ājñā.* The *piṅgalā* starts from the right side of the *mūlādhāra* and passes through the right nostril to the *ājñā* (*fig.* 1.26). A third view describes each of these two *nāḍīs* as two bows on each side of the central channel (*fig* 1.27). Each bow starts at the level of the scrotum (*muṣka*) and ends at the level of the collar bone (clavicle or *jatru*). We also do not agree to the second and the third view.

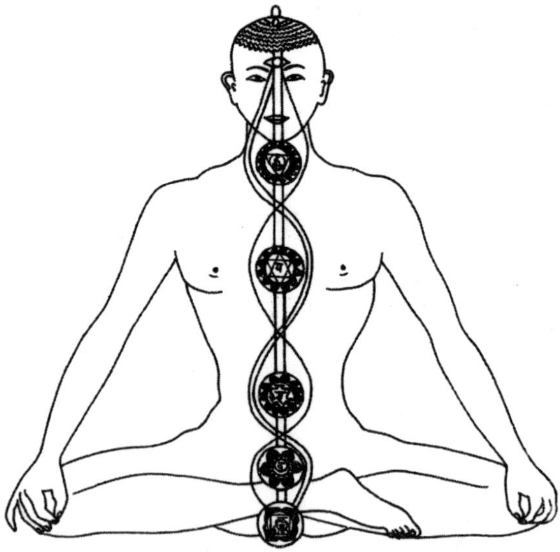

fig.* 1.25 The intertwining of the *iḍā* and the *piṅgalā* around the *suṣumṇā* at each *cakra.

***fig.* 1.26 The courses of the *iḍā* and the *piṅgalā* on the left and the right side of the *suṣumṇā*, respectively, from the *mūlādhāra*, through the respective nostril, to the *ājñā*.**

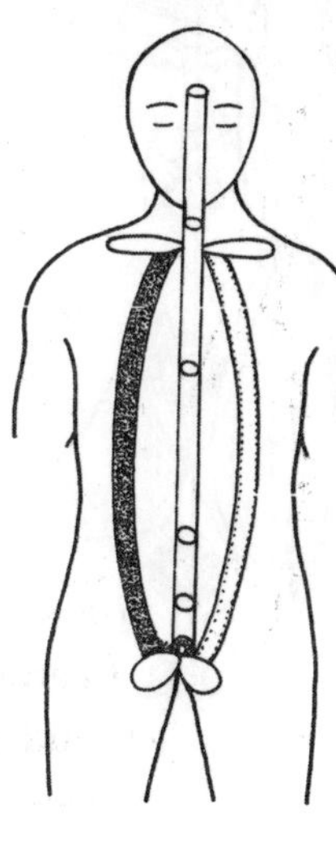

***fig.* 1.27 The *iḍā* and the *piṅgalā* as two bows on the left and the right side of the *suṣumṇā*, respectively, starting from the level of the scrotum and ending at the level of the collar bone.**

The *iḍā* and the *piṅgalā* traverse *almost* straight paths to the level of the *ājñā* where they form a confluence (*triveṇī*) with the *suṣumṇā*. We have used the word 'almost' for the reason that these three *nāḍī*s meet at the *anāhata* on the way. They form three knots (*granthi*s) along the entire path they travel from the *mūlādhāra* to the *ājñā*. The first knot known as the *brahmagranthi* is at the *mūlādhāra*. The second knot formed at the *anāhata* is the *viṣṇugranthi*. The third and the last knot is formed at the *ājñā*. It is known as the *rudragranthi*. The three knots and the courses of the *iḍā* and the *piṅgalā* are illustrated in *fig.* 1.28.

The confluent channel formed at the *ājñā* ascends upward as a single *nāḍī*. It reaches the *sahasrāra* finally to terminate at the *brahmarandhra*. Thence, by a certain flexure, it goes to the

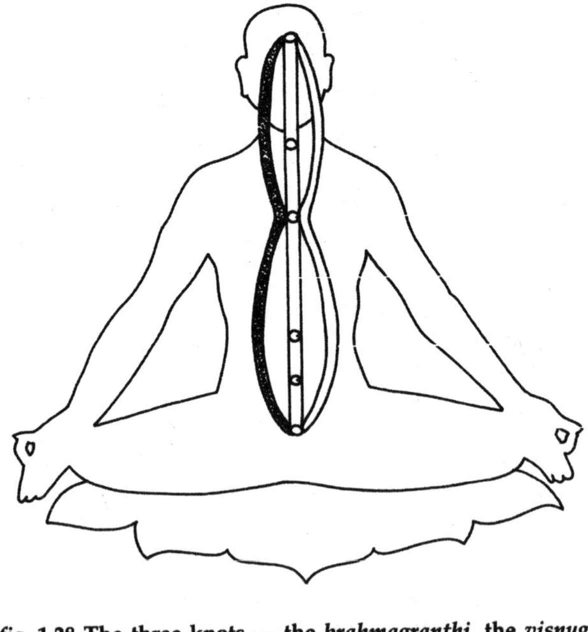

***fig.* 1.28 The three knots — the *brahmagranthi*, the *viṣṇugranthi* and the *rudragranthi*.**

right side of the *ājñā cakra,* whence it proceeds to the left nostril. Similarly, by a second flexure, it moves down to the left side of the *ājñā cakra,* whence it proceeds to the right nostril. The courses of these *nāḍīs* have been illustrated in *fig.* 1.29.

It may be mentioned here that the brain is divided into two hemispheres, right and left. Nerves emerging from the right hemishphere innervate the left side of the body. Reverse is the case for the right side of the body that is innervated by nerves emerging from the left hemisphere. The flexures (right and left) of the confluent *nāḍī* at the *sahasrāra* follows a similar pattern.

Out of the 3,50,000 *nāḍīs,* fourteen are major. Three of them, the most important ones, have already been described.

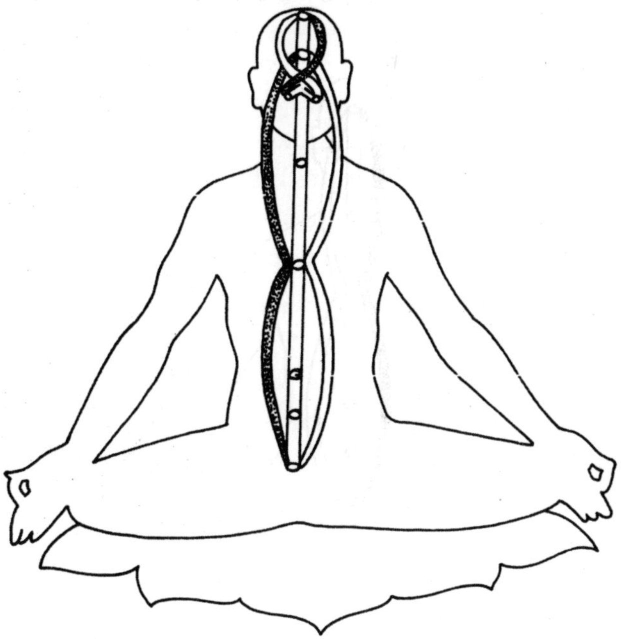

***fig.* 1.29 The confluent *nāḍī* at the *ājñā*, its straight course to the *brahmarandhra*, its flexure and downward courses to the nostrils through the *ājñā* by changes of sides.**

The rest eleven are : *gāndhārī, hastijihvikā, kuhū, sarasvatī, pūṣā, śaṅkhinī, payasvanī, vāruṇī, alambuṣā, viśvodarī* and *yaśasvinī.* All these *nāḍī*s rising from the *mūlādhāra,* go to the various parts of the body — the tongue, the eyes, the ears, the armpit, the fingers, the abdomen, the scrotum, the anus, the feet and the toes.

With this, ends the brief description of the subtle body. The Indian concept of mind cannot be dissociated from the subtle body and the causal body. It may further be emphasized that mind in Indian philosophy and psychology is not a structure of the gross body, that it is not the Western 'soul' and that it is not the Vedāntic self (*ātmā*). A group of subtle structures and sub-structures constitute the mind which itself is material (albeit subtle) and insentient. With the reflection of the fundamental Consciousness (*Brahman* or *Ātman*), the insentient mind is rendered conscious. In the dualism of René Descartes, mind (spirit or soul) does not interact with matter or body. That is not the case, however, in Indian psychology which regards psychosomatic interaction as the interaction between subtle matter and gross matter, both being matter according to the Sāṅkhya concept.

In a book on *Yoga-Nidrā,* we had to clarify the concept of mind, conscious mind and the Unconscious, the *cakra*s and the related *nāḍī*s. Internal *nyāsa* is practised in the advanced type of *yoga-nidrā* and, hence, is the necessity of the acquaintance with the *cakra*s. Auto-suggestion is made through a resolve (*saṅkalpa*) to print an impression on the Subconscious or the Unconscious or to erase an impression from it. For producing a better effect in the process, the flow of *Prāṇa* in the *nāḍī*s should be unimpeded without obstruction anywhere, and the *cakra*s should be activated simultaneously. Since *yoga-nidrā* directly involves the Subconscious and the Unconscious, a discussion on depth psychology becomes necessary.

INDIAN VERSUS FREUDIAN DEPTH PSYCHOLOGY

We would first present some salient features of Indian depth psychology and, in the context of that framework, we would compare and contrast it with the Freudian system.

Personality in Indian Psychology

The concept of 'personality' in Indian psychology is not the same as that in Western psychology. The personality of an individual is the sum total of his/her life pattern and behaviour. The *saṁskāra*s of the past lives (not inherited from parents, but carried over in one's own causal body through reincarnations), his genotype inherited from his mother and father, his nurture and his *pauruṣa* (the will and effort to fight adversities and create opportunities) combinedly influence the making of the personality. The word 'nurture' stands for three types of influences, namely, the planetary and stellar positions at the time of birth, the familial, social and global influences (environmental influences) and the training and education one receives.

Indian psychology recognizes three types of personalities, namely, *sāttvika, rājasika* and *tāmasika*.[65] These three are not discrete. There is hardly any person of purely *sāttvika* or *rājasika* or *tāmasika* traits. Every person has different permutations and combinations of the *guṇa*s — *sattva, rajas* and *tamas*. The type of personality is named according to the quantitative dominance of any of the *guṇa*s. It is inferred from this that there are different grades of personalities, all of which can be represented in a bell-shaped normal curve of error. To attain liberation (*mokṣa*), one has to transcend these three *guṇa*s, or to speak in the language of the *Gītā*,[66] one has to become

---

65. *BG*, XVII.
66. *Ibid*, II.45.

nistraiguṇya (devoid of the three *guṇas*).

The Sāṅkhya concept of *Prakṛti* and her three constituent *guṇas* may be presented first and then the Vedāntic concept may be compared and contrasted. The Sāṅkhya *Prakṛti* is the primordial (unmanifested or *avyakta*) Nature that is constituted of three *guṇas*, namely, *sattva, rajas and tamas.*[67] She is without a beginning and an end, and co-eternal with the multiple *puruṣas.*[68] She is insentient whereas the *puruṣas* are sentient.[69] She is active whereas the *puruṣas* are inactive.[70] Both the *Prakṛti* and the *puruṣas* are in proximity and they co-operatively work as in the parable of the lame and the blind men.[71] *Prakṛti* is rendered sentient by virtue of the reflection of the *puruṣa* on her.[72] The three *guṇas* are in equipoise (*sāmyāvasthā*) in the period of no creation.[73] When this equilibrium is disturbed, creation or, more befittingly, evolution ensues.[74] The Sāṅkhya has the doctrine of transformation (*pariṇāma-vāda*),[75] according to which *Prakṛti* is transformed into *Mahat* or *Buddhi*[76] from which everything of the universe evolves sequentially. Since *Prakṛti* is made up of three *guṇas*, all the evolutes of *Prakṛti* are also constituted of these *guṇas*, although not necessarily in equal proportions.

The Vedānta conceives of *Brahman* which is eternal, timeless, with and without space, formless, attributeless and

---

67. *SPS*, I.126; I.136; VI.39; *SK*, 11.
68. *Ibid.*, I.149; I.152; V.72; VI.45; *SK*, 18.
69. *Ibid.*, I.145; III.59; *SK*, 11.
70. *Ibid.*, I.26; III.20; III.59; V.129; *SK*, 11.
71. *SK*, 21.
72. *SPS*, I.96-97; I.99; I.164; II.35; VI.27-28.
73. *Ibid.*, I.61.
74. *Ibid.*, VI.42.
75. *Ibid.*, I.61; I.75.
76. *Ibid.*, I.61; I.71.

actionless. *Māyā* or *Mūla-Prakṛti* (the primordial, unmanifested nature) is the Power (*Śakti*) of *Brahman*. But the former is not a second entity, she being inseparable from the possessor of Power in the analogy of fire and heat. *Brahman*, when *nirupādhikam* (devoid of *upādhi* or limiting adjunct) is attributeless (*nirguṇa*) and functionless (*niṣkriya*). The same *Brahman*, with *Māyā* as the *upādhi*, takes the role of *Īśvara* (God) who is with attributes and who functions through *Māyā*. *Īśvara* is the *Puruṣa* and the single *Puruṣa* (the masculine aspect of Divinity). *Prakṛti* or *Māyā* is the single Power (*Śakti*) of the *Puruṣa*. The Vedāntic *Prakṛti* is also constituted of three *guṇas*, namely, *sattva, rajas* and *tamas*. Both *Puruṣa* and *Prakṛti* are beginningless, endless and co-enternal. The universe evolves as a result of their union. But this evolution is empirical; it is not the transformation of *Prakṛti*. The universe is not a product out of the precursor matter of *Prakṛti*. The Vedānta rejects *Brahma-pariṇāma-vāda* (tranformation of *Brahman* into the universe) and *Māyā-pariṇāma-vāda* (transformation of *Māyā* into the universe). *Māyā* projects a Supermind (*Virāḍ*) from which the universe evolves empirically. This phenomenon is known as *adhyāsa* or *vivarta-vāda*. According to this doctrine, the substratum (*adhiṣṭhāna*) is *Brahman* only, which is changeless, unmodifiable and constant. The one appears to be many with forms, attributes and functions. The many are not nothing. They are empirically *real*, although not absolutely. The triple process of evolution, sustenance and involution, finally leading to dissolution of the universe in *Māyā* is brought about by the Chairpersonship of the Divine Father (*Īśvara*) and the activity of the Divine Mother (*Māyā*).

We accept the Vedāntic doctrine of the cosmic evolution. How do we account for the three *main* types of personalities then?

In the Vedic and the Vedāntic cosmogony, the one and

the only one Lord of the universe played the role of Brahmā for creating the universe. He did it through his *Śakti* (Power) who is known as Sarasvatī (the one and the only one Divine Mother who is known by this name for the purpose of creation). The *Śakti* of God, by any name (Sarasvatī, Lakṣmī, Kālī or Gaurī) is constituted of three *guṇa*s namely, *sattva, rajas* and *tamas*. In the beginning, Mother Sarasvatī played her *vīṇā*. The three strings of her *vīṇā* vibrated to produce the *udgītha* (*CU*, I.1.1), the *oṅkāra dhvani* (*AUṀ*, ॐ). This sound resolved into many types and numbers of cosmic notes to produce everything of the universe. The *oṅkāra dhvani* is still being produced and the process will continue in future until the termination of the cosmic cycle. This results in the continuing evolution. *Virāḍ* or the Cosmic Mind (the supermind) first manifested as a result of the vibration or *nāda* (the vibration of the three strings — *sattva, rajas* and *tamas*) of the *vīṇā* of Mother Sarasvatī. A *bindu* or the singularity of modern cosmology evolved from *Virāḍ*. The *bindu* is the cosmic egg. The Vedic concept of *nāda* gives birth to the first superstring theory of the world.

The Śaiva philosophy and the Tantra lay much importance on the *bindu* and the *nāda* in explaining cosmology and cosmogony. The *tāṇḍava* dance of Lord Śiva, with the beating a drum (*ḍamaru*) confirms the vibration (*spanda*) theory of the genesis and the annihilation of the universe. The symbol of Mother Kālī, looking terrifying and vigorously dancing on the chest of Father Śiva, supports the theory of vibration and the concept of the inactive Divine Father and the active Divine Mother, the Father still being the substratum and the foundational base.

The primal sound *AUṀ* (ॐ) is monosyllabic (*ekākṣara*), consisting of three letters (*varṇa*s), namely, *A, U* and *Ṁ*. The first letter, *A*, stands for the *guṇa sattva*; the second letter, *U*, stands for *rajas*; and the third letter, *Ṁ*, stands for *tamas*. All the three letters, when combined, stand for All Existence (*Sat*), both manifested and unmanifested, both absolute (*pāramārthika*) and empirical (*vyāvahārika*). The symbol *AUṀ* (ॐ) is devoid of all the three attributes (*guṇas* : *sattva, rajas* and *tamas*). It is a verbal representation (*vācaka*) for *Brahman*.

It has already been stated that the Vedānta rejects the doctrine of transformation (*pariṇāma-vāda*). Neither *Brahman* nor *Māyā* is transformed into the universe. Neither Brahmā nor Sarasvatī is transformed into the universe. That being so, none of the three *guṇa*s of the Divine Mother can directly be transmitted to any created entity of the universe. Nevertheless, the universe being a product of *Virāḍ,* a mental projection of the Mega-Mind, each created entity has been constituted of the mental images of the *guṇa*s, blended in different quantities and proportions, of course.

The words *sattva, rajas* and *tamas* were originally used by the Sāṅkhya. Purity, serenity, steadfastness, altruism, goodness, benignness, whiteness and auspiciousness are the meanings associated with the *sattva-guṇa.* Restless activity, unsteadiness, strong propensities, rat-race for more wealth and power, self-centredness, seeking for bodily pleasure and sensual gratification, efforts for dominance and prominence, redness and sanguinity are the characteristics of *rajas-guṇa.* Inertia, slothfulness, inactivity, a mentality for the *status quo,* pessimism, blackness and darkness, sadism, jealousy, cruelty, violence, self-centredness, malignant sensuality and excessive attachment for sensual gratification are the characteristic traits of *tamas-guṇa.* The three *guṇa*s are *descriptive* terms in the Vedānta psychology in contrast with the Yoga and the Sāṅkhya psychology where *Prakṛti-pariṇāma-vāda* is involved.

The *Bhagavadgītā* has also described personality by the use of two terms — *daiva* and *āsura*.[77] The former word means 'divine' and the latter 'demoniac'. The self in man is intrinsically God Himself. The animality in man is antithetical to the divinity in him. Knowledge and ignorance rule a man and shape his personality. Thus, man is bipolar — *daiva* and *āsura*. There are different proportions of *daiva* and *āsura* traits in different individuals. According to this scheme, types of individuals are not two only. They are innumerable, depending on the relative quantities of these traits in the total individuality. With the exception of the *jīvanmukta* (liberated, although still living), every individual person has some *daiva* and *āsura* qualities. A person is good when his *daiva* nature predominates; he is bad when his *āsura* nature predominates; he is average with almost equal proportions of these two.

The Cause of Personality Difference

What causes an individual to be *sāttvika* or *rājasika* or *tāmasika*? Why are some persons more *daiva* and others more *āsura*? Why are some persons *pravṛtti-mārgī* (followers of the path of worldly attachment and sensual indulgence) and why are some others *nivṛtti-mārgī* (followers of the path of detachment and renunciation) ? What is the seminal cause of evil ?

Avidyā (ignorance) is the cause of evil. The lack of informational knowledge about the world and the deficiency in the erudition of scriptures do not contextually convey the meaning of Vedāntic *avidyā*. It is the lack of the knowledge of the Reality. It is the lack of the knowledge that discriminates good from bad, 'should' from 'should-not'. It is the lack of the realization of *Brahman* (*brahmopalabdhi*) and of the realization that everything and everybody of the universe are not different from *Brahman*.

---

77. *BG*, XVI.

The traditional Vedāntic explanation for the origin of evil is the bad *karma* of an individual. The doctrine of *karma* inextricably goes with the doctrine of reincarnation. All the karmic impressions of the past and the present life are imprinted in the *karmāśaya* (reservoir of *karmas*) which is a component of the causal body of an individual. Rebirth continues so long as the residual karmic traces are present in the *karmāśaya*. With the complete erasure or obliteration of the karmic traces, the *karmāśaya* dissolves and this leads to the cessation of rebirth and the consequent liberation (*mokṣa*).

The *karmas* may be good or bad. All accumulated *karmas* of the past lives are stored in the *karmāśaya* and this store is the *sañcita karma*. A person is born to consume a portion of the *sañcita karma* in the current life. This is the *prārabdha karma*. The *karmas* of the present life are cumulatively added to the *karma*-ledger to bear fruit in the future lives. This is the *āgāmī karma.*

The bad actions of a person lead to the accumulation of bad *karmas*. The good actions of a person lead to the accumulation of good *karmas*. The individual is fully responsible for his/her good or bad actions, and God does not play any role in this process except the placement of the *jīvātmā* with its causal body in a proper womb at a proper time, commensurate with the type of *karma*. Even this placement is *natural* (*svabhāvataḥ*) without the *direct* doership of God. As we understand, a process is natural if it follows the laws of Nature or the divine laws.

Pure Consciousness (*Viśuddha Cit* or *Brahman*) is all-pervasive. Everything, non-living or living, micro or macro, gets induced consciousness as a result of the proximity of *Brahman*. The level of induced consciousness is qualitatively and quantitatively variable, depending upon the evolved apparatus of the mind, since through the apparatus (structures like neurons and the brain) only is consciousness expressed. The source of consciousness (*vidyā*) is common. What is the source of *avidyā* then ? Why should one person have more *vidyā* (knowledge) and why should another more *avidyā* ? *Avidyā* is the cause of evil. How do we account for the inequal distribution of *avidyā* in different individuals ?

The Vedānta has an answer to the question posed here. The cosmic cycles are beginningless. Even on the total dissolution of the cosmos in a single cycle, every unliberated individual with his causal body and karmic store potentially and latently stays in *Virāḍ* that undergoes dissolution in *Māyā*. In the next creation, an individual's potential existence is manifested. Thus, the karmic inequalities among individuals are explained.

We do not reject the explanation given in the foregoing paragraph. But, we are not fully satisfied with it. *Ahaṅkāra*, the subtle component of the *antaḥkaraṇa* (the internal subtle structure of the mind-complex), has the freedom to function, subject to the condition that this freedom has limitations. Will is the combined functional attribute of the *buddhi-ahaṅkāra-manas* complex. Due to the freedom of will, a person can do good actions or bad actions of mental, vocal and physical nature. Good actions generate good *karmas* whereas bad actions bad *karmas*. *Buddhi*, in *sāttvika* state, is transparent, in *rājasika* state translucent and in *tāmasika* state opaque.

Buddhi, with dirt on it, cannot efficiently discriminate good from bad. The *vijñānamaya kośa* (intellectual sheath) becomes non-functional or wrongly functional. In such a state, it cannot guide the *ahaṅkāra* and the *manas* in a right direction. Thus, *avidyā* is created by an individual himself. More and more of *avidyā* leads to more and more of evil, and that, in turn, leads to the generation of more and more of bad *karma-saṁskāras*.

So far have we explained the genesis of the personality type on the basis of the *karma-vāda*. Nature and nurture also play important roles in determining the personality type. The genes inherited from the mother and the father, the planetary configuration at the time of birth and subsequent planetary environment made available in the life, the family, the social and the global environments and the education-*cum*-training are the other factors that play important roles in shaping the personality of an individual. There is, however, a difference of opinion on this point. According to one view, all these factors independently exert their effects although there are interactions too; the resultant effect decides the type of the personality. A second view is in favour of the primacy of the *karma* which plays a decisive role in generating the other factors. We have a tendency to lean on the second view.

Personality Types in Western Psychology

In Western psychology, behavioural psychology has much to do with personality traits. The typing of personalities has been done in more than one ways. One typing that has gained much popularity classifies personalities into type A and type B.

Persons of type A show a temperament characterized by an excessive drive and competitiveness, an unrealistic sense of time urgency, unrealistic and inappropriate ambition, a reluctance to provide self-evaluation, a tendency to emphasize quantity of output over quality and an unquenched thirst for fame, power, dominance and self-aggrandisement. Type A behaviour is predisposed to psychosomatic diseases, coronary disease and hypertension.

Type B personality has a temperament characterized by a relaxed, easy-going approach to life, a focus on quality over quantity, low competitiveness, a tendency for self-reflection and living a life of contentment.

The Sheaths: the Sites of Memory and Saṁskāras

All the non-living objects are in possession of three sheaths (*kośa*s) only, namely, the material sheath (*annamaya kośa*), the vital sheath (*prāṇamaya kośa*) and the mental sheath (*manomaya kośa*). With the disintegration or conversion of any non-living entity, nothing of the preceding object survives except the material (energy) substance. It has no *karma* and *karmāśaya* in a causal body. This also happens in the plant kingdom. The evolution of the intellectual sheath (*vijñānamaya kośa*) and the blissful sheath (*ānandamaya kośa*) takes place in the animal kingdom. With the evolution of the nervous system, these two *kośa*s ascend in structure and quality from a rudimentary state in primitive animals to an advanced state in the human species. Each human being has an advanced *karmāśaya* in the causal body and the *vāsanā-saṁskāra*s are printed on the *karmāśaya.*

The word *saṁskāra-piṇḍa* is a collective term that stands for all the *saṁskāra*s printed and stored. *Saṁskāra*s are stored both in the Subconscious and the Unconscious. The former is in the mental sheath and the latter in the blissful sheath. The *karmāśaya* (reservoir of *karma*s) is located in the Unconscious of the blissful sheath. The karmic impressions or the *vāsanā*s are stored here. *Karma* is a technical term in Indian philosophy. It does not mean 'action'. Any action done by one, like eating, sleeping, playing or talking, is not printed in one's *karmāśaya.* Actions, good or bad, that profoundly affect the *antaḥkaraṇa* (the inner subtle organ of the mental complex) are recorded in the *karmāśaya*. This recording is analogous to the audio-visual recording on magnetic tapes, although this simile is not 100 per cent appropriate.

The *vāsanā-saṁskāra*s are generated by strong desires, aspirations, feelings, emotions, sentiments, sorrowful events, ecstatic events, love, hatred, violent activities, jealousy, caprice, avarice, lustful desires — either fulfilled or unfulfilled, anger, delusion, sadistic activities and destructive actions. They leave tracings on the *karmāśaya*, which is also called the *vāsanāśaya*. All *vāsanā*s are *saṁskāra*s, but the reverse is not true.

The *karmāśaya* is three-dimensional. It has length, breadth and depth. It is like a multi-volume book, each volume being thick. Some *saṁskāra*s are recorded on the superficial pages whereas some others are buried in the deep layers. The *karmāśaya* is the Unconscious of the *antaḥkaraṇa*.

The mental sheath contains the Subconscious which records some *saṁskāra*s that are not *vāsanā*s. This sheath also contains the memory (*smṛti*). The mental sheath is in the subtle body (*sūkṣma* or *liṅga śarīra*) whereas the blissful sheath is in the causal body (*kāraṇa śarīra*). The recordings of the non-*vāsanā* *saṁskāra*s and the memory have a similarity. But *saṁskāra*s and *smṛti* (memory) are not identical, and their storing sites, albeit the same mental sheath, do not superimpose each other.

New information is encoded; the encoded information is stored in memory; and the stored information is retrieved as and when needed. These three are important aspects of the working of memory. There are two types of memory, namely, short-term memory (STM) and long-term memory (LTM). Before information gets access to STM, it can be held for a brief time (a few seconds) in the sensory channels (visual, auditory, olfactory, gustatory, tactile). This storage function of the sensory channel is called the sensory register. This sensory register transmits information to STM which can store it up to about thirty seconds. The STM becomes LTM through a process known as consolidation. Two brain structures, namely, amygdala and hippocampus, located in the deeper part of the temporal lobe, are involved in the cosolidation of STM into LTM. The amygdala in general and the hippocampus in particular are indispensable in the formation of *new* LTM. These two structures, however, are not the storing sites of the long-term memory. Already formed LTM is not lost if these two structures are damaged. According to ancient Indian psychology, LTM is not stored in the brain, but in the *manomaya kośa* of the subtle body. Some psychologists are of the view that information stored in LTM stay there for a long time. Some others hold that they are never lost and permanently stay in LTM. We agree to this second view. When memory fails, it happens due to retrieval problems, and not due to loss of stored information.

When Indian psychology refers to memory (*smṛti*), it generally speaks of the long-term memory (LTM) stored in the mental sheath (*manomaya kośa*), without any reference to the *karmāśaya* in the causal body. It has already been said that the *karmāśaya* is the Unconscious in Indian psychology.

Freudian Mind versus Yoga-Vedānta Mind

The three components of personality in the psychoanalytic theory of Sigmund Freud are the id, the ego and the superego.[78] Only about 10 per cent of the personality remains conscious and the rest 90 per cent unconscious. The id occupies a major portion (about 75 per cent) of the total personality. The whole of the id is unconscious. Out of the remaining personality, the ego is major and the superego is minor in size. Both the ego and the superego share all the three levels of Freudian consciousness, unequally, of course. Freud's levels of consciousness (awareness) are: the *conscious*, the *preconscious* and the *unconscious*. We are aware of certain things around us and certain thoughts. This is what Freud terms *conscious*. His *preconscious* level refers to our memories or thoughts that are easily available with a moment's reflection. The *unconscious*

78. C.T. Morgan, *et al.*, p. 578.

of Freud contains memories, thoughts and motives which we cannot easily call up.

In the Indian psychological system, the mental store pertaining to the *karmāśaya* is the *acetana manas* (the Unconscious) and that pertaining to the *smṛti* (memory) consists of the *cetana manas* (the conscious mind) and the *avacetana manas* (the subconscious mind). The term 'subconscious mind', as an equivalent for the unconscious, has been very much popularized. This is, however, not correct. In no circumstances can the 'subconscious' be a synonym for the 'unconscious'. The Indian *avacetana* and the Freudian *preconscious* are not identical or even similar too. It is to be emphasized here that the Indian unconscious and the Freudian unconscious are different.

The Freudian unconscious is a domain of the psyche encompassing the repressed id functions, the primitive impulses, and desires, the memory, images and wishes that are too anxiety-provoking to be accepted into consciousness. The Freudian unconscious is assumed to be populated by two varieties of psychic entities, those that were once conscious but had been exiled from awareness and those that were never in consciousness.

A clarification is necessary for the expression 'exiled from consciousness'. The Freudian concept of 'repression' has a relevance here. It is a hypothesized mental process or operation that functions to protect the individual from ideas, impulses and memories which would produce anxiety, apprehension or guilt, were they to become conscious. It is an ego function. Firstly, primitive, forbidden impulses are blocked and prevented from ever reaching consciousness. Secondly, anxiety-producing mental content is forcefully removed from consciousness and prevented from re-emerging. Thirdly, elements that might serve to remind the person of that which has been previously repressed are themselves repressed. The first two types are known as primary repression; the third type is known as secondary repression. Any type of repression is a form of 'psychological defence'. It is a process whereby an individual 'expels' from his consciousness thoughts, recollections and emotional experiences unacceptable to him, and transfers them to the sphere of the *unconscious*. Nonetheless, what is repressed is not deactivated but continues to have a lively existence in the unconscious, now and then making itself felt through projections in disguised symbolic form in dreams, parapraxes, psychoneurosis and anxiety and fear with no *apparent* reasons.

What has been said by Freud on repression is acceptable to Indian depth psychology. It is a fact that *ahaṅkāra* throws any feeling — hostile, mentally agonising and anxiety-provoking — to the subconscious and the unconscious (both of Indian types) where it is buried. It is, however, to be noted that *ahaṅkāra* and Freud's ego are not identical, although they are apparently similar. Freud does not recognize anything like a subtle body or causal body. He does not accept the doctrine of re-incarnation and the doctrine of *karma*. According to his psychological theory, the psyche of an individual is formed subsequent to his conception in the mother's womb and/or in the post-natal life. His psyche vanishes consequent to his demise. The ancient Western concept of the psyche was identical to the soul. Freud rejected the soul. His psychology is atheistic. He uses the terms 'psyche', 'id' 'ego', 'superego' and 'unconscious' to describe some psychological phenomena. These are not anatomical structures. They have no locations. They cannot be identified with any structure of the brain or the spinal cord. On the contrary, *buddhi, ahaṅkāra, manas* and *citta* are subtle structures in the subtle body, and the *karmāśaya* which is the unconscious in the Indian depth psychology is a subtle structure in the causal body.

Ahaṅkāra is self-cognising, self-preserving and self-defending. It gives the I-sense and cognises the 'I' *versus* the not 'I' . Any virus, bacteria, protozoa, foreign body — living or non-living, on entering the body, is immediately recognized as not-I by the *ahaṅkāra*. Not only does it take cognizance of the not-I, but also it takes action to fight against the not-I and to defend the 'I'.

What has been said in the preceding paragraph pertains to biological phenomena.. Similar is the case with psychological phenomena, especially with reference to self-defence. And repression is one of the multiple mechanisms that the *ahaṅkāra* adopts for self-defence. In Freud's theory, both ego and superego have the conscious, the preconscious and the unconscious in unequal proportions. In Indian depth psychology, however, the ego and the superego are not in possession of the unconscious.

What is the nature of the superego in Indian depth psychology? The *buddhi* which is a subtle structure in the subtle body is the superego. All the mental structures in Indian psychology are insentient as such. But they are rendered sentient by the reflection of the Self (or the self) that is the fundamental Consciousness. Induction takes place due to the proximity of the all-pervading Self. In reality, the *buddhi*, lighted and made transparent by the *jīvātmā*, is the superego.

Freud's id and the unconscious of Indian psychology are not identical. There is no id's equivalent in Indian depth psychology. Here we would give a brief description of the id, the ego and the superego of Freud before we accept or reject his id.

In the Freudian tripartite model of mind, id, ego and superego are the three components of personality. Each of these has its own functions; but the three interact to govern behaviour.

The id is the original source of personality, present in the newborn infant, from which the ego and the superego later develop. It is the primitive, animalistic, instinctual element. The major instinctual drives are sex and aggression. It provides the energy source (libido) for the operation of all the three systems. Its libidinous energy demands immediate satisfaction. It is the deepest component of the psyche, the true unconscious. Being entirely self-contained and isolated from the world about it, it is bent on achieving its own ends. It operates on the pleasure principle and is the ultimate hedonist. It endeavours to avoid pain and obtain pleasure. It seeks immediate gratification of primitive, pleasure-seeking impulses regardless of external situations and moral standards of the parents and the society.

The id attempts to reduce tension by forming a mental image or hallucination of its desires. It thereby does wish-fulfilment. Freud believes that we conjure up objects and events in our dreams to fulfil some impulses of the id in disguised way through symbols. He also thinks that psychotic patients do their wish-fulfilment through hallucinations, although without any consideration of realities.

Freud theorises that the id attempts to reduce tension and anxiety by expressing the impulse in disguised form so as to avoid social disapproval and condemnation by the supergo. This is one defence mechanism. Repression which has already been discussed is another defence mechanism. Through it, the impulse is pushed out of awareness into the unconscious.

In contrast with the unrealistic demands of the id, the ego obeys the reality principle. Its approach is realistic and logical. It delays gratification of the id instincts until conditions are appropriate. It exerts restraining influence on the id. It is the executive of the personality. It mediates between the demands of the id, the realities of the situations and the demands of the superego.

The superego is the component of the psyche that is the watch dog for values and morals of the society as taught to the child by the parents and others. It judges whether an action is right or wrong in accordance with the morals taught. It strives for perfection. It develops in response to parental rewards for *good* actions and punishments for *bad* actions.

The id and the superego are diametrically on opposite poles. The ego mediates between them. Usually in the normal person, the three components of personality work as a team, and such a person produces integrated behaviour. Sometimes, however, they are at loggerheads with one another, and in such situations, the personality is disintegrated and the behaviour becomes abnormal.

It has already been said that the id is the first component that develops in the child first. This happens in the first six years after birth. Freud calls these periods psychosexual stages. During each stage, the pleasure-seeking impulses of the id focus on a particular region of the body and on activities of that region.

The first year of life is the oral stage, during which the infant derives pleasure from sucking by putting the thumb or anything else into the mouth. The second year of life is the anal stage, during which gratification is derived from withholding or expelling faeces. The phallic stage spreads from about age three to age six. During this period, children begin to derive pleasure from fondling their genitals.

Freud's notion of infantile sexuality, just described, is the foundation of his psychology and psychoanalytic theory.

Freudianism becomes vaguely adultomorphic in assigning sexuality as the motivator of man throughout the life. Freud has become a pan-sexualist, for assigning a sexual base to all sensuality, all pleasure and all sorts of human behaviour.

We do not agree to the pan-sexuality of Freud. We also do not agree to his concept of infantile sexuality. We do not believe in the existence of Freud's id, especially with reference to its formation during the infanthood and its sovereign influence on the total behaviour in the adulthood.

Instincts are not as bad as we think. They are ontogenically and phylogenically protective, well-meaning, necessary and desirable provisions provided by the Provident. The baby's sucking instinct is a feeding instinct for ontogenic survival. It is not a sexual instinct. Freud's so-called anal stage of psychosexual development with regard to 'the gratification derived from withholding or expelling faeces' may be an instinctual performance of the *aśvinī mudrā* (equine gesture) to avoid constipation. We reject the view that the infant has anything to do with sex.

We do recognize the sex-instinct in animals and man. It is a programmed and in-built phyolgenic instinct in life to avoid the extinction of the species by ensuring reproduction. It manifests prior to or on the onset of puberty and wanes subsequent to menopause in females and after fifty years of age in males (the declining phase dragging to the age of senility). The sex instinct operates in unison with and in consonance with the development and functioning of the endocrine system of the body. The effective functioning of the sex-instinct is dependent upon the secretion of the sex-hormones in a balanced way. During Freud's time, neuro-chemistry, hormone-chemistry, neuro-transmitters, gene-chemistry (molecular biology) and other aspects of biochemistry and psychochemistry did not develop much. He speculated id and the connected infantile sexuality and the unconscious. He built his suprastructure of psychology on a vacuum foundation.

Pātañjala Yoga Darśanam does admit the role of pleasure and pain in the psychology of animals and human beings.[79] Man does that which gives pleasure. He tries to avoid that which is painful. The preponderance of sensitive nerve-endings on the lips, in the anal region and the genitals are responsible for the genesis of physical pleasure, when handled or otherwise made functional. The infant may experience the pleasure as a result of trial and error or as a result of the working of the feeding instinct such as sucking. These infantile behaviours are not to be necessarily tagged to sex-psychology in the infant.

Patañjali enlists five *kleśas* (hindrances).[80] These are *avidyā* (the *saṁskāras* deposited in the unconscious), *asmitā* (the *saṁskāras* out of clinging to the 'I'), *rāga* (the *saṁskāras* out of seeking for pleasure), *dveṣa* (the *saṁskāras* out of the painful experiences of life) and *abhiniveśa* (the *saṁskāras* out of clinging to life or out of fear of death).

Thus, the Yoga psychology gives priority to the unconcious by listing it first among the five *kleśas*. It also does lay importance on the ego by listing it as the second one. But the Yoga *asmitā* refers to the *ahaṅkāra* in the subtle body and not to the descriptive term in Freudian psychology. It may be noted that the terms *buddhi, ahaṅkāra, manas* and *citta* in the Sāṅkhya, Yoga and Vedānta are not merely descriptive terms. They are not attributive and functional words only. They are subtle structures with specific functions in the subtle body. They are component organs in the subtle, inner mental complex (*antaḥkaraṇa*).

79. *PYD*, II.7 (*sukhānuśayī rāgaḥ*); II.8 (*duḥkhānuśayī dveṣaḥ*).

80. *Ibid.*, II.3 (*avidyāsmitārāgadveṣābhiniveśāḥ kleśāḥ*).

The Fredudian id has nothing good in it. Sexuality, libido, aggression and repressed feelings are the main constituents of id. It forms the main component of the Freudian unconscious that affects the conscious in a profound way. Anything repressed in the unconscious is not buried for ever; neither is it annihilated. It stays at the bottom of the psyche in its depth and troubles the surface of the psyche or the awareness in bizarre ways.

The unconscious of Indian psychology is structurally and functionally different, however. Before we specify the yogic unconscious, we would dilate the concepts of *saṁskāra, saṁskāra-piṇḍa, vāsanā, karmāśaya* and *vāsanāśaya*.

The Conscious and the Unconscious of Yoga-Vedānta

With reference to awareness, the Yoga psychology classifies mind into two divisions, namely, the conscious and the unconscious.

Three types of mental datas are present in the conscious mind (*cetana manas*). The datas of which we are normally aware in our wakeful state belong to the surface conscious mind. The datas which escape our awareness momentarily and come to the surface with some difficulty, or with some associative technique, or spontaneously at some other time, belong to the sub-surface conscious mind. This mind is equivalent to the preconscious of Freud and is the *prākcetana* of Yoga-Vedānta. The subconscious (*avacetana*) of Yoga-Vedānta is the bottom layer of the conscious mind. The datas of the subconscious do not easily rise to the surface level in our wakeful state. They, however, play an important role in our dreaming, while we are asleep. The mind, in dreams, makes use of the stored data of the subconscious, edits them and creatively synthesizes events which we call dreams. Less often, the datas of the unconscious are also used. Some dreams are just the creations of the sleeping mind. Some others are mentally created for wish-fulfilment which could not be attained in the real life. A few dreams are premonitory too.

The conscious, the preconscious and the subconscious datas latently lie in the *manas* or the *manomaya kośa* (mental sheath). The site of memory (*smṛti*) is the mental sheath (*manas*).

The unconscious of Yoga-Vedānta has its site in the causal body (*kāraṇa śarīra*) or the blissful sheath (*ānandamaya kośa*). This site is known as the *karmāśaya* (resorvoir of karmic *saṁskāras*). The natures of *smṛti* and *saṁskāra* are similar,[81] with a single difference, of course. Whereas the site of *smṛti* is the mental sheath, that of *saṁskāras* is both the mental and the blissful sheaths. The memory site is in the subtle body and the site of the *vāsanā saṁskāra* is in the causal body. It is, however, to be emphasized that both *smṛtis* and *saṁskāras* cannot exist without sites (*āśaya*).[82]

Saṁskāras are stored cumulatively through many births, the past ones and the present.[83] Freud does not accept the doctrine of reincarnation and, hence, his unconscious is limited to the present life only. Furthermore, the Freudian tripartite mind is non-locational. Freud does not recognize any body other than the gross. His id, ego and superego do not reside in any anatomical structure of the nervous system or any other system of the gross body.

The term *saṁskāra* has been mentioned in Pātañjala Yoga a number of times.[84] The latent deposits in our subconscious and unconscious mind are called *saṁskāras* in the Yoga-Vedānta

81. *PYD*, IV.9 (*jātideśakālavyavahitānāmapyānantaryaṁ smṛtisaṁskāra-yorekarūpatvāt*).

82. *BSŚB*, II.2.30 (*saṁskārāśca nāśrayamantareṇāvakalpante*).

83. *PYD*, II.12; IV.8-11.

84. *Ibid.*, I.18; I.50; II.15; III.9-10; III.18; IV.9; IV.27.

psychology. All *vāsanās* are *saṁskāras*, but all *saṁskāras* are not *vāsanās*. The storage of *saṁskāras* is roughly likened to that of data in a magnetic tape, although the exact mechanism of the encoding, storage and retrieval of the mental data is not yet known to us. All the stored *saṁskāras* in the subconscious and unconscious mind of an individual are given a collective name *saṁskāra-piṇḍa*.

Saṁskāras can be typed. These types are mainly three in number, namely, cognitive (*jñānaja*), affective (*kleśaja*) and conative (*kriyāja*).[85]

The cognitive *saṁskāras* are the mental datas that are received through the five *akliṣṭa vṛttis*[86] (non-affective modes), namely, *pramāṇa*[87] (sense-percetion), *viparyaya*[88] (*mithyā-jñāna* or illusory knowledge), *vikalpa*[89] (hallucinatory knowledge), *nidrā*[90] (dream knowledge) and *smṛti*[91] (knowledge from memory). They are imprinted on the mental sheath of the subtle body.

The conative (*kriyāja*) *saṁskāras* have their roots in the volitional activities of a person. Some of them are imprinted in the mental sheath and, thus, reside in the subtle body. Some others are imprinted in the causal body and, thus, become part of the unconscious. Which ones of them form the conscious (including the preconscious and the subconscious) and which ones form the unconscious are dependent upon the qualitative and quantitative effects they exert on the affliction or non-

85. *PYDVB*, II.15.
86. *PYD*, I.5-6.
87. *Ibid.*, I.7.
88. *Ibid.*, I.8.
89. *Ibid.*, I.9.
90. *Ibid.*, I.10.
91. *Ibid.*, I.11.

affliction of the mind. The non-afflictive mental impressions stay in the subtle body; the afflictive ones go to the causal body. To cite some examples, the volitional attempt to rape a woman or murder a man generates *saṁskāras* to be imprinted in the causal body. The volition for becoming a good poet or for discovering an effective drug for the cure of cancer generates *saṁskāras* to be stored in the subtle body.

The affective (*kleśaja*) *saṁskāras* are generated by the five *kleśas*[92] (afflictions), namely, *avidyā*[93] (lack of right knowledge), *asmitā*[94] (egoity, I-sense or *ahaṅkāra*), *rāga*[95] (passion and craving for pleasure due to excessive attachment and strong desire), *dveṣa*[96] (aversion due to painful experiences) and *abhiniveśa*[97] (clinging to life and fear of death). These *saṁskāras* become the latent deposits in the causal body (*kāraṇa śarīra*); they reside in the *ānandamaya kośa* (blissful sheath) in which the individual self (*jīvātmā*) sits. The *saṁskāras* stored in the causal body are the *vāsanās*[98] and the site of their storage is called the *vāsanāśaya*. All the *vāsanās* printed and stored in the blissful sheath or the causal body form the unconscious of the Yoga-Vedānta psychology.

The cognitive (*jñānaja*) *saṁskāras* do not leave any latent deposits in the causal body. The afflictive sub-type of the conative (*kriyāja*) *saṁskāras* leave latent deposits in the causal body whereas the non-afflictive conative ones do not. All the affective (*kleśaja*) *saṁskāras* use the causal body as their

92. *PYD*, II.3.
93. *Ibid.*, II.4-5.
94. *Ibid.*, II.6.
95. *Ibid.*, II.7.
96. *Ibid.*, II.8.
97. *Ibid.*, II.9.
98. *Ibid.*, IV.8; *BSŚB*, II.2.30 (*api ca vāsanā nāma saṁskāraviśeṣāḥ*).

reservoir. All *saṁskāras* that lie in the causal body are *vāsanās* that are not easily available to the conscious. Notwithstanding this fact of the non-availability of the deeply buried *vāsanās* (the unconscious) for the conscious, the former does not remain as an inert mass and does affect the latter in a profound way.

The Meaning of *Karma* in Yoga-Vedānta

The literal meaning of *karma* is 'action' or 'work'. However, in Yoga-Vedānta, it has another technical meaning. The *vāsanā* prints in the causal body are technically known as *karma*. The area of the causal body that serves as the reservoir of *karmas* is called *kārmāśaya* (the word *āsaya* meaning 'reservoir'). In the *Pātañjala Yoga-Darśana*, we come across the words *karma*[99] and *kārmāśaya*[100] a number of times.

What generates *karma* ? How does it behave as a seed (*bīja*) ? What is its ground (*bhūmi*) where the seed lies in a latent condition ? How does the seed germinate ? How are the seeds or the roots of the sprout burnt ? These topics will be discussed now.

The five *kleśas* (afflictions/hindrances), namely, *avidyā* (ignorance, or knowledge of *X* as *Y*), *asmitā* (I-sense, the agency for self-centredness), *rāga* (passionate desire for pleasure), *dveṣa* (aversion or anxiety to escape from pain) and *abhiniveśa* (clinging to life and fear of death), generate *karma*.[101] Secondly, any conative (*kriyāja*) *saṁskāra* that re-inforces *kleśas* and synergistically works with them generates *karma*. Actions associated with lustful desire and ever unquenched thirst (*kāma* or *tṛṣṇā*, Buddha's *tanhā*), anger and especially mixed with

99. *PYD*, IV.7-8.

100. *Ibid.*, II.12-13; IV.6; *PYDVB*, I.5; II.13; II.15; IV.6; IV.30.

101. *Ibid.*, II.12.

violence and aggressiveness (*krodha, hiṁsā*), greed (*lobha*), delusion (*moha*), pride and arrogance (*mada*) and envy (*mātsarya*) are factors favourable for the germination of *karma*. Vyāsa, the commentator of the *Pātañjala Yoga-Darśanam*, has enumerated a number of factors that generate diverse types of *karmāśaya* such as *rāgaja* (generated by passionate attachment to sensual pleasure), *dveṣaja* (generated by painful experiences), *mohakṛta* (caused by infatuation), *lobhakṛta* (caused by greed), *hiṁsākṛta* (caused by violence), etc.[102] No *karmāśaya* can be formed without *kleśa*s and rebirth is not possible without *karmāśaya*.

The actions of *yogī*s are non-productive of either good or bad *karma*s. They are non-white (*aśukla*) and non-black (*akṛṣṇa*). The actions of non-*yogī*s are of three types, namely *śukla* (literally white, standing for actions of virtues), *kṛṣṇa* (black, standing for actions of vices) and mixed (both good and bad).[103] Here lies an important difference between the Freudian Unconscious and the Unconscious of the Yoga-Vedānta. Everything of the Freudian Unconscious is bad. It is constituted mainly by infantile sexuality and repressed ideas. There is nothing good in it. In contrast, the Unconscious of the Yoga-Vedānta contains karmic imressions that are good, bad and good and bad, We may take a couple of examples of good *karma*s. A social worker has devoted his whole life for the uplift of the poorer sections of people. He is not fully satisfied with the results obtained. He has a strong desire to continue the work and get success thereof. He expires before completing the work. His Unconscious (*karmāśaya*) would contain some *karma* that is *śukla* in nature and unknowingly he would develop strong propensity for doing social work in his next life. We may take a second example. A poet gets immense pleasure in

---

102. *PYDVB*, II.15.

103. *PYD*, IV.7.

composing poems. He desires and strives for becoming a still better poet. His Unconscious (*kārmāśaya*) would contain *karma* that is *śukla* in nature. In his next life, he would unknowingly develop strong propensity for becoming a poet.

The *yogī*, through the practice of special techniques of *yoga*, burns or uproots the *kleśas*, and erases his good as well as bad (*kuśalākuśala*) *karmāśaya*. Such a *yogī* becomes liberated even though he is living (*jīvanmukta*).[104] He has still *dhyānaja citta* (mind generated by meditation). But this mind is devoid of *kārmāśaya*.[105]

The *kārmāśaya*, located in the causal body or the blissful sheath, may be compared with the ground. Vyāsa uses the term *citta-bhūmi* (the ground of mind).[106] The five *kleśas* serve as the roots (*mūla*). The *vāsanā-saṁskāras* are the seeds (*bīja*). So long as the seeds are unburnt and the roots are not completely uprooted and destroyed, rebirth with transmigration of the self is inevitable.[107]

Any *karma* must come to fruition, resulting in birth, length of life and kinds of experiences of pleasure and pain.[108] In this context, Patañjali uses the word *vipāka* for the 'fruition of the *karmas*'.

Repression is an important concept in Freudian depth psychology. It is a mental process or operation that functions to protect the individual from ideas, impulses and memories which would produce anxiety, apprehension or guilt were they to become conscious. Feelings that are unpleasant are thrown down to the Unconscious and deeply buried there. This process

---

104. *PYD*, IV.30.
105. *Ibid.*, IV.6.
106. *PYDVB*, I.24.
107. *Ibid.*, II.13.
108. *PYD*, II.13.

operates at an unconscious level. Its very operation lies outside of conscious awareness. What is repressed, however, is not deactivated but continues to have a lively existence at the unconscious level, making itself felt through projections in disguised symbolic form in dreams, parapraxes and psychoneuroses.

What has been said about repression in the foregoing paragraph can be accepted in general by the Yoga-Vedānta psychology, with one salient difference, of course. The unpleasant feelings are repressed by the *ahaṅkāra* (*almost* equivalent to the ego), outside the awareness of the individual, to the Subconscious (*avacetana*) and not to the Unconscious (*acetana*). It has already been pointed out that the Unconscious is part of the causal body whereas the Subconscious is part of the subtle body. The Conscious, the Preconscious and the Subconscious are components of the conscious mind and all of them are located in the *manomaya kośa* (mental sheath) which is part of the subtle body. Memory (*smṛti*) is located in the *manas* of this sheath. It is likened to the sedimentary rock with many stratifications. The bottommost strata is the Subconscious. The surface strata is the Conscious. A very thin strata lies beneath the Conscious; this is the Preconscious. The analogy is not fully correct, however. Whereas fresh sedimentation does not occur at the bottom level of the rock, repression materializes at the bottom level of the conscious mind (the Subconscious) due to the subtle nature of the mind *vis-a-vis* the gross nature of the sedimentary soil. Freud does not recognize the Subconscious. His tripartite mind consists of the Conscious, the Preconscious (the Foreconscious) and the Unconscious. Unpleasant feelings are repressed into the Unconscious in Freudian psychology.

With this much comparative discussion on the depth psychology of Sigmund Freud and that of the Yoga-Vedānta, we would present the psychoanalytic theory of Freud as compared and contrasted with the therapeutic theory of *Yoga-Nidrā*.

Freudian Psychoanalysis

Psychoanalysis is a theory of human behaviour. It has a set of techniques for exploring the underlying motivations of human behaviour. It is a method of treatment of various mental disorders. The core components of psychoanalysis are free association, rich interpretation and transference.

Freudianism has a focus upon the Unconscious, specially the role of unconscious processes as motivators of behaviour. It lays importance on the sexual and the aggressive human behaviour, regarded by it as the basic biological progenitors of behaviour. According to Freud, all behaviour stems from two opposing groups of instincts, namely, the life instincts and death instincts. The energy of the life instincts is libido. The death instincts may be directed inward or outward. In the former case, the result may be suicide or other self-destructive activities. In the latter case, the result is aggression on others. Thus, Freud believed in two basic human motives — sex and aggression. Freudianism has a strong presumption that early childhood experiences are the causes of later adult behaviours. It has an abiding concern with the cognitive and the symbolic. Freudian psychoanalysis rummages down through the layers of the psyche to seek understanding and explanation. The psychoanalytic therapy is meant for producing changes in behaviour, thought and feeling.

Freud infers the unconscious motives from behaviour expressed. Wishes and impulses we are unaware of are often expressed in dreams. Unconscious mannerisms and slips of speech may reveal motives hidden in the Unconscious.

Symptoms of mental illness are often shown to serve the unconscious needs.

Free association is a psychoanalytical technique to discover the unconscious impulses and conflicts. By this technique, mental patients are asked to let their thoughts run free, without censorship, reporting them as and when they occur. For the flow of thoughts without inhibition, they are advised to relax on a couch and look away from the psychoanalyst. The patient goes on reporting. The analyst detects unexpected trains of thought, sudden memory lapses and unusual statements that provide cluses to unravel the patient's Unconscious where his repressed thoughts, feelings and conflicts lie.

Freud's another pathway to reach the Unconscious is dream analysis. He is of the opinion that id urges and unconscious conflicts push for expression when we are asleep. This expression is not direct, but through dreams by the use of disguised forms. Many analysts believe that we use certain common symbols in dreams to stand for particular ideas. In spite of this commonness, the use of symbols in dreams has many subjective elements. It is to be admitted that dream interpretation is a difficult art.

Psychoanalysis aims at bringing unconscious conflicts to the individual's awareness. The analyst interprets the patient's reportings of free association and his dreams. Thereby the analyst diagnoses the unconscious conflicts of the patient to whom the diagnosis is revealed. The defence mechanisms that the patient has been using to control anxiety are explained to him/her. The analyst advises the patient to deal with the problem in a more realistic and adaptive way.

Critique of Psychoanalysis

It is not claimed that Freudian psychoanalysis has everything wrong in it. Nevertheless, the fact that the foundation of Freudian psychoanalysis is very shaky has to be recognized.

The Freudian Unconscious, which is not a structure, neither anatomical nor physiological, is a psychological, descriptive term only. It is formed by id in infanthood. It is unscientific to speak of store of ideas and feelings without reference to any location and any structure.

Human behaviour is based on a number of factors rather than the life instincts (sex and libido) and the death instincts (aggressiveness). The *karma*s cumulatively collected through the past and the present lives minus those already undergone fruition (*vipāka*) exert a tremendous effect on the psychology of an individual person. His genotype inherited from his parents has a sizeable effect on his psychological behaviours. The environment to which the individual is exposed *throughout* the life plays a significant role in shaping his behavioural pattern. In this context, 'environment' is a comprehensive term that includes a number of sub-factors. The childhood nurture (even the intra-uterine nourishment of the foetus and the mental condition of the mother in the intra-uterine life of the foetus), the parental relations, the family conditions, education and training received, influences of the society, religious influences, cultural milieu, political influences, friends and company one gets, marital relationship, job relationship, events in own life and the lives of kith and kin, events of success and failure in one's life, events of fulfilment and frustration and many others are covered by the term 'environment' for the present discussion. Freud's claim that only infantile sexuality and aggressiveness are the only factors that shape the adult behaviour through the Unconscious is summarily rejected. We do not agree with him on the point that there is anything like infantile sexuality.

The psychological process of repression is a fact. But it is not limited to childhood only. This process is operative throughout the life. In the Freudian scheme, all childhood unpleasant feelings and ideas are thrown to the Unconscious and deeply buried there. According to the Yoga-Vedānta, unpleasant feelings and ideas, throughout the life, are buried in the deeper strata of the Conscious (the Subconscious). Mental prints, deep or surface, are subtle components of the *manas* which is in the mental sheath (*manomaya kośa*), a component of the subtle body (not the causal body).

Freudian psychoanalysis has some limitations. The subject may not be able to recollect and portray the Unconscious. He may not co-operate with the analyst. Hence, is the genesis of Freud's 'transference'. In such situations, Freud's technique of free association is very much constrained.

Dream analysis is a technique which is not *very* dependable. The subject may not be able to recollect the details of the dreams and correctly reproduce. His use of symbols in dreams may have much subjective meanings. The analyst's interpretation may not be correct too. Moreover, most of the dreams do not originate from the *karmāśaya* and most dreams may not be indicators of the psychopathology of an individual.

It is a fact that some dreams have their roots in the *karmāśaya* and also in the Subconscious of the Yoga-Vedānta. It is also a fact that some dreams are premonitory. When a person has some unfulfilled desire imprinted in the *karmāśaya* or in the Subconscious, and it is not feasible to fulfil that desire in the real life, the ego (*ahaṅkāra*) tries to create that phantasy in dreams. It imagines a world of its own, creates it and enacts a drama for the wish-fulfilment.

Most dreams, however are neutral to psychopathology. They may not be meaningful with special reference to the

Unconscious and also they may not be premonitory. Every night, during sleep, we dream. Most of the dreams are forgotten. Only a few dreams are remembered and they too may be partially rather than wholly.

Why do we dream ? Some causes of dreams have already been given. Most dreams, however, are created by the *manas* and the *ahaṅkāra* innocently, just because the *manas* is reluctant to be idle and anxious to create events out of the data printed in the Subconscious and the Unconscious. The mind and the ego are not inactive while we are asleep. They cannot use our conscious apparatus in our sleeping state. The external sense-doors are closed. No information reach the *manas* and the ego from the external world in the sleeping state. In such a state, the ego uses the memory store present in the *manas* (*manomaya kośa*) of the subtle body for getting mental data which are synthesized from piece-meal state, censored, edited and composed. Thus, is created a mental drama in which the ego itself participates as an actor/actress. The mental data are collected from different strata of the memory, including the bottom layer called the Subconscious. The data are joined together in different permutations and combinations to create the drama which may be a comedy or a tragedy, a drama pleasant and enjoyable or terrifying and distasteful.

The ego can also use some latent deposits in the *karmāśaya* for the mental drama enacted during dreaming. These datas may belong to experiences of this life or of previous lives. But one significant note to be made is this that nothing unexperienced in this life or previous lives can be the components of the dream story.[109] Of course, the component may not be factually true sense-data. Anything unreal, read, listened, believed and culturally imbibed, might have been

109. *PYD*, I.11 (*anubhūtaviṣayāsampramoṣaḥ smṛtiḥ*).

imprinted in the Unconscious and the Subconscious. Such fictitious datas that have already been printed in the mind can be components of the dream-story.

Freud's Unconscious is the Subconscious of the Yoga-Vedānta. The Unconscious of the latter is the *karmāśaya* that holds karmic impressions. Psychoanalysis can hardly probe into the karmic impressions and bring them to the surface level of the Conscious. At best, psychoanalysis may be able to raise the dormant subconscious impressions to the conscious level. It may further be noted here that both the Unconscious and the Subconscious of the Yoga-Vedānta hold latent mental deposits of divine (*daiva*) and demoniac (*āsura*) nature, in varying ratios, of course. Persons possess qualities of altruism, kindness, forgiveness, sympathy, love, etc. Only sexuality and violence (aggressiveness) are not the only mental traits. Sex plays an important role in life. But it is not everything in life. There are persons who have sublimated sex and have lived a super-conscious life. Vyāsa's Bhīṣma in the *Mahābhārata* was not a neurotic. Even the devil has a conscience. The most die-hard criminal whose mind seems to harbour 100 per cent hatred, cruelty, aggressiveness and violence has some eclipsed love, affection, kindness and softness. Sigmund Freud, the great psychologist, did not take these facts into cognizance.

Psychoanalysis and the subsequent psychological counselling provide an important tool for psychotherapy. But this tool becomes ineffective in erasing, uprooting and burning the seeds and roots of the *karmāśaya* that prepares the seed-bed for the psycho-frame of an individual.

Very often the hostile and unfavourable environment of an individual cannot be changed. He or she has to live in the conditions imposed on him/her. In such a situation, psychoanalysis has very little to do. On the contrary, the Yoga-Vedānta has definitely effective methods that can enable the individual to cope with the adversities. If and when one cannot avoid the tempest, one has to learn how to live with it.

The Yoga-Vedānta prepares the mind to *enjoy* by renunciation[110] and to always have full contentment.[111] Such a mind is not affected by frustration. It is ever full and never empty, partially or fully.[112] In the midst of physical cyclone, the *yogī*'s mind is still and undisturbed. It is attuned to be free from contradictions and conflicts (*dvandva*).[113] It has equanimity over opposites like pleasure and pain, success and failure.[114] Success does not make it overjoyous; neither does failure make it distressed and depressed.[115] Such a yogic mind is prepared not to be affected by success or failure and by opposing conflicts.

The acceptance of the fundamental positivity in the Yoga-Vedānta helps avoiding or coping with the negativity in life. The *yogī* is supersaturated with that positive which is the Reality. A supersaturated yogic mind does not allow a partial or a total vacuum or even a low pressure. Hence, the question of the occurrence of a mental storm is ruled out. Amid physical storms, the *yogī* remains undisturbed in his mind. He has a support (*ālambana*) which is infinitely strong. And the support and he are not *essentially* different. This support is absent in Freudian psychology.

THE PSYCHOLOGICAL BASIS OF YOGA-NIDRĀ

Unlike the psychoanalytic theory in which conflicts of the

---

110. *IU*, 1 (*tena tyaktena bhuñjīthā*).
111. *PYD*, II.32.
112. *BG*, II.70.
113. *Ibid.*, IV.22; VII.28.
114. *Ibid.*, II.38; II.50; II.55-56; II.72.
115. *Ibid.*, V.20.

Unconscious are brought to the Conscious, *yoga-nidrā* does not make any such attempt. Of course, there are yogic techniques by practising which an adept and perfected *yogī* can get a direct vision of the *saṁskāras* imprinted in the mind of the *yogī* himself and also in that of any other person.[116] *Yoga-nidrā* can be practised by persons who may not be adept in *yoga* and there is no indispensability to know the Unconscious and bring its conflicts to awareness in order that benefits from *yoga-nidrā* may be obtained.

Yoga-nidrā tries to print an idea in the Subconscious or the Unconscious. In special situations, it also tries to erase an idea out of the Subconscious or the Unconscious. The former action is positive; the latter action is negative. A *saṅkalpa* (resolve) is printed. By repeated practice, the printing is reinforced so that the *saṅkalpa* is recorded in the Subconscious or the Unconscious or both. In the process of erasure, an undesirable mental print, already nested in the Subconscious or the Unconscious, is removed through the fresh printing of a desirable *saṅkalpa* as a substitute of the already printed undesirable idea. In this process, the already nested idea is erased first and the new idea is printed next. Of course, both these functions take place synchronously. It is a compound process of erasing-cum-printing.

The waking state is not very conducive to the receptivity of the Subconscious or the Unconscious. In the state of deep sleep (*suṣupti*), it is not practicable to repeat the *saṅkalpa* and stamp it on the Subconscious or the Unconscious. One's awareness is not operative in the sleeping state. Hence, an ideal state is created by a special technique of *yoga-nidrā.* This ideal *yoga-nidrā* state is neither wakeful nor sleeping. It is a state intermediate between the waking and the sleeping ones.

---

116. *PYD*, III.18-19.

It is a twilight area, similar to the junction between night and day in the early morning or between the sunset and the evening, when the sun is below the western horizon.

That the Subconscious and the Unconscious profoundly influence the Conscious is recognized by the theory of *yoga-nidrā*. In a *hidden* way, the *ahaṅkāra* (ego) influenses the conscious mind and the organs of the body by using the *saṅkalpa* stored in the Subconscious of the *manas*. The latter action, that is, influencing the organs, tissues and cells of the body to alter their anatomical, physiological, biochemical, immunological and even genetic functions to the desired advantages of the hoslistic organism, is done in a hidden way without the mediation of the Conscious.

The ordinary person's behaviour is very much influenced by pleasure and pain. He has passion (*rāga*) for pleasure. He has aversion (*dveṣa)* to pain. To get rid of some bad habits, such as smoking, alcoholism, drug-addiction, etc., *yoga-nidrā* makes use of aversion therapy which is designed to make a subject averse to an existing habit.

The Sanskrit word *preya* means 'pleasurable'. A person is instinctually attracted towards that which is *preya*. But, what is *preya* may not necessarily be *śreya* (good, useful and beneficial). It is ideal to do what is both *preya* and *śreya*. But, in the absence of this ideal condition, what is *śreya* is to be preferred to what is *preya*.[117] This is a very difficult task for individuals who have strong propensities (*pravṛtti*) for indulgence and sensual gratification. Some of them can sublimate if they are exposed to favourable situations. They may divert their energy of the primitive impulse into a culturally higher activity. *Yoga-nidrā*, by its repeated *saṅkalpa*-therapy, can inject the idea of sublimation by which the subject

117. *KTU*, I.2.1-2.

overcomes the gravitating influence of *pravṛtti* (strong propensity for attachment and indulgence).

TECHNIQUE FOR THE INDUCTION OF THE YOGA-NIDRĀ STATE

To induce the *yoga-nidrā* state, the person is to lie in *śavāsana*. He closes his eyes, relaxes his body and mind. How does this help ? The *manas* receives no visual stimuli. The external world is mostly cut off. A tense body and active mental thoughts keep the *manas* over-occupied. Relaxation of body and mind helps relax the *manas*. When the afferent pathway to the *manas* is *mostly* blocked, the efferent pathway from the *manas* to different parts of the body and the external world remains still, without traffic. By this, the Conscious is *almost* inactivated. If the Conscious becomes active, the Subconscious becomes passive, and *vice versa*. This first technique, described here, may be summarized as 'blocking the afferent pathway to the Conscious'.

The second technique may be given the name 'destabilizing the Conscious through gliding and sliding'. The *manas* is allowed to glide and slide with reference to space and time. This movement is smooth, rapid in a sequential pattern. By this, the *manas* shifts locationally and temporally. This is what we call 'shifting of consciousness'. In the temporal type of the shifting of consciousness, the stream of time flows with changing scenarios.

The next exercise in the process of the flow of consciousness involves variation in visual images of objects like flowers, trees or tree-leaves, animals and birds. The next one is the shifting of consciousness from scenario to scenario, pertaining to Nature.

By the practice of these techniques, the conscious component of the *manas* is brought to a state which is half-awake and half-sleepy. This is a state which is intermediate between the state of wakefulness and the dream state. This is what we call the *yoga-nidrā* state in which the Subconscious component of the *manas* acquires enhanced receptivity to suggestion or auto-suggestion. And the *saṅkalpa* in *yoga-nidrā* is an auto-suggestion. An active or hyperactive conscious mind acts like dirt on a mirror. Once this dirt is removed, the underlying subconscious receives the light of suggestion or auto-suggestion.

SAṄKALPA (RESOLVE)

The *saṅkalpa* should be a simple sentence, not too lengthy, with straightforward meaning. It is a command and, hence, should preferably be in imperative mood. Any language that appeals the heart most should be used. The sentence may also be affirmative or negative in some special cases. In the case of 'do', an affirmative resolve is used. In the case of 'don't', a negative resolve is used. Taking the case into consideration and deeply thinking over it, the sentence should be constructed judiciously. The *saṅkalpa* is not normally changed during the course of the auto-therapy. Occasionally, two or three sentences may be used for a single *saṅkalpa*; but very often one sentence is preferred. More than three sentences should not be used for a *saṅkalpa*.

A single therapy may be for three months, six months or one year. Ordinarily, a period less than three months is not recommended. The practice may be done once or twice a day. If once, the time before going to sleep is ideal. After the termination of one therapy, a second therapy may be taken up if a second problem is faced. But, ordinarily, more than one problem should not be tackled during a therapy period.

Yoga-nidrā may be practised for getting *mokṣa* (liberation). For this purpose, the therapy period covers the whole life, even after being *jīvanmukta* (liberated, although living). For liberation, *yoga-nidrā* may be combined with Pātañjala Yoga techniques.

The idea of the *saṅkalpa* is recorded in the Subconscious. It becomes a memory (*smṛti*), but not the ordinary memory-store, made available to the Conscious. This layer of the deep *manas* makes the *ahaṅkāra* (ego) conscious of executing the auto-command. The *ahaṅkāra* executes the command through the agency of the Conscious and the physique — its genes, cells, tissues and organs. The execution, however, is unconscious. The physiological functions, the biochemical functions, the restoration of hormonal balance, the healing process, the immunological responses, the activation of the defence mechanism of the body, the retardation of the ageing proceses and sundries may suitably be modulated by the *ahaṅkāra* for the benefit of the total organism, all being done without the awareness of the organism itself.

If *yoga-nidrā* is used for the final goal of liberation and not for any mundane purpose, the *yoga* is to be more comprehensive and rigorous. For such a goal, Patañjali's prescription of *yama*[118] and *niyama*[119] is to be strictly adhered to and his *saṁyama*[120] comprising *dhyāna, dhāraṇā* and *samādhi* is to be rigorously practised. What is the special role of *yoga-nidrā* then ? For attaining *kaivalya* or *brahma-nirvāṇa, yoga-nidrā* accelerates the speed of success. It works synergistically.

There is a concept of *pratiprasava* (involution; the opposite process of evolution) in Pātañjala Yoga.[121] In the process of involution, the *manas*, the five subtle organs of perception,

118. *PYD*, II. 30 (*ahiṁsāsatyāsteyabrahmacaryāparigrahā yamāḥ*).

119. *Ibid.*, II.32 (*śaucasantoṣatapaḥsvādhyāyeśvarapraṇidhānāni niyamāḥ*).

120. *Ibid.*, III.4.

121. *Ibid.*, II.10.

the five subtle organs of action and the five *tanmātras* get dissolved in *ahaṅkāra*. Finally *ahaṅkāra* is dissolved in *buddhi*. This backward pathway of sequential dissolution is known as *pratiprasava*. The forward pathway of evolution is: *buddhi* *ahaṅkāra* *manas*, senses and *tanmātras*. Thus, the *citta* is formed from *asmitā* or *ahaṅkāra*.[122] But *ahaṅkāra* evolves from *buddhi*. With reference to an individual, we use the *buddhi*. For the cosmic purpose, it is *Buddhi* or *Mahat* which is one only. The Sāṅkhya *Buddhi* or *Mahat* is synonymus with the Vedic *Virāḍ*. That being so, we have to explain the individual differences existing among the mind-stuffs of individual persons. The Cosmic *Buddhi* or *Mahat*, when encased (*upādhi*) in an individual body is the individual *buddhi* from which the ego (*ahaṅkāra*) evolves. The ego has freedom of action (within limits, of course). It develops propensities (*pravṛtti*). The *pravṛtti*s vary from person to person and, hence, is the variation among the *citta*s.[123] *Pravṛtti*s lead to *kleśa*s that, in turn, lead to *karma*s. So long as the *karmāśaya* persists, the individual *citta* persists in a dormant state even after the total dissolution (after the Cosmic *Buddhi* or *Mahat* is completely dissolved in the Primordial Nature or *Prakṛti*) to re-emerge in the next cosmic cycle. If the *karmāśaya* is erased prior to the cosmic involution (*pratiprasava*), the individual *buddhi* loses its own identity and merges in the Cosmic *Buddhi* or *Mahat* which dissolves in the *Mūla-Prakṛti* or *Māyā* in the total dissolution (*mahāpralaya*).

Pātañjala Yoga has its own method of erasing, uprooting or burning the *karmāśaya*. *Yoga-nidrā* uses a composite *saṅkalpa* (resolve) comprising three statements for the attainment of liberation. The first is: Let the *karma*s be erased (*karmani naśyantu*). The second is: Let the involution accelerate

122. *PYD*, IV.4 (*nirmāṇacittānyasmitāmātrāt*).

123. *Ibid.*, IV.5 (*pravṛttibhede prayojakaṁ cittamekamanekeṣām*).

(*pratiprasavastvarito bhavatu*). The third is: I am *Brahman* (*ahaṁ brahmāsmi*). Thus, for the purpose of liberation, *yoga-nidrā* is not a substitute for the Pātañjala Yoga. It is a supplement only and not an insignificant supplement.

Alternative *saṅkalpa*s have been suggested in the third chapter of this book for attaining liberation. They have been designed in accordance with the psychological temperament of the person who practises *yoga-nidrā*.

NYĀSA AS A TECHNIQUE FOR THE SHIFTING OF AWARENESS

*Nyāsa*s have their origin in the *Tantra*. These are techniques for the shifting of awareness from one spot to another, from one idea to another and from one imagery to another. In addition to the shifting of awareness in *nyāsa*, there is another important process that is operative. All parts of the gross body and the subtle body are divinized while doing Tantric *nyāsa*.

There are many kinds of *nyāsa*, some short, some long. All those kinds will not be given here. For the purpose of *yoga-nidrā*, only the external and the internal varieties will be given. The external variety pertains to the gross body and the internal variety to the subtle body. In this context, we would introduce the Sanskrit word *mātṛkā*. Literally, it means 'a mother' or 'a divine mother'. In Tantra, it refers to the petals of the six *cakra*s on which a divine mother (different aspects of the one and the only one Divine Mother) presides. Each divine mother is designated by a letter of the Sanskrit alphabet. The external variety of *nyāsa* is known as *bahirmātṛkā nyāsa* (*bahir* = external) and the internal variety of *nyāsa* the *antarmātṛkā nyāsa* (*antar* = internal).

Both the *antarmātṛkā nyāsa* and the *bahirmātṛkā nyāsa* will be given in detail in the addenda following the third chapter of this book.

PRESCRIPTIONS AND PROSCRIPTIONS FOR A YOGĪ

Yoga basically concerns the *citta* (mind-stuff). Waves emanated from it are the *vṛttis*. Yoga causes the cessation of the emanation of the *vṛttis*.[124] As long as *vṛttis* persist to exist, they would generate *kleśas*. As long as *kleśas* are operative, they would generate *vṛttis*. This vicious circle is broken by *yoga*. Hence, the prerequisite for a yogic life is the purification of the *citta* (*citta-śuddhi*). One cannot expect to have clean feet as long as one stands in mud. One must come out of the mud and wash his feet and must not repeat the muddling activity. This is ahieved by the *yama* and the *niyama* of Pātañjala Yoga.

The *yamas* are five in number.[125] All of them are proscriptive. They are: Non-violence (*ahiṁsā*) in thought, speech and action, truthfulness (*satya*), non-stealing or non-acceptance of unearned cash or kind (*asteya*), non-indulgence in sexuality (*brahmacarya*) and non-accumulation of property (*aparigraha*).

The five *niyamas* are prescriptive.[126] They are: Cleanliness (*śauca*) of body, speech and mind, contentment (*santoṣa*), readiness for undertaking any suffering for a noble cause (*tapaḥ*), study of scriptures on *Brahman* and allied matters (*svādhyāya*) and complete surrender to God (*īśvara-praṇidhāna*).

Yoga-nidrā can be done without *yama* and *niyama*, and some benefits can be had. But the benefits could be maximized if the person lives a yogic life. A yogic life has the implied meaning that it is a life which is wedded to ethical living, purity of body and mind and humanitarianism.

Yoga recommends a moderate living. The *yogī* avoids excess of eating and excess of fasting and dieting, excess of sleeping and resting and excess of excercise and over-activity

124. *PYD*, I.2 (*yogaścittavṛttinirodhaḥ*).
125. *Ibid.*, II.30.
126. *Ibid.*, II.32.

(both physical and mental) and excess of anything pertaining to the body and mind. He avoids *indulgence* in sex. Unless he is a mendicant, the householder *yogī* may not altogether avoid sex, and here also the middle path is the golden path. He avoids foods that are harmful to health. He avoids drinking and smoking.

A *yogī* avoids mental tension. In certain circumstances, complete avoidance of tension may not be feasible for an average person who is not an adept in *yoga*. In such situations, he should try to minimize tension. He should take note of the *realities* of life. Over-ambition in day-dreaming is to be avoided. *Yoga* does not prescribe inaction: but it prescribes detached action, action without attachment (*āsakti*) to the fruits thereof. If detachment (*anāsakti*) is practised, a person is not overwhelmed with joy by getting success and not distressed in sorrow on failure. There are many sorrowful incidences in life, quite unavoidable, like accidents and death of kith and kin. One should develop the self-power to tolerate the unfavourable situations and avoid frustration. What cannot be cured must be endured. This motto should be practised in life. One should train oneself to accept the inevitable without grudge. Actions should be oriented to avoid enmity. Self-centredness is to be forsaken. Altruism is to be adopted as a philosophy of life. Human values are to be cherished. One should not be afraid of facing the roughness of life while enjoying its smoothness. Optimism in life in the midst of tempestuous peril is a yogic trait. All these traits can be acquired by a strong faith in God and by a faith that every entity of the universe, non-living or living, is a manifestation of the Power (*Śakti*) of *Brahman*. There would be no storm if there is no depression. There would be no depression if the mind is full, without letting any chance of creating a vacuum, partial or total.

It should be remembered that *yoga-nidrā* is a yogic technique to condition the mind so that some mental and physical mal-adjustments can be set in order: but it is not a panacea for curing every malady. It is not a magical formula to sanctify every immoral action and licentious behaviour of a person. There is no substitute for goodness.

ĀSANAS AND PRĀṆĀYĀMAS PRELIMINARY TO YOGA-NIDRĀ

Yoga-nidrā is practised in *śavāsana* (corpse pose). This is the only *āsana* that is indispensable for *yoga-nidrā*.

Muscular tension and joint stiffness are great obstacles to *yoga-nidrā*. For bringing about physical relaxation prior to *yoga-nidrā*, it is advisable to do some *āsanas*. The following *āsanas* are recommended:

A. Biginners who have little practice of *āsanas* and those who cannot devote more time may do *prāṇamuktāsana*. Of course, *śavāsana* is unavoidable since this is the pose in which *yoga-nidrā* is practised.

It may be pointed out here that our *prāṇamuktāsana* is the *pavanamuktāsana* of some *yogīs*. Swāmī Satyānanda Sarasvatī uses the name *pavanamuktāsana*.[127] We prefer the name *prāṇamuktāsana* to *pavanamuktāsana*. Although one of the meanings of *pavana* or *vāyu* is *prāṇa*, people are to confuse it with the physical air or wind. Secondly, many *yoga* books describe an *āsana* with the name *pavanamuktāsana* which helps the expulsion of wind from the bowels and stimulates intestinal peristalsis for the relief of constipation.

127. Swāmī Satyānanda Sarasvatī, 1983, pp. 15-27.

B. Advanced *yoga*-practitioners and those who can spend more time may do the following *āsanas*:

1. *Sarvāṅgāsana* (shoulderstand pose)
2. *Halāsana* (plough pose)
3. *Matsyāsana* (fish pose)
4. *Paścimottānāsana* (the back-stretching pose)
5. *Bhujaṅgāsana* (cobra pose)
6. *Śalabhāsana* (locust pose)
7. *Vajrāsana* (thunderbolt pose).

C. A shorter alternative to series B is *Sūrya-Namaskāra* (six to twelve rounds). It would loosen the joints and muscles and massage the internal organs.

D. Another still shorter alternative is *naukāsana* (the boat pose). The practice of this *āsana* three to five times provides a general physical relaxation which prepares the body for *yoga-nidrā.*

After doing the *āsanas* and before the *yoga-nidrā, prāṇāyāma* should preferably be done. For getting the most benefits from *yoga-nidrā,* the flow of *prāṇa* in the *nāḍīs* should be free and unimpeded.

One should sit in *vajrāsana* and do *ujjayī prāṇayāma* with *so'ham* (He is I) *mantra-japa* (*ajapā japa*). One should think of the flow of *prāṇa* in the *vajrā-nāḍī* of the *suṣumṇā.* During inhalation, the *prāṇa* flows downward to the *mūlādhāra* while thinking of *saḥ* (*so*). During exhalation, the *prāṇa* flows upward while thinking of *aham* (*ham*). If this *prāṇāyāma* is practised in the *vajrāsana,* any previous practice of *vajrāsana* in the *āsana* series may be avoided.

Nāḍī-śodhana prāṇāyāma with or without retention

(*kumbhaka-sahita* or *kumbhaka-rahita*) may be done as a better alternative to *ujjayī prāṇāyāma*. For this purpose, *padmāsana* or *siddhāsana* may be the ideal *āsana*.

With this, we end the chapter on the theory of *yoga-nidrā*. Readers who are not interested in the theory may skip over this chapter and go through the second chapter which deals with the practice only.

2

Practice of Yoga-Nidrā

In this chapter, we will deal with the practice of *yoga-nidrā*, without any direct reference to its theory. The detailed procedure will be described step by step so as to enable the practitioner to follow the techniques without the guidance or assistance of a second person or an instructor. Some *yoga-nidrā*-teachers recommend the guidance of an instructor when the practitioner is a beginner. As an alternative, they recommend taping the sequential instructions and making use of a record-player in the beginning stage. We are of the opinion that the practitioner can do himself without taking help of an instructor or a record-player. Before the actual practice, he may go through the instructions a number of times and remember the sequence of the shifting of consciousness. The shifting of consciousness should be rapid and the sequence should be unaltered in all sessions. The maintenance of the sequence should be strictly followed. However, it may be pointed out that there would be no harm if the sequence is disturbed a little in the beginning stage. In the course of practice, the sequence will be memorized and everything will be conditioned.

STEPS PREPARATORY TO YOGA-NIDRĀ

Yoga-nidrā should be done twice a day, in the morning and the evening. The morning session may be adjusted sometime between 4 a.m. to 6 a.m. The evening session may be any time between 6 p.m. to 8 p.m. or before going to sleep. If one has no time to practise *yoga-nidrā* twice a day, one may do it once a day. One may select the morning or the evening time according to one's convenience. If once a day and just before the bedtime are preferred, one may accommodate one's time of *āsanas* and *prāṇāyāmas* suitably. Those who take early supper may finish doing *āsanas* and *prāṇāyāma* before the supper time. Those who take late supper may do *āsanas* and *prāṇāyāmas* any time during the evening hours before taking supper. In the worst inconvenience, *āsanas* and *prāṇāyāmas* may be done in the morning and the night *yoga-nidrā* may be practised just before going to sleep. For *vajrāsana* and *ujjayī prāṇāyāma*, of course, there is no restriction. They can be practised even immediately after a full meal. *Yoga-nidrā* should preferably be practised at least three hours after a full meal. Anyone who has to do *yoga-nidrā* before the bedtime is advised to take early supper. A person who cannot avoid a late supper may practise *yoga-nidrā* after supper and before going to sleep, with some disadvantages which are not very serious. But it may be emphasized that *āsanas* and *prāṇāyāmas* other than *vajrāsana* and *ujjayī* must be avoided within three hours after a full meal. It may further be emphasized that one may straight away go for *yoga-nidrā* without prior *āsanas* and *prāṇāyāmas*.

The clothing should be minimum and adjustable to the ambient temperature and varying weather conditions. However, it should be loose and light and, in no circumstances, heavy and tight. The feeling of comfort is an indication with regard to the appropriateness of clothing.

The room where *yoga-nidrā* is practised should be calm and quiet. It should be airy, but without draught. It should be dimly lighted or not lighted at all, depending on the circumstances. The temperature of the room should be comfortable. The room should be noise-free and free from mosquitoes and other insects. If practicable, the presence of other persons in the room may not be allowed. The entry of noise into the room from the sources of radio, television and other extraneous objects may be avoided as far as practicable.

PRĀṆA-SAÑCĀLANA KRIYĀ

What is called *pavana-muktāsana* by some *yogīs* is our *prāṇa-sañcālana kriyā*. It is not an *āsana*. It is a series of exercises that facilitate the removal of obstructions at joints and the free flow of *prāṇa* (neither air nor wind) in the *nāḍīs*. In our *prāṇa-sañcālana kriyā*, some of the steps of *pavana-muktāsana* have been omitted, some others have been modified, and some have been added.

Base position

There are three base positions for this series of exercises. In base position A (*fig*. 2.1), the person sits with legs extended in front of the body, with hands placed on the floor by the side of the trunk and behind the hips. He leans backwards and takes the support of the straight arms. In base position B, he sits on a hard bed or an armless chair or a stool, with feet flat on the ground. In base position C, he stands on a hard floor, without a support or with a support against a table or a wall.

***Kriyā*-1: *Padāṅguli-namana* (*toe-bending*).** Do this *kriyā* in either position A or B. If you take position B, raise the front parts of the feet, with the heels still on the floor. Keep the feet rigid. Move the toes of both the feet forwards and backwards (*fig*. 2.2). Repeat about ten times.

***Kriyā*-2: *Gulpha-namana* (*ankle-bending*).** Do this *kriyā* in either position A or position B, with feet raised from the floor. Move both the feet backward and forward as much as possible, bending them from the ankle joints (*fig*. 2. 3). Repeat about ten times.

***Kriyā*-3: *Gulpha-cakrāyaṇa* (*ankle-rotation*).** Do this *kriyā* in

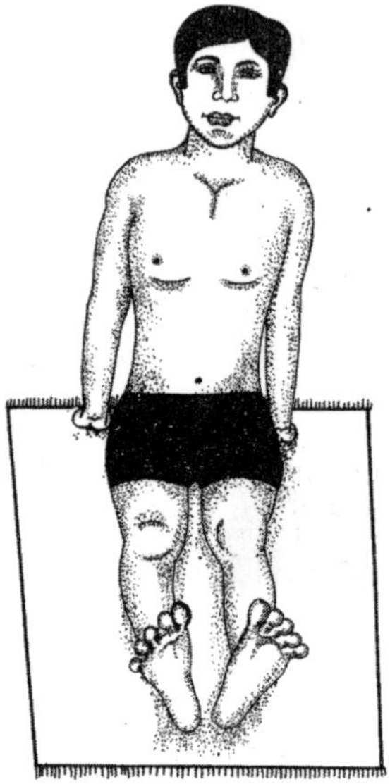

fig. **2.1 (a)**

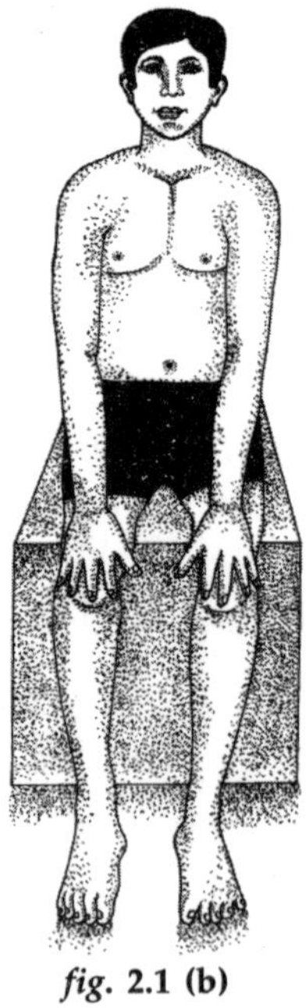

fig. **2.1 (b)**

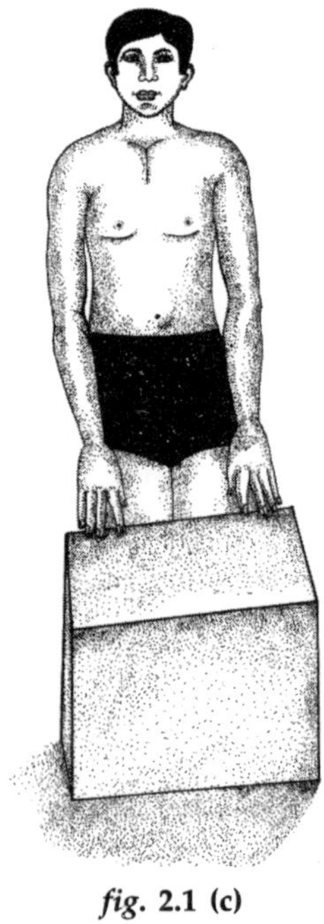

fig. **2.1 (c)**

fig. **2.1 (a, b & c) Base positions for *prāṇa-sañcālana-kriyā*.**

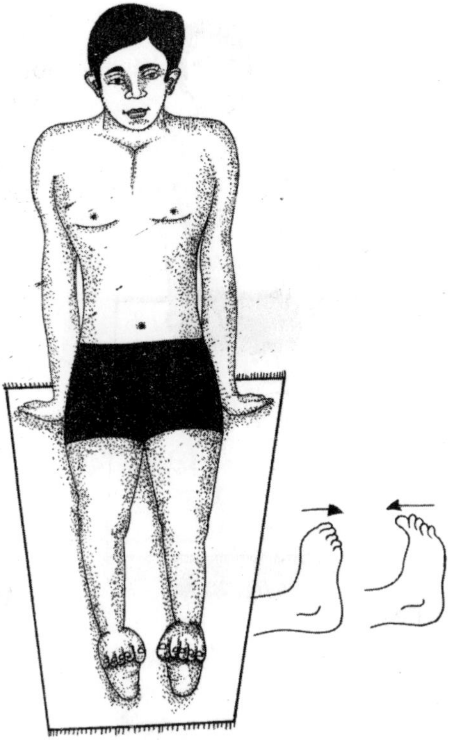

fig. 2.2 ***Pādāṅguli-namana*** **(toe-bending).**

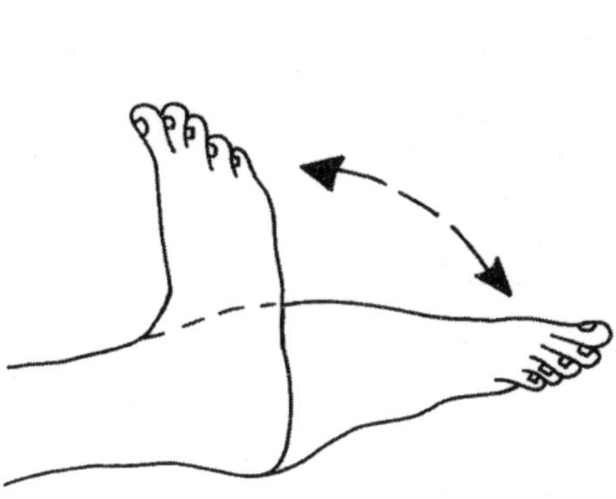

fig. 2.3 ***Gulpha-namana*** **(ankle-bending).**

either position A or position B. Separate the feet about 30 cm apart. Keep the heels in contact with the floor while raising the rest parts of the feet. Rotate the right foot clockwise (*dakṣināvarta*) about ten times, with the ankle as the lever (*fig.* 2.4). Then rotate anticlockwise (*vāmāvarta*) the same number of times. Repeat the rotating with the left foot. Finally, rotate both feet together first clockwise and then anticlockwise.

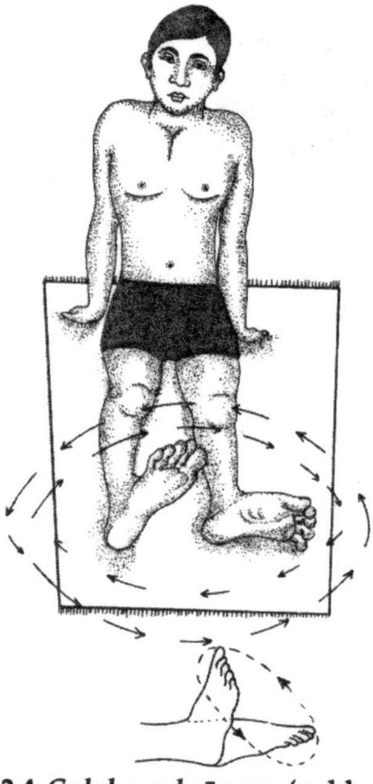

***fig.* 2.4 *Gulpha-cakrāyaṇa* (ankle-rotation).**

***Kriyā-4: Gulpha-ghūrṇana* (*ankle-crank*).** Do this *kriyā* in either position A or position B. Place the right ankle on the left thigh. Catch hold of the right toes with the left hand. With the help of the left hand, rotate the right foot clockwise about ten times and then anticlockwise about ten times (*fig.* 2.5). Repeat the same procedure for the left foot with the right hand after placing the left ankle on the right thigh.

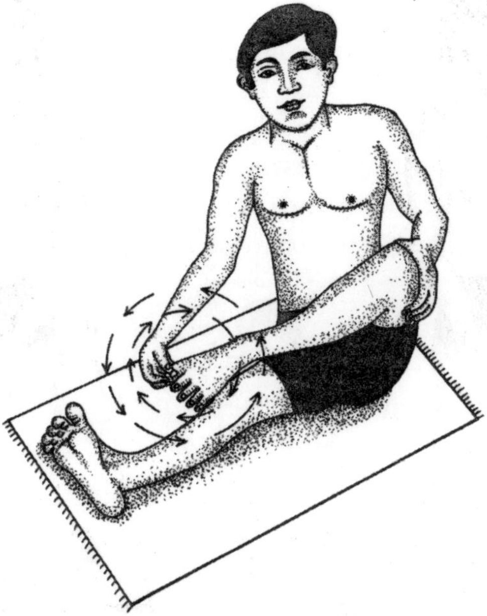

fig. 2.5 ***Gulpha-ghūrṇana* (ankle-crank).**

***Kriyā*-5: *Jānu-namana* (*knee-bending*).** Do this *kriyā* in either position A or position B. In position B, the leg to be handled is raised so that the level of the foot is higher than that of the bed or the armless chair or the stool. Bend the right leg at the knee and clasp your hands under the right thigh. Stretch your right leg in front and bring it back so that the right heel comes near the right buttock. While stretching forward, the right heel and toes do not touch the ground, the hands are under the right thigh and both arms are straightened. While bringing the right heel towards the right buttock, the right leg is bent at the right knee and both the hands are folded at the elbows.

For bending the left knee, the same procedure is to be repeated, with the change of sides, of course. Knee-bending, in each case, is to be done about ten times (*fig.* 2.6).

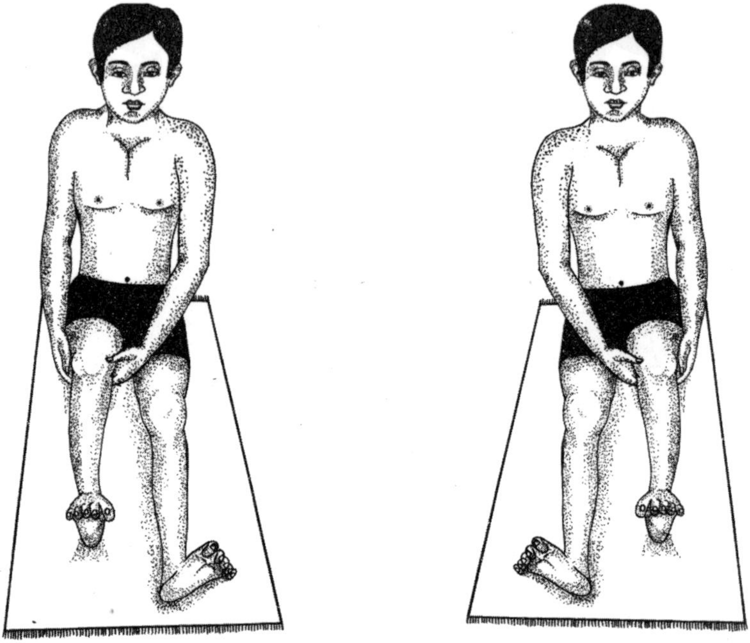

fig. **2.6** ***Jānu-namana*** **(knee-bending).**

***Kriyā*-6: *Jānu-ghūrṇana* (*knee-rotation*).** Assume the position as in *kriyā*-5. Bend the right leg at the right knee and clasp your hands under the right thigh. Hold the right thigh near the trunk. Rotate the right lower leg in a circular motion about the right knee (*fig.* 2.7). Do about ten times clockwise and about ten times anticlockwise.

With the change of sides, repeat the same procedure for the left leg.

***Kriyā*-7: *Śroṇi-dolana* (*hip-swinging*).** Sit in position A. Fold the right leg at the knee and place it on the left thigh. Hold the right foot with the left hand and place the right palm on the right knee. By pressure of the right hand on the right knee, move the bent right leg up and down (*fig.* 2.8). See that the right knee touches the floor in the downward movement. Do this excercise for about three minutes.

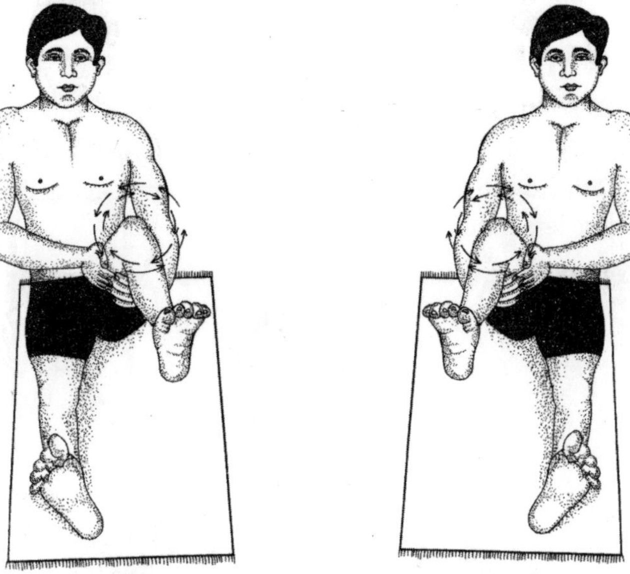

fig. **2.7 (a & b)** ***Jānu-ghūrṇana*** **(knee-rotation).**

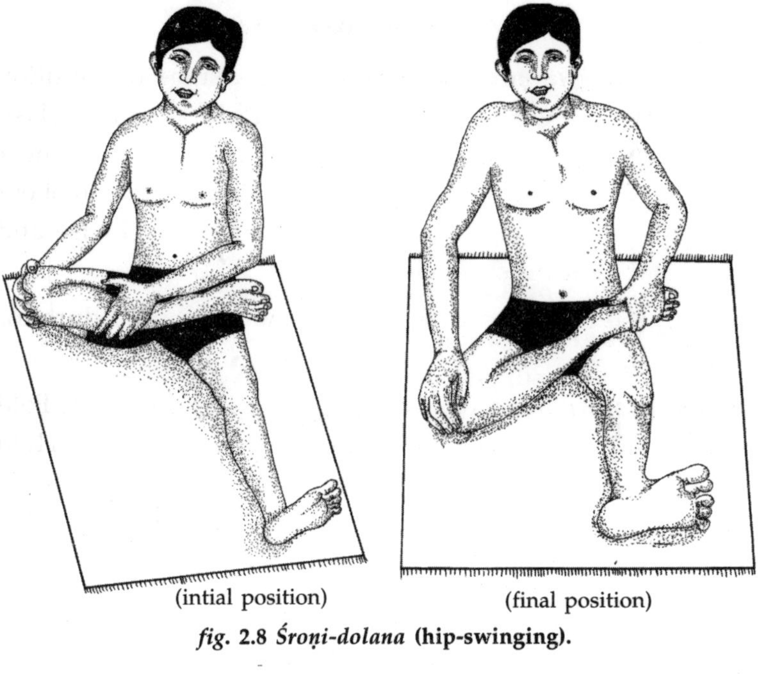

(intial position) (final position)

fig. **2.8** ***Śroṇi-dolana*** **(hip-swinging).**

By changing the sides, repeat the same procedure for the left hip.

***Kriyā*-8: *Śroṇi-cakra* (*hip-circling*).** Remain in the same position as in *kriyā*-7 for *śroṇi-dolana*, except the hand positions as shown in *fig*. 2.9. Rotate the right hip in a circle, ten times clockwise and then ten times anticlockwise.

Repeat the procedure for the left hip.

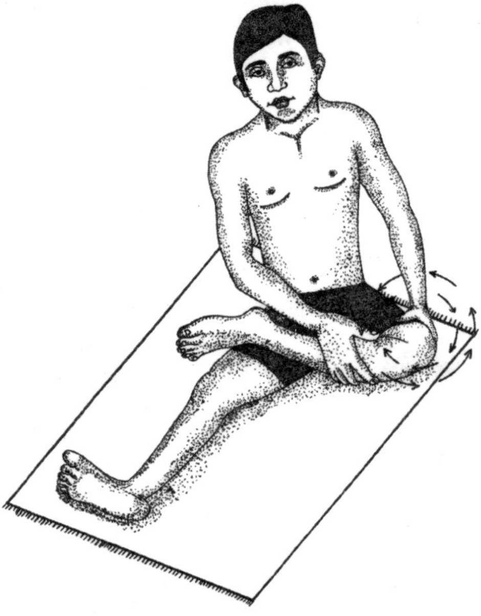

***fig*. 2.9 *Śroṇi-cakra* (hip-circling).**

***Kriyā*-9: *Śroṇi-ghūrṇana* (*hip-rotation*).** Do this *kriyā* in position C with a support. Raise the right leg from the ground level. Rotate the right hip in horizontal circles ten times clockwise and ten times anticlockwise (*fig*. 2.10). Do the Same thing with the left hip.

***Kriyā*-10: *Kāka-pādacāra* (*crow-walking*).** Squat on the floor on the toes, with the rear parts of the feet raised. Place the palms of the hands on the respective knees. Now start crow-

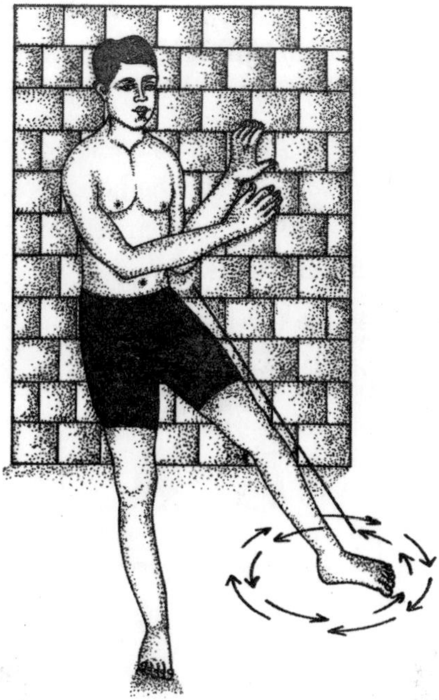

fig. **2.10 *Śroṇi-ghūrṇana* (hip-rotation).**

walking (*fig*. 2.11). The right foot for the forward step flatly rests on the ground while the left foot rests on the toes only and its knee is lowered. Then the left foot makes the forward movement, flatly resting on the ground, while the right foot rests on the toes only, with lowered knee. This alternate process continues.

Crow-walking is an exercise which well prepares the legs for meditational *āsanas*.

Persons who have poor blood circulation to the legs are immensely benefitted by crow-walking.

Crow-walking removes constipation. The patient should take two glasses of water and then crow-walk for one minute. Taking water and crow-walking should be repeated three to four times.

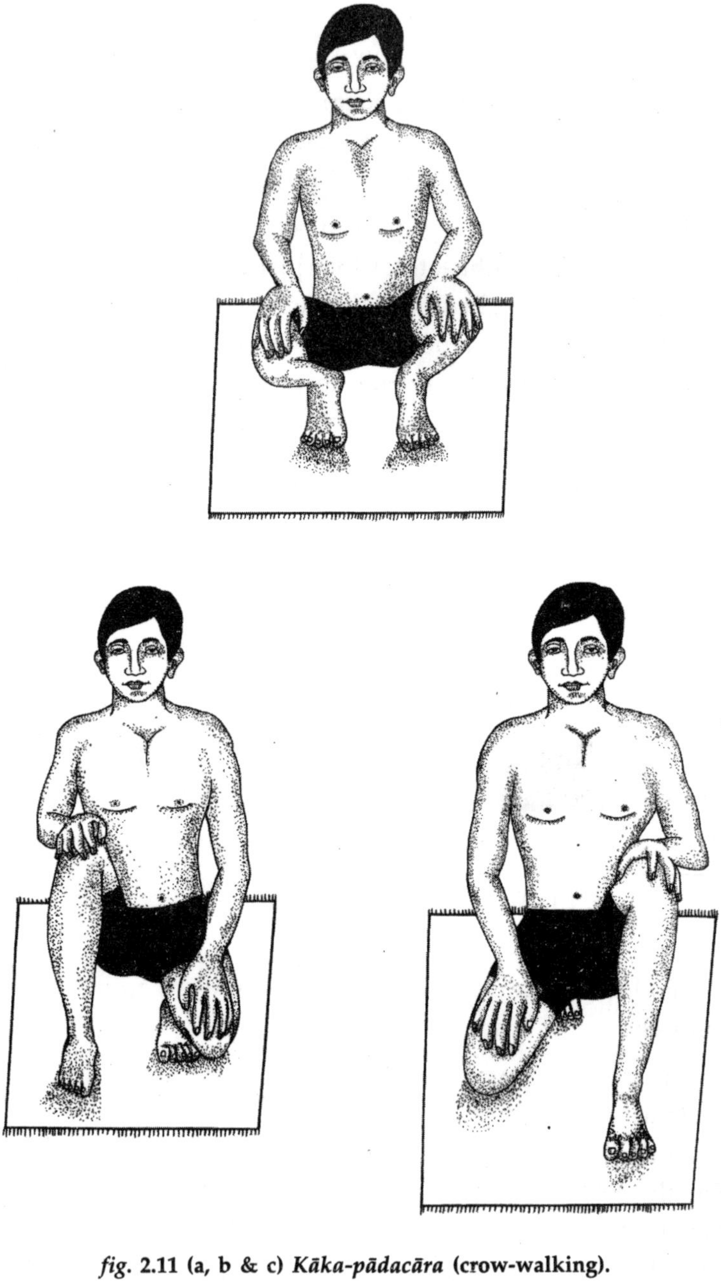

fig. **2.11 (a, b & c)** ***Kāka-pādacāra*** **(crow-walking).**

All obstructions to the flow of *prāṇa* in the lower half of the body are removed if crow-walking is done regularly.

***Kriyā*-11: *Meru-pārśva-vakrāsana* (*lateral spinal twist*).** Do this *kriyā* either in a sitting or a standing position.

Sit in *sukhāsana*. Place the right palm on the external part of the left thigh with a grip on it. Place the dorsal side of the left hand on the right lateral loin just above the right hip. In this posture the right forearm touches the abdomen in front and the left forearm touches the lower back behind. Twist the head to the left and back. Stay in this posture for about three minutes. The final twisting posture has been demonstrated in *fig.* 2.12.

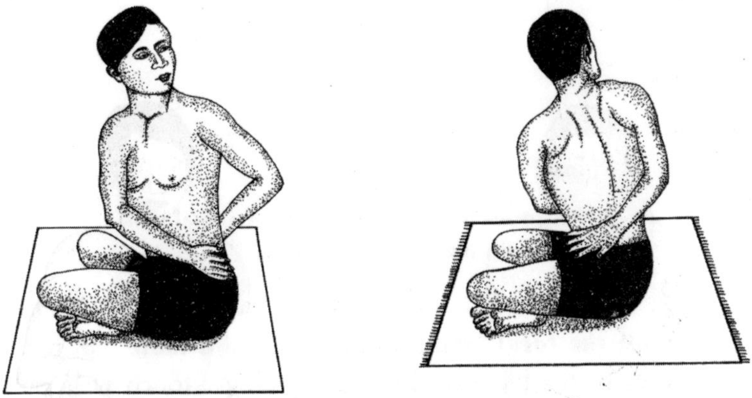

***fig.* 2.12 *Meru-pārśva-vakrāsana* (lateral spinal twist) in the sitting posture.**

Follow the some procedure for the right spinal twisting with change of sides.

In the standing posture (*fig.* 2.13), the procedure is the same as in the sitting one except one deviation. The palm-grip is on the lateral loin above the hip instead of the lateral thigh. For the left twisting, the right palm is placed above the left hip. For the right twisting, the left palm is placed above the right hip.

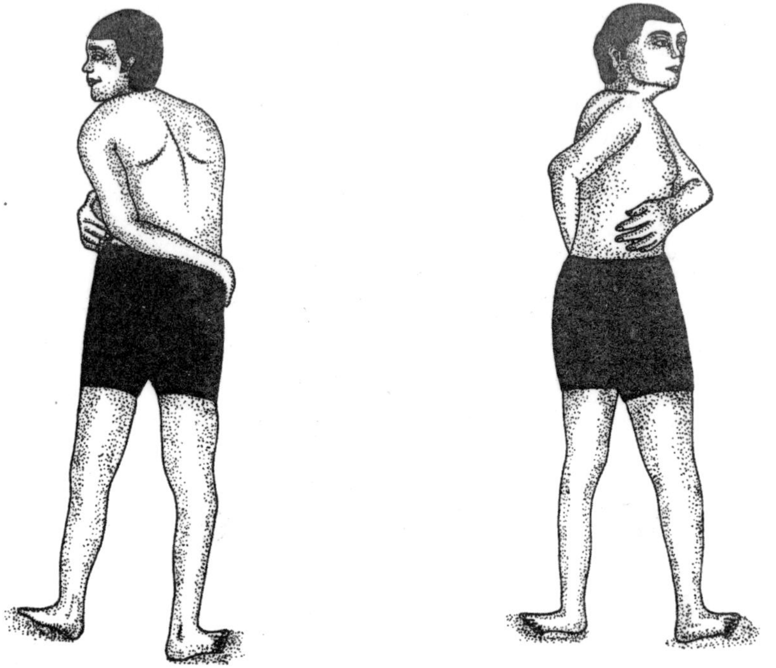

***fig.* 2.13 *Meru-pārśva-vakrāsana* (lateral spinal twist) in the standing posture.**

***Kriyā*-12: *Ūrdhvamukhī tāḍāsana* (*backward bending while standing on the toes*).** Stand by the side of a table or a wall. Get support of the table or the wall by a *light* touch with both the hands. Raise the back parts of the feet and stand on the toes. Raise the head upwards and backwards as far as possible. In this attempt, the spine should have a concavity in the middle of the back, the abdomen should bulge forward and the abdominal muscles (*retus abdomini*) should be stretched. The posture of *ūrdhvamukhī tāḍāsana* has been illustrated in *fig.* 2.14.

***Kriyā*-13: *Meru-dolana* (*spine-swinging*).** Stand erect with both hands fully stretched to the respective sides. Swing to the left while the right hand moves upwards (*fig.* 2.15a). Then swing to the right while the left hand moves upwards. Continue this

fig. **2.14** ***Ūrdhvamukhī tāḍāsana***
(backward bending while standing on the toes).

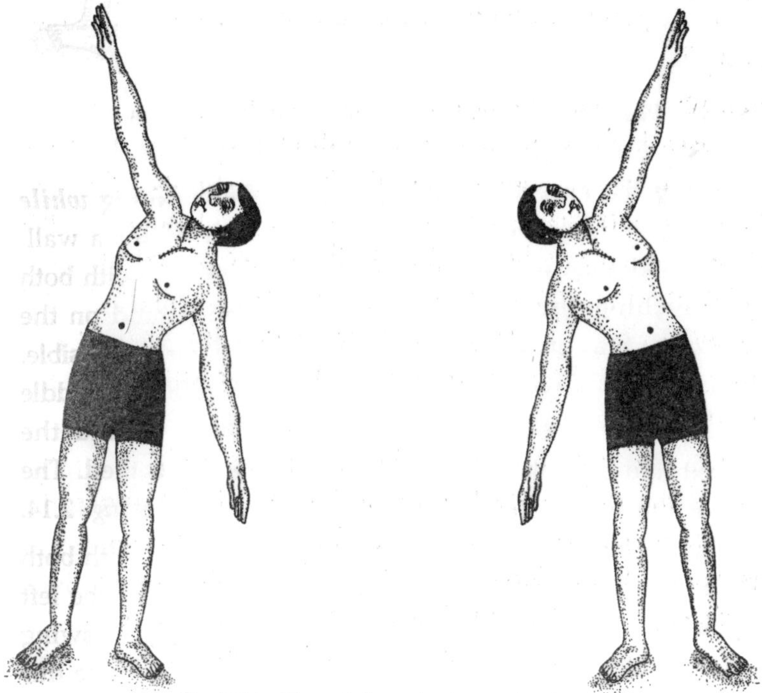

fig. 2.15a *Meru-dolana* (spine-swinging)
in a standing position.

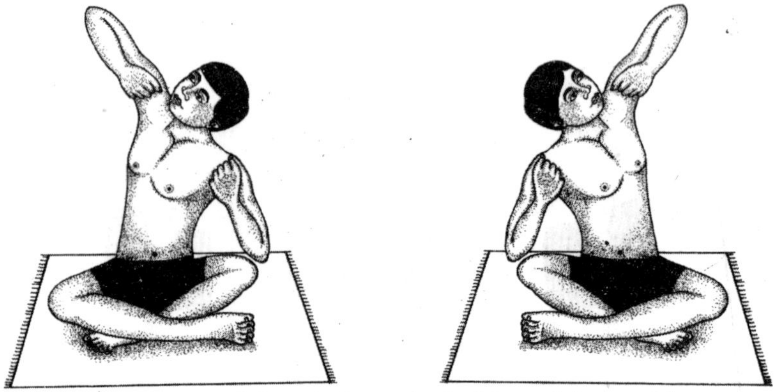

fig. **2.15b *Meru-dolana* (spine-swinging) in a sitting position.**

process alternately for about three minutes. The trunk and the head should move to one side or the other simultaneously.

If you do this *kriyā* in a sitting position, fold both the hands at the elbows so that the fingers touch the collar-bones. The rest of the procedure is the same as in the standing position (*fig.* 2.15b).

***Kriyā*-14: *Pavana-muktāsana (wind-releasing āsana, the leg-lock pose)*.** Lie flat on the ground with face upwards. Fold the right leg at the knee-joint. Hold the lower right leg below the right knee with clasped hands. Press the right thigh against the right abdomen while slightly lifting the chest and the head and stretching the right foot at the ankle forward and downward. Stay in the posture (*fig.* 2.16a) for a while and release. Repeat three times. Repeat the same process for the left leg.

Next fold both the legs at the knee joints. Hold the upper parts of the lower legs below the knees with handlock (by gripping the left wrist with the right hand) and press the folded legs against the abdomen while the anterior part of the body (the chest and the head) is lifted from the floor and the feet at the ankles are stretched forward and downward (*fig.* 2.16b). Repeat this *āsana* thrice.

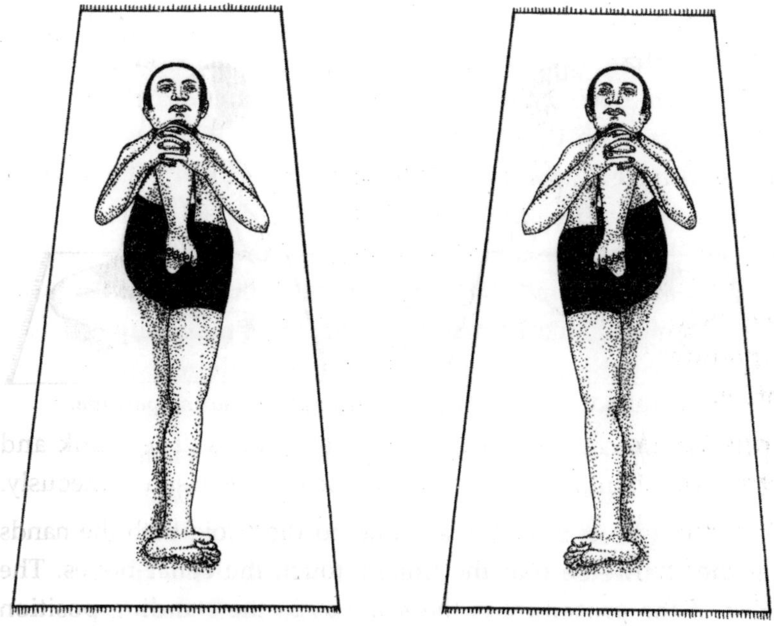

fig. **2.16a** ***Pavana-muktāsana*** **(wind-releasing** ***āsana,*** **the leg-lock pose), the right and the left leg separately.**

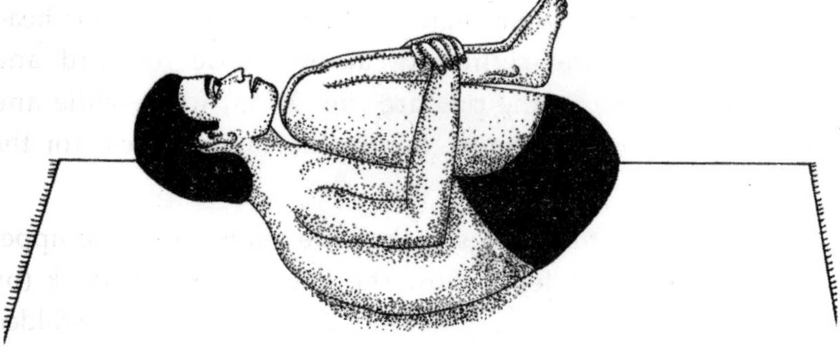

fig. **2.16b** ***Pavana-muktāsana*** **(wind-releasing** ***āsana,*** **the leg-lock pose), both legs together.**

***Kriyā*-15: *Meru-agra-vakrāsana (front spinal bending)*.** Sit in *sukhāsana*. Straighten the arms and place the palms on the floor about 25 cm behind the buttocks. Lift your torso. Let it make a curvature with its convexity towards the front, while the face is directed upward and backward and both the knees touch the floor (*fig*. 2.17). The palms, the dorsal parts of the feet and the lower legs between the kness and the ankles touch the floor and transmit the body weight to the ground. In this *āsana*, attempt should be made to bring about maximum convex curvature of the spine towards the front. Repeat the *āsana* thrice.

***Kriyā*-16: *Muṣṭika-bandhana-unmocana (hand-clenching and opening)*.** Assume the base position A or B. Hold both the arms straight in front so as to keep them in line with the shoulders. Stretch out the fingers, keeping them apart from one another, making them tense and directing them towards the sides and towards the backs of the palms (*fig*. 2.18).

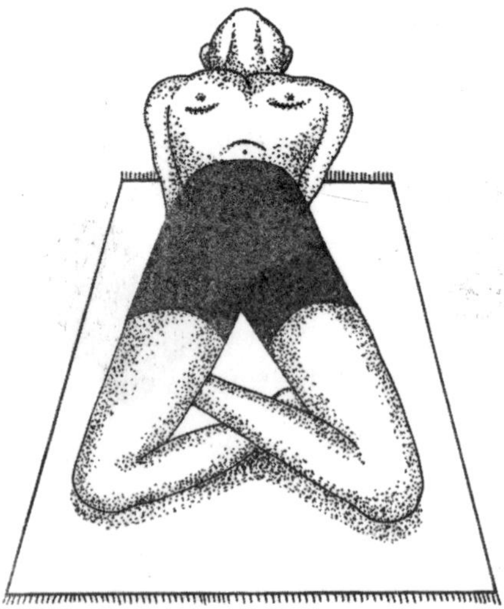

fig. 2.17 ***Meru-agra-vakrāsana* (front spinal bending).**

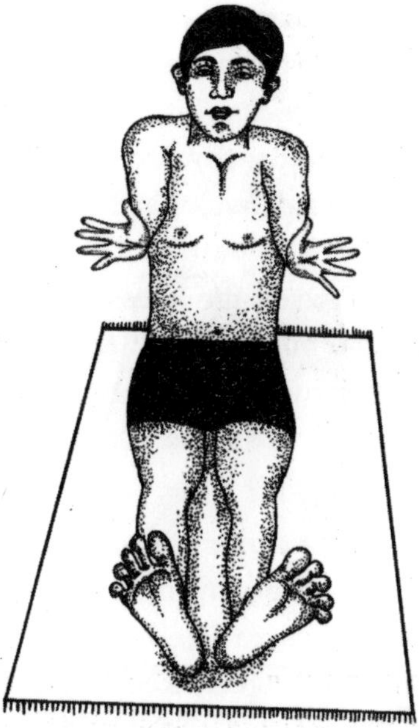

***fig.* 2.18 *Muṣṭika-bandhana-unmocana* (hand clenching and opening), lateral stretching of hands.**

Close the fingers over the respective thumb and make tight fists (*fig.* 2.19).

Repeat the alternate process of stretching and tensing the fingers and closing them into fists about ten times.

***Kriyā*-17: *Maṇibandha-namana* (*wrist-bending*).** Stay in position as in *kriyā*-16. Bend the hands at the wrists with upward-pointing fingers, as if you are pressing the palms against a wall (*fig.* 2.20). The fingers should be vertically up and face away from you.

Next, bend the hands at the wrists with downward-pointing fingers (*fig.* 2.21). The fingers should be vertically down and face towards you.

Repeat the alternate bending about ten times.

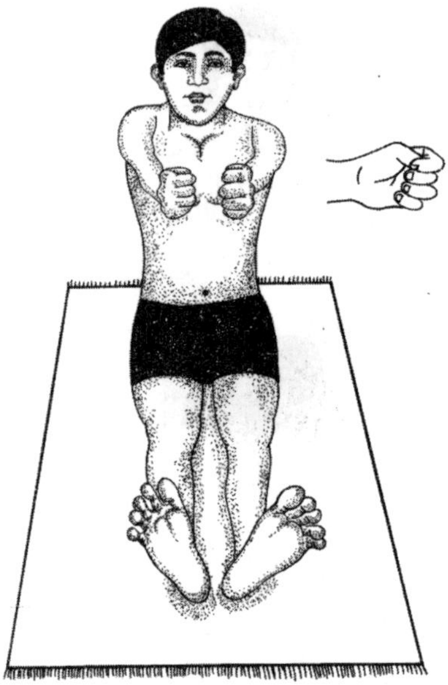

fig. **2.19** ***Muṣṭika-bandhana-unmocana*** **(hand clenching and opening), closing the figures in tight fists.**

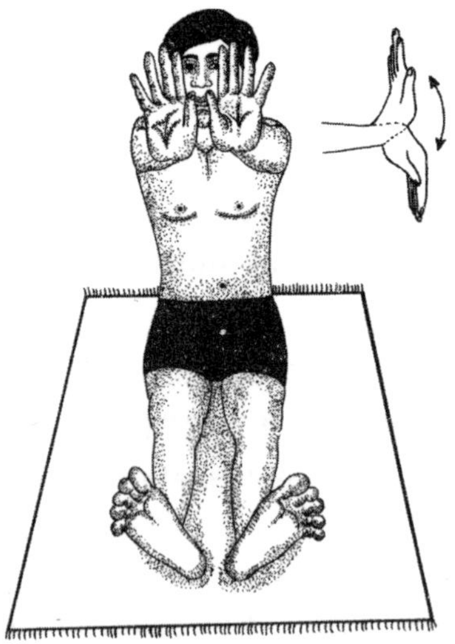

fig. **2.20** ***Maṇibandha-namana*** **(wrist-bending), with upward pointing fingers.**

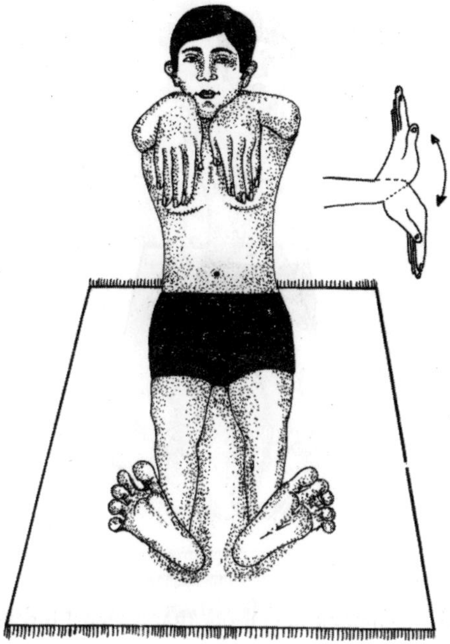

fig. **2.21** ***Maṇibandha-namana*** **(wrist-bending), with down-ward pointing fingers.**

***Kriyā*-18: *Maṇibandha-cakra* (*wrist-joint rotation*).** Stay in position as in *kriyā*-16, but with only the right arm extended. Clench the right fist with the thumb inside. Rotate the right hand (fist) about the wrist, first clockwise ten times and then anticlockwise ten times (*fig.* 2.22).

Repeat the procedure for the left hand.

Finally, do the wrist-joint rotation by extending both the arms forward with both fists clenched and rotating both the fists together around their respective wrists (*fig.* 2.23). Rotate ten times clockwise and ten times anticlockwise.

Lower the arms and relax a while before commencing the next *kriyā*.

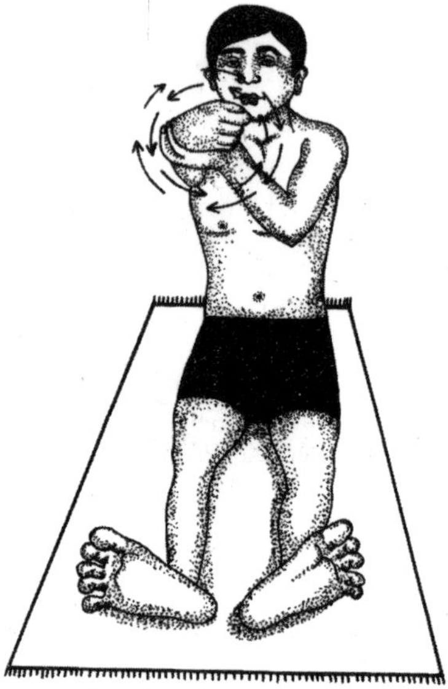

fig. **2.22** ***Maṇibandha-cakra*** **(wrist-joint rotation) of each hand.**

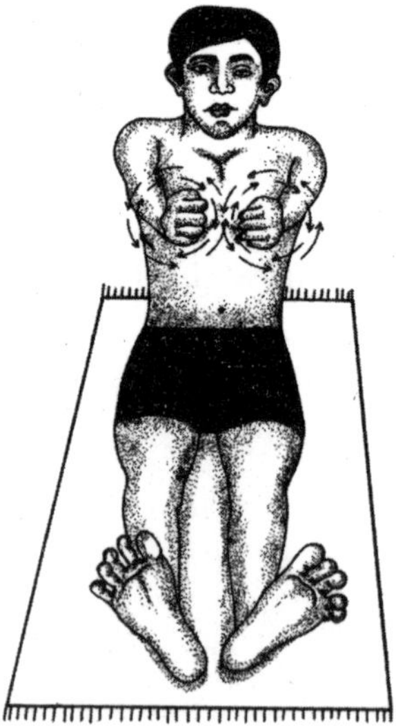

fig. **2.23** ***Maṇibandha-cakra*** **(wrist-joint rotation) of both hands done simultaneously.**

***Kriyā*-19: *Kūrpara-namana* (*elbow-bending*).** Assume position A or B or C (standing without a support). Hold both arms outstretched in front with palms up. Bend both arms at the elbows so that the fingers touch the respective shoulders. Then straighten the arms (*fig.* 2.24a & b). Repeat the bending and the straightening operations ten times.

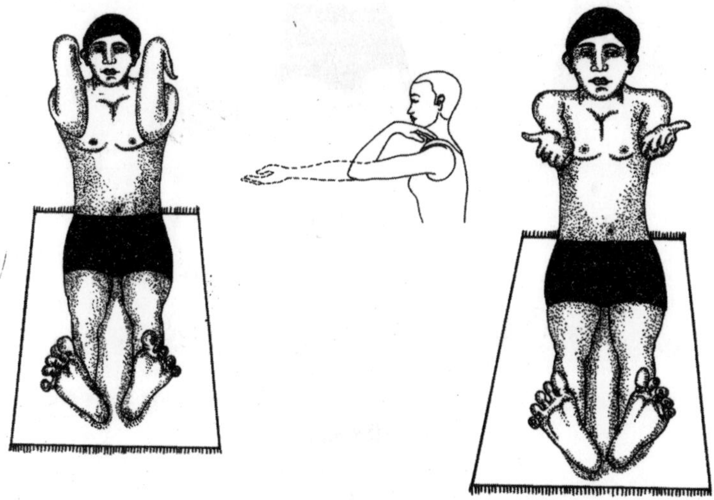

***fig.* 2.24a & b *Kūrpara-namana* (elbow-bending) with forward extension of arms :**
(a) Bending the arms at the elbow. (b) Forward stretching the arms.

Next, extend the arms sideways with palms up. Follow the same procedure as for the forward stretching (*fig.* 2.25a & b).

***Kriyā*-20: *Skandha-cakra* (*shoulder-socket rotation*).** Stay in the same position as for *kriyā*-19, with both arms extended in front or sideways. Fold the arms at the elbows so that the fingers touch the respective shoulders. Maintain this posture and make circular movements of both the shoulder joints simultaneously (*fig.* 2.26). While making the circular

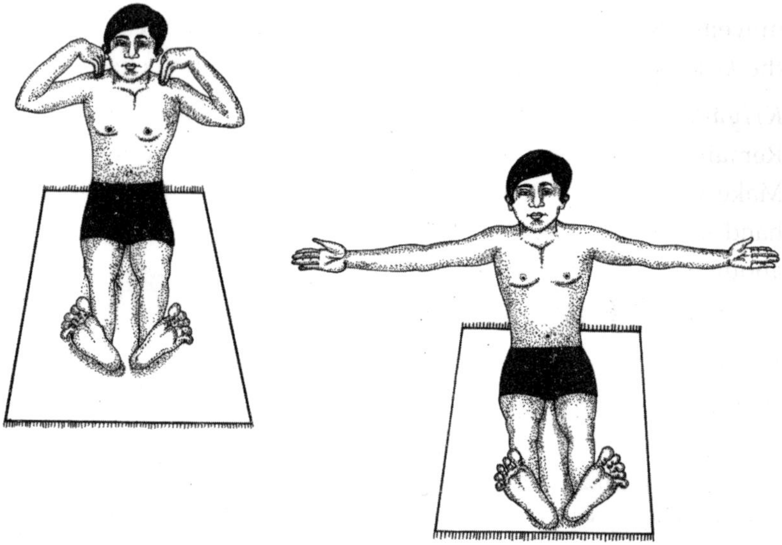

fig. **2.25a & b** ***Kūrpara-namana*** **(elbow-bending) with lateral extension of arms :**
(a) Bending the arms at the elbow. (b) Stretching the arms sideways.

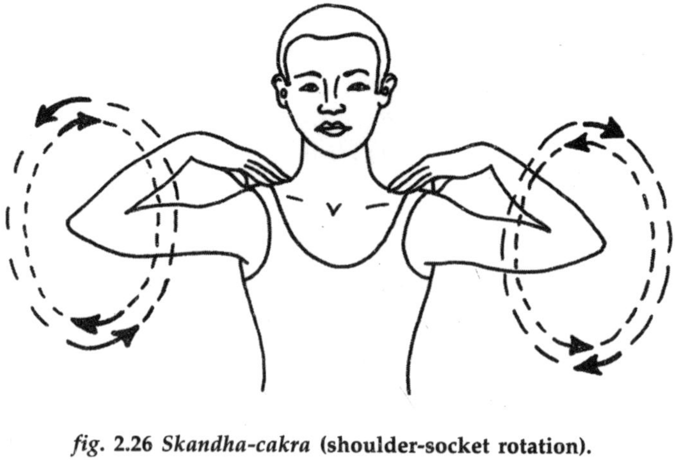

fig. **2.26** ***Skandha-cakra*** **(shoulder-socket rotation).**

movements, bring the elbows in contact with the chest. Repeat the *kriyā* ten times clockwise and ten times anticlockwise.

***Kriyā*-21: *Bāhu-mūla ghūrṇana* (*shoulder joint circling*).** Remain in position C (standing position without a support). Make vertically circling movements of the right arm with the hand in a lightly clenched fist (*fig.* 2.27). Make such movements about ten times clockwise and then anticlockwise.

Repeat the same procedure for the left hand.

***Kriyā*-22: *Bāhu-dolana* (*arm-swinging*).** Do this *kriyā* in standing position without a support. Move both the arms with open palms, facing downwards, to the front and to the back in swinging motion (*fig.* 2.28). In the front swinging, take the hands to an extreme upward position. In the back swinging, take the hands to an extreme backward position. Repeat the *kriyā* for about three minutes.

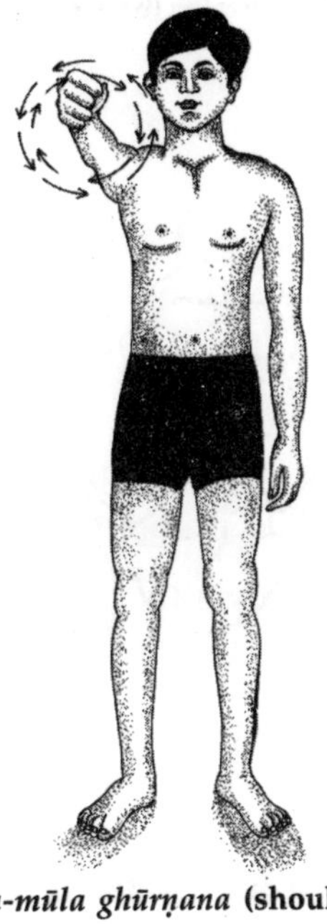

***fig.* 2.27 *Bāhu-mūla ghūrṇana* (shoulder-joint circling).**

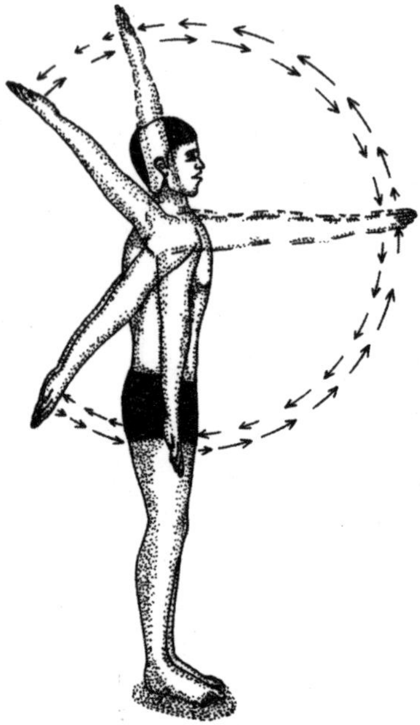

fig. **2.28** ***Bāhu-dolana*** **(arm-swinging).**

***Kriyā*-23: *Grīvā-sañcālana* (*neck movement*).** Do this *kriyā* in any of the three basic positions. Gently move your head backwards and forwards (*fig.* 2.29a & b). Repeat about ten times.

Next, slowly and gently tilt your head to the left and to the right (*fig.* 2.30a & b). Do it about ten times.

Finally, very slowly and gently make a circling movement of the head clockwise about ten times (*fig.* 2.31). Then do the same thing anticlockwise.

In addition to the benefits accrued from *prāṇa-sañcālana-kriyā* for facilitating *yoga-nidrā*, this *kriyā* is very useful for the relief of hypertension and for vitalising a devitalized body.

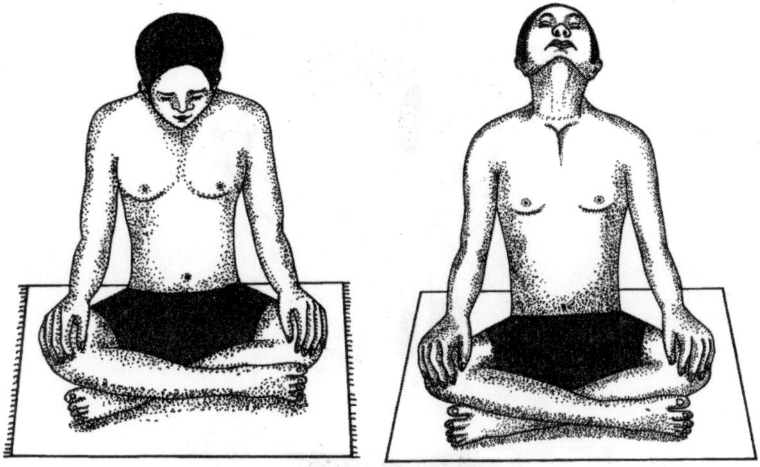

fig. **2.29 a&b** ***Grīvā-sañcālana*** **(neck movement)**
(a) Forward movement of the neck.
(b) Backward movement of the neck.

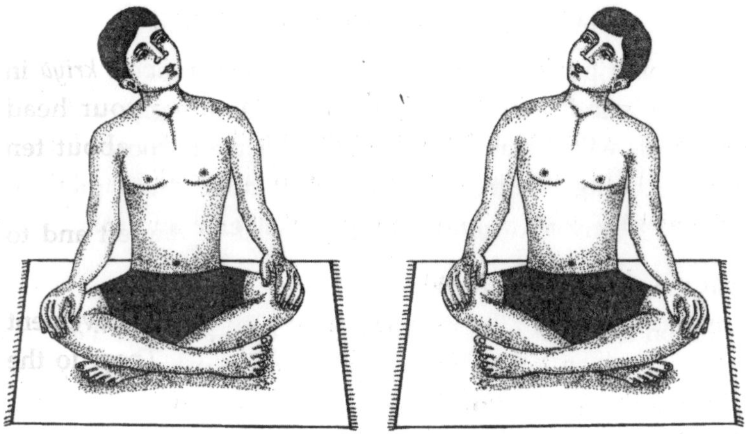

fig. **2.30 a&b:** ***Grīvā-sañcālana*** **(neck movement).**
(a) Tilting the neck to the right.
(b) Tilting the neck to the lift.

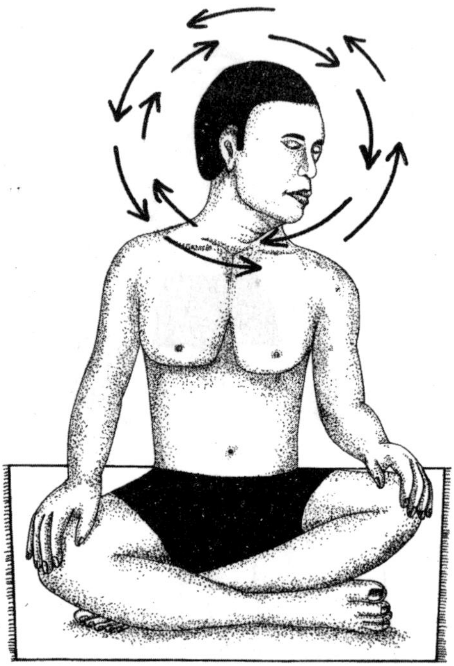

***fig.* 2.31 *Grīvā-sañcālana* (neck movement) : Circling movement of the head.**

ĀSANAS (USEFUL FOR *YOGA-NIDRĀ*)

Yoga-nidrā is practised in *śavāsana* (the corpse pose). Hence, this *āsana* is indispensable for the practice of *yoga-nidrā*. The other *āsana*s which may be dispensable for the purpose of *yoga-nidrā* are being recommended here. If done, the beneficial effects of *yoga-nidrā* would multiply in degree and quality.

Śavāsana (the corpse pose)

Lie flat on the back with face upwards, with arms on the sides of the body and palms facing medially upwards. Keep the heels slightly apart, with the feet in a V-shape. Close the eyes (*fig.* 2.32).

Relax your whole body. Make all parts of the body immobile. Relax the mind. Bring it to either a thoughtless

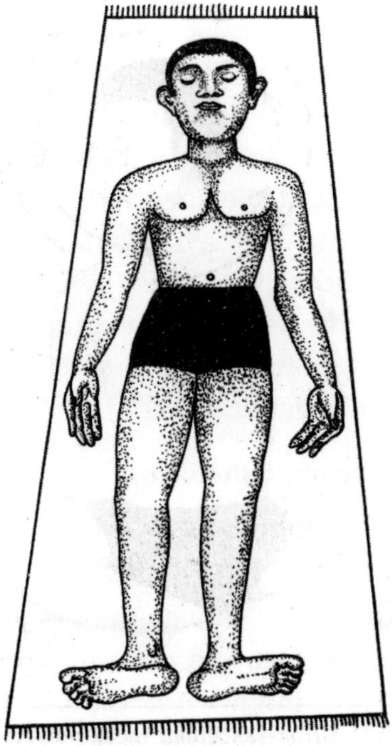

fig. **2.32 *Śavāsana* (the corpse pose).**

condition or a condition of breath-consciousness. (In *yoga-nidrā,* the mind will not be thoughtless; the awareness will rapidly shift.) *Ajapā-japa* may be accompanied with breath-consciousness. *Praṇava-japa* may also be done in both inhaling and exhaling. Let your inhalation and exhalation be slow, steady, rhythmic and natural.

Remain in this *āsana* comfortably for five to ten minutes or even longer.

Padmāsana (the lotus pose)

If *nāḍī-śodhana prāṇāyāma* is done before the practice of *yoga-nidrā,* the posture recommeded is *padmāsana* or *siddhāsana* or *svastikāsana.*

For the practice of *padmāsana,* sit on the floor with the legs stretched in front. Fold the right leg at the knee and place the right foot on the top of the left thigh. See that the sole of the right foot faces upwards and the right heel touches the pelvic bone. Fold the left leg at the knee and place the left foot on the top of the right thigh, the left sole facing upwards and the left heel touching the pelvic bone (*fig.* 2.33). Sit in an erect position by keeping the head, neck and torso in a vertical line perpendicular to the ground level. In an ideal *padmāsana,* both the knees touch the ground.

Siddhāsana (the accomplished pose)

Siddhāsana is necessary in the practice of *yoga-nidrā* if *nāḍī-śodhana prāṇāyāma* is done prior to the yogic sleep.

To sit in *siddhāsana,* first sit with the legs stretched forward. Fold the left leg at the knee and place the sole of the left foot flat against the right thigh while the left heel presses the perineum (*sīvana*). Next, fold the right leg at the knee and

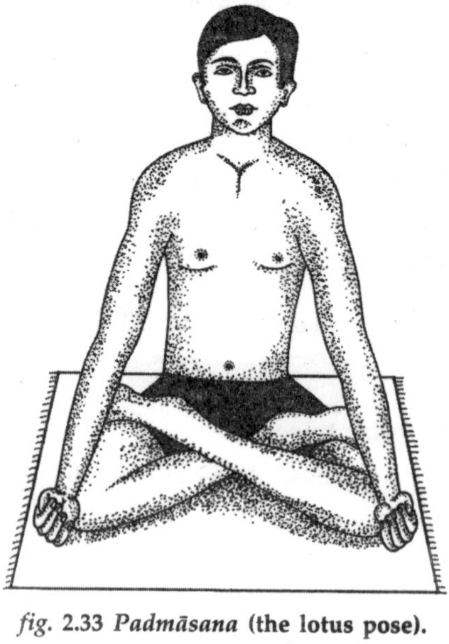

fig. 2.33 *Padmāsana* (the lotus pose).

place its foot on the top of the left calf, with the right sole flat against the left thigh. Press the pelvic bone with the right heel directly above the genitals. See that the toes of each foot are logded between the calf and the thigh muscles of the opposite leg (*fig.* 2.34).

It may be noted here that, in *siddhāsana,* the weight of the body is transmitted to the ground through the two buttocks. Hence, one should sit on the buttocks and not on the heels.

This *āsana* can be practised with either leg upward. It is done with *cin-mudrā* or *jñāna-mudrā.*

Siddhāsana is practised by men only. Women practise *siddha-yoni-āsana* instead of *siddhāsana*. The procedure is the same except one deviation. The heel of the lower leg is placed inside the labia majora of the vagina.

The spine should be erect while sitting in *siddhāsana* or *siddha-yoni-āsana*.

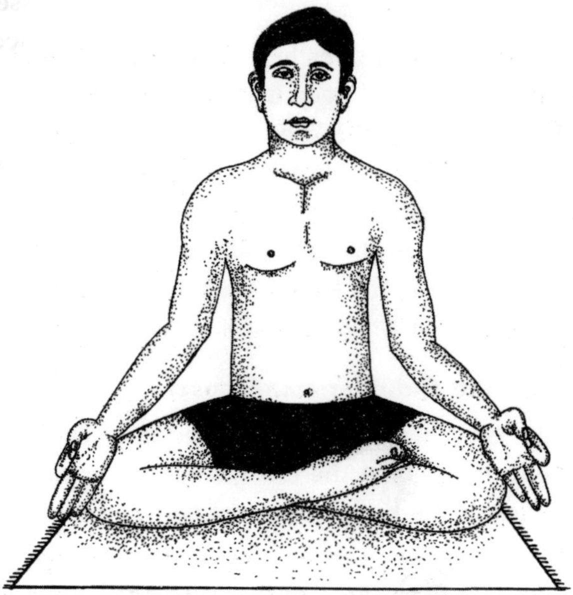

***fig.* 2.34 *Siddhāsana* (the accomplished pose).**

Svastikāsana (the auspicious pose)

Fold the left leg and place the left foot adjacent to the right thigh muscles.

Fold the right leg and place the right foot in the space between the left thigh and the left calf muscle.

The toes of each foot lie between the thigh and the calf of the opposite leg.

The hands can be placed on the respective knees in *cin-mudrā* or *jñāna-mudrā*. They may also be placed on the lap in *bhairava* or *bhairavī-mudrā*.

For illustration, see *siddhāsana*. In *siddhāsana*, the left heel presses the perineum, whereas, in *svastikāsana*, it does not press.

Sukhāsana (the easy pose, the comfortable pose)

This *āsana* is not necessary for *yoga-nidrā*. It is a component of *meru-agra-vakrāsana* which is one of the *prāṇa-sañcālana kriyā*s and, hence, is given here.

Sit with both the legs stretched in front of the body. Fold the left leg at the knee and keep its foot under the right thigh. Then fold the right leg at the knee and keep its foot under the left calf muscle, the right ankle remaining under the left ankle. Finally, adjust the position of the left foot under the right calf to maintain symmetry in the levels of the two knees (*fig*. 2.35). In the regular *sukhāsana*, the hands are placed on the respective knees, or on the lap in *bhairava-mudrā*.

Sarvāṅgāsana (the shoulder-stand pose)

Lie flat on the back, with the arms by the sides and palms on the floor. Fold the arms at the elbows. Place the palms at the respective sides of the body at a level between the chest and the abdomen. Using the arms as levers, raise the legs and the trunk to a vertical position. Use the arms bent at the elbows

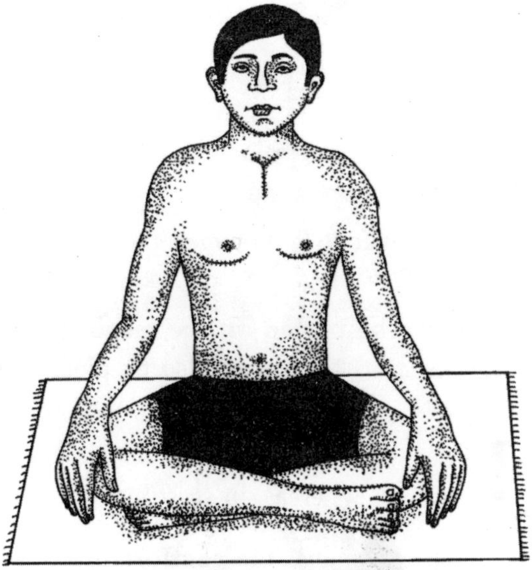

fig. **2.35** ***Sukhāsana*** **(the easy pose).**

as props (*ālamba*). The bending of the trunk should be at a level below the shoulders. Adjust the position of the palms so that the chin presses against the chest (*fig*. 2.36). The higher the position of propping hands, the more ideal the right angle of the legs and the torso at the shoulders. Stay in this *āsana* for about five minutes.

Halāsana (the plough pose)

Lie on the back with the face upwards, the arms by the sides of the body and the palms facing downwards. Slowly raise the legs to a vertical position while keeping them straight. Bend the trunk and lower the legs over the head until the toes of both the feet touch the floor. Keep the legs without bending at the knees. Bend the arms at the elbows and place the hands on the back as in *sarvāṅgāsana*. Remain in this final pose (*fig*. 2.37) for a comfortable period and then return to the starting position.

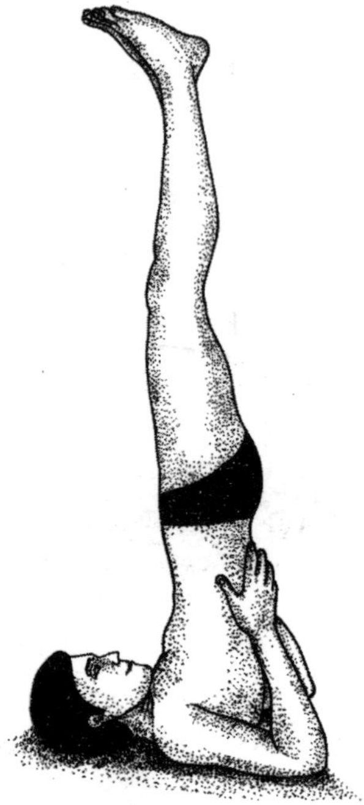

fig. **2.36** ***Sarvāṅgāsana*** **(the shoulder stand pose).**

fig. **2.37** ***Halāsana*** **(the plough pose).**

Matsyāsana (the fish pose)

Matsyāsana is practised after *halāsana* or *sarvāṅgāsana*. Sit in *padmāsana*. Bend backwards, while supporting the body with the forearms and elbows. Let your trunk and head lie on the floor. Fold the arms at the elbows and keep the hands flat on the floor by the sides of the head, with palms downwards and fingers and thumbs pointing towards the shoulders. Using the palms as the lever, bend upwards to make a convexity of the spine in the upward direction, while the crown of the head touches the ground. Hold the big toes and rest the elbows on the floor. Arch the back as much as possible. Remain in this pose (*fig.* 2.38) for a half of the duration of *sarvāṅgāsana*.

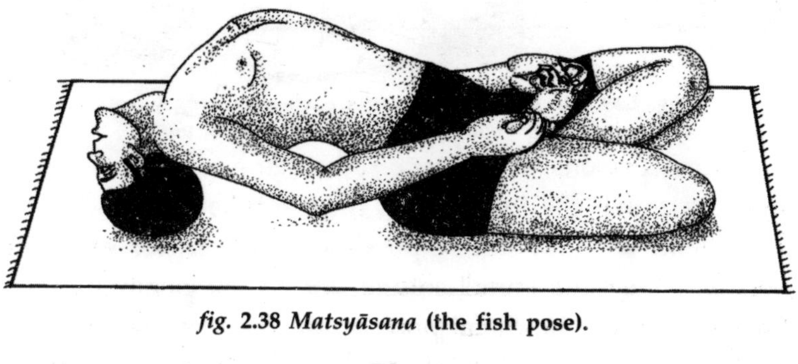

fig. **2.38** ***Matsyāsana*** **(the fish pose).**

Paścimottānāsana (the back-stretching pose)

Sit on the floor, with the legs stretched in front and the lower arms on the thighs. Slowly bend your trunk forward while your hands slide along the top of the legs. When you bend down, bend the head between the hands. Grasp the big toes with the respective thumbs and index and middle fingers. Touch the knees with the forehead. Do not bend the legs at the knees. Remain in this final pose (*fig.* 2.39) for a comfortable length of time. Slowly return to the starting position.

This *āsana* may also be practised in the standing posture.

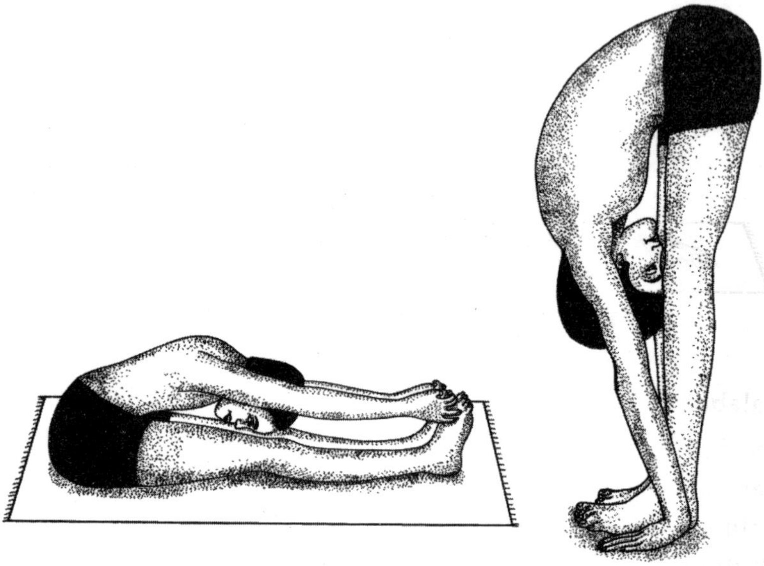

fig. **2.39** ***Paścimottānāsana*** **(the back-stretching pose).**

Young persons with elastic spine can easily grasp the big toes and touch the knees with their forehead in their very first attempt. It may not be possible, however, for grown-up persons with rigid spinal column during the beginning days. They may hold the distal parts of the legs, or the ankles, or the heels as near as possible to the feet. Even for them, the final pose will be attained in the due course of practice.

Bhujaṅgāsana (the cobra or the serpent pose)

Lie on the floor, with face downwards, legs straight and feet extended. Place the palms flat on the floor under the shoulders, with fingers pointing towards the head. Slowly raise the head and the shoulders off the ground; bend the back and the head upwards and backwards as much as possible until the arms are straight. Keep the pubis as near to the ground as possible. Hold this final pose (*fig.* 2.40) as long as it is comfortable for you.

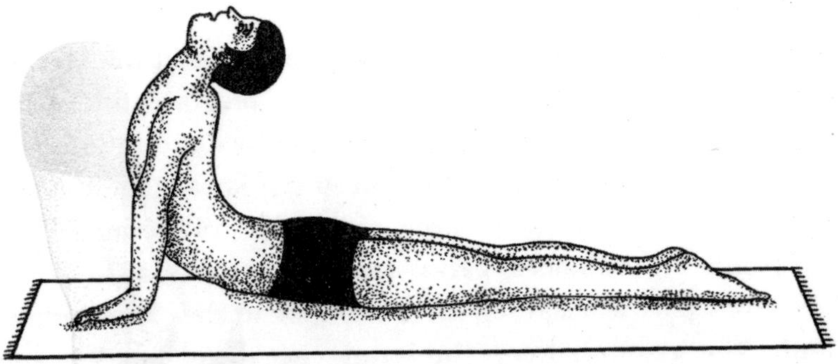

fig. **2.40** ***Bhujaṅgāsana*** **(the cobra or the serpent pose).**

Śalabhāsana (the locust pose)

Lie full length on the floor, with the face downwards, the hands under the thighs, with palms facing upwards. Use the palms as lever to raise the legs and the lower abadomen. Without bending the legs, raise the legs and the lower abdomen as high as possible (*fig.* 2.41). Return to the starting position and repeat the practice five times.

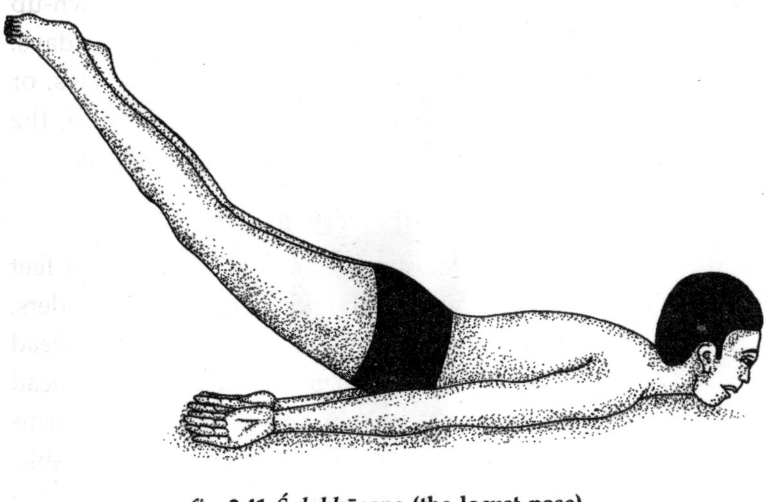

fig. **2.41** ***Śalabhāsana*** **(the locust pose).**

Vajrāsana (the thunderbolt pose)

Sit with both the legs folded at the knees so that the feet are stretched backwards, the soles of the feet are under the buttocks on both sides of the anus, the toes are interlocked and the calves touch the thighs. Keep the knees together and heels apart, positioning the heels at the sides of the hips. Place the palms on the knees, palms facing downwards (*fig*. 2.42). The front part of each leg from the toes to the knee should touch the ground. Keep the trunk, neck and head in one vertically straight line.

The *vajrā nāḍī* flows from the *kanda* (bulb) at the *mūlādhāra*. It is a *nāḍī* inside the *suṣumṇā*. The *vajrāsana* stimulates the flow of *prāṇa* through the *vajrā*.

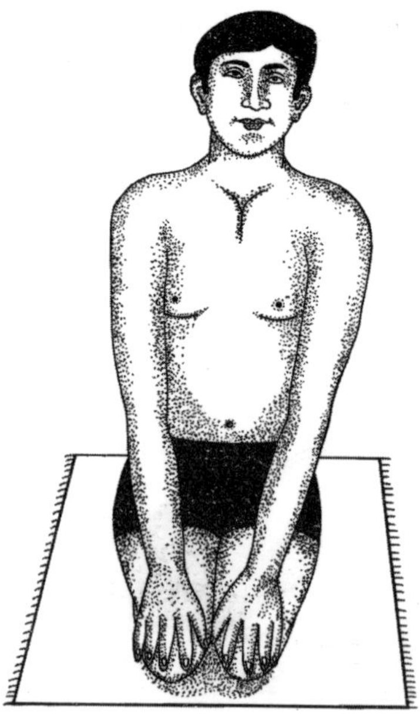

fig. **2.42** ***Vajrāsana*** **(the thunderbolt pose).**

The *maṇipūra cakra* controls the legs. The pressure on the knees, ankles, the upper sides of the feet and the soles exerts a feedback effect on the *maṇipūra* that takes care of the digestive organs and digestion, the locomotive limbs and the visual sense-organs.

Naukāsana or Nāvāsana (the boat pose)

Sit on the floor with legs stretched in front, arms straight and palms on the floor. Raise the legs without folding at the knees, raise the straightened arms with palms downwards at a level with the feet and keep your trunk, neck and head in an inclined position in between the horizontal floor and the perpendicular to it (at 45^0 angle to the floor). The level of the raised head and feet should not exceed about 30 cm off the ground. The level of the arms and the toes should be the same and they should be in one line (*fig*. 2.43).

Maintain the balance of the body on the buttocks only. Do not allow any part of the spine to touch the floor.

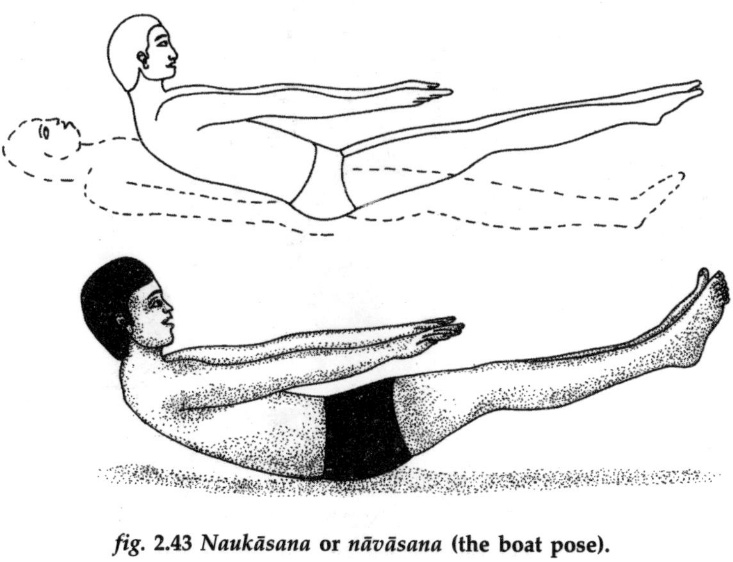

***fig*. 2.43 *Naukāsana* or *nāvāsana* (the boat pose).**

Stay in the final position for a comfortable length of time. Slowly return to the starting position. Repeat this *āsana* five times.

Makarāsana (the crocodile pose)

Lie flat on the floor with the back up and abdomen down. Raise the head and the shoulders. Keep the elbows on the floor. Rest the mandible on both the palms of the hands (*fig.* 2.44).

Close the eyes. Relax the whole body. Breathe naturally and rhythmically. Fix your awareness on the natural inhalation and exhalation. Maintain the *āsana* as long as possible.

You may practise the basic form of *ujjayī prāṇāyāma* (without *khecarī mudrā* and without retention) while you are

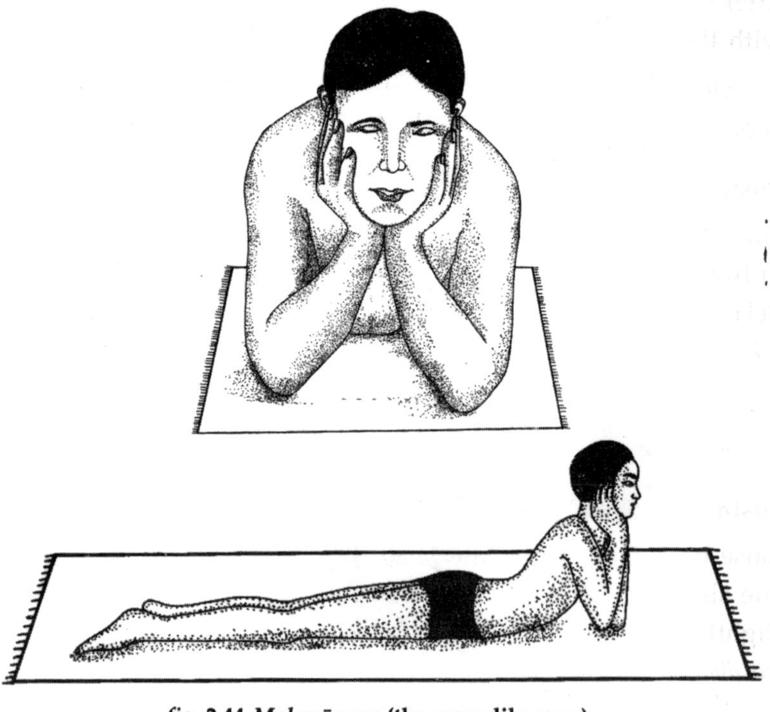

fig. **2.44** ***Makarāsana*** **(the crocodile pose).**

in the *makarāsana*. Thereby you will benefit a lot especially if you have any of the health problems of slipped disc, lumbar spondylitis, cervical spondylitis, other spinal disorders, asthma, other pulmonary ailments, hypertension and mental tension.

SŪRYA NAMASKĀRA (SALUTATION TO THE SUN)

Sūrya namaskāra comprises a series of twelve postures, each of which corresponds to one of the twelve signs of the zodiac. One round of *sūrya namaskāra* is completed by practising the twelve postures twice.

While practising each of the twelve postures, a *mantra* is uttered verbally or mentally. The *mantra*s are meant to salute the sun. Alternatively, *bīja mantra*s (seed-syallables) are also uttered. Non-Hindus or agnostics or atheists may dispense with these *mantra*s if they like.

Sūrya namaskāra is not traditionally regarded as part of *yoga* practices.

Posture 1 : Praṇāmāsana (the prayer pose)

Stand erect, with the feet together. Keep the palms together in front of the chest at the level of the *anāhata cakra* (*fig*. 2.45). Relax the body and breathe normally. Do *dhāraṇā* on the *anāhata cakra*.

Mantra: *o'ṁ mitrāya namaḥ* (Salutations to the friend of all).

Alternative *bīja mantra* : *o'ṁ hrāṁ*.

Posture 2: Hasta Uttānāsana (the raised arms pose)

Raise both arms above the head, keeping them separated by one shoulder's breadth. Bend the head and the upper torso slightily backward (*fig*. 2.46). Inhale while raising the arms. Do *dhāraṇā* on the *viśuddhi cakra*.

fig. **2.45** ***Sūrya-namaskāra*****:** ***praṇāmāsana*** **(the prayer pose).**

fig. **2.46** ***Sūrya-namaskāra*** **:** ***hasta-uttānāsana*** **(the raised arms pose).**

Mantra : *o'ṁ ravaye namaḥ* (Salutations to the shining one).

Alternative *bīja mantra*: *o'ṁ hrīṁ.*

Posture 3 : Padahastāsana (the hand to foot pose)

Bend forward until the fingers or hands touch the ground on either side or in front of the feet, while the forehead touches the knees. In this bending position, keep the legs straight (*fig.* 2.47). Exhale as you bend forward. Do *dhāraṇā* on the *svādhiṣṭhāna cakra.*

Mantra: *o'ṁ sūryāya namaḥ* (Salutations to the one who induces activity).

Alternative *bīja mantra*: *o'ṁ hrūṁ.*

Posture 4 : Aśva Sañcālanāsana (the equestrian pose)

Stretch the right leg back as far as possible. Simultaneously bend the left leg while keeping the position of the left foot unaltered. Rest both the palms on the ground at the level of the left foot on either side. Keep the arms straight. The right

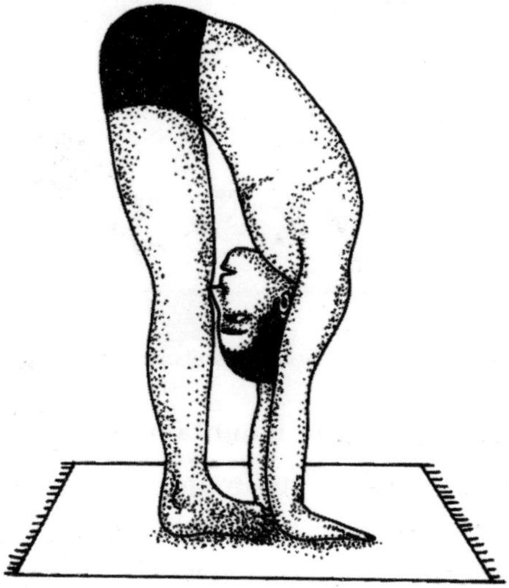

***fig.* 2.47 *Sūrya-namaskāra* : *pādahastāsana* (the hand to foot pose).**

knee should touch the ground. Tilt the head backward while gazing directly upward. In this final position (*fig*. 2.48), the back is slightly arched. The weight of the body is borne by the two hands, the left foot, the right knee and the toes of the right foot. While taking this posture, *dhāraṇā* is done on the *ājñā cakra*.

Mantra : *o'ṁ bhānave namaḥ* (Salutations to the one who illumines)

Alternative *bīja mantra* : *o'ṁ hraiṁ*.

***fig*. 2.48 *Sūrya-namaskāra* : *aśvasañcālanāsana* (the equestrian pose).**

Posture 5 : Parvatāsana (the mountain pose)

Start this posture from the equestrian pose. Straighten the left leg and place the left foot beside the right foot. Raise the buttocks to a position as high as possible. Lower the head so that it lies between the two arms. Now you have formed a triangle, the ground being the base, the two legs being one side and the trunk, neck and head being the other side. In the final position (*fig.* 2.49), the legs and arms should be straight and the heels in contact with the ground. While you are in this posture, do *dhāraṇā* on the *viśuddhi cakra*.

Mantra : *o'ṁ khagāya namaḥ* (Salutations to the one who moves in the sky).

Alternative *bīja mantra* : *o'ṁ hrauṁ*.

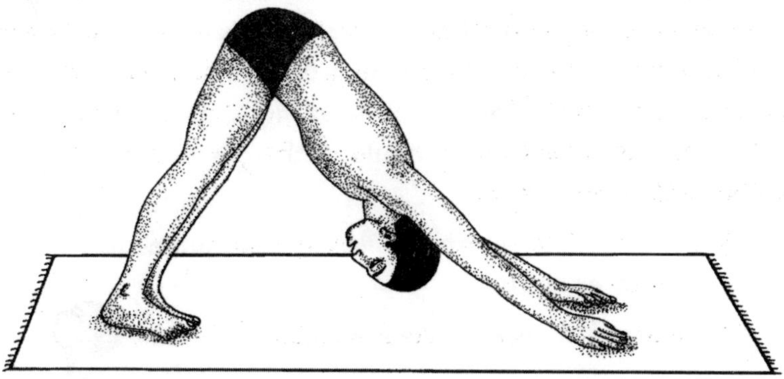

***fig.* 2.49 *Sūrya-namaskāra* : *parvatāsana* (the mountain pose).**

Posture 6: Aṣṭāṅga Namaskāra (Salute with eight limbs)

Now begin from the *parvatāsana*. Lower the body to the ground so that in the final position (*fig.* 2.50), only the toes of both the feet, the two knees, the chest, the hands and the chin touch the ground, with the hips and the abdomen slightly raised off the ground. While in this posture, respiration should be stopped and *dhāraṇā* done on the *maṇipūra cakra*.

Mantra: *o'ṁ pūṣṇe namaḥ* (Salutations to the nourisher.)

Alternative *bīja mantra* : *o'ṁ hraḥ*.

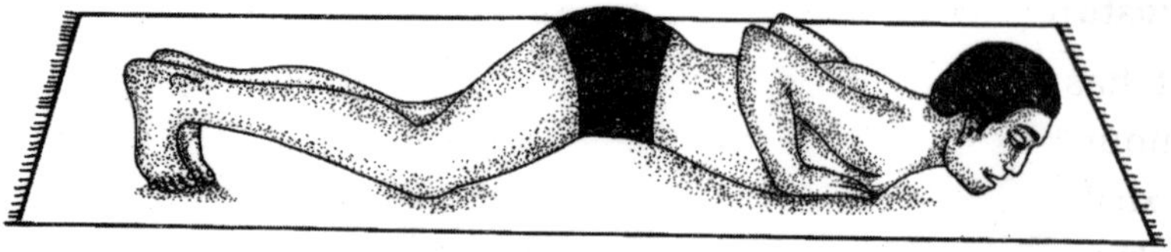

fig. **2.50 *Sūrya-namaskāra* : *aṣṭāṅga namaskāra* (salute with eight limbs).**

Posture 7 : Bhujaṅgāsana (the serpent pose)

Start this pose from *aṣṭāṅga namaskāra*. Straighten the arms and thereby raise the body anterior to the waist. Bend the head backwards. By this, the back is arched. This is a backward bending posture. Inhale while raising the trunk, neck and head and arching the back. The final position (*fig.* 2.51) of this posture is the same as *bhujaṅgāsana*. While in the posture, do *dhāraṇā* on the *svādhiṣṭhāna cakra*.

Mantra : *o'ṁ hiraṇyagarbhāya namaḥ* (Salutations to the golden embryo).

Alternative *bīja mantra* (seed syllable): *o'ṁ hrāṁ*.

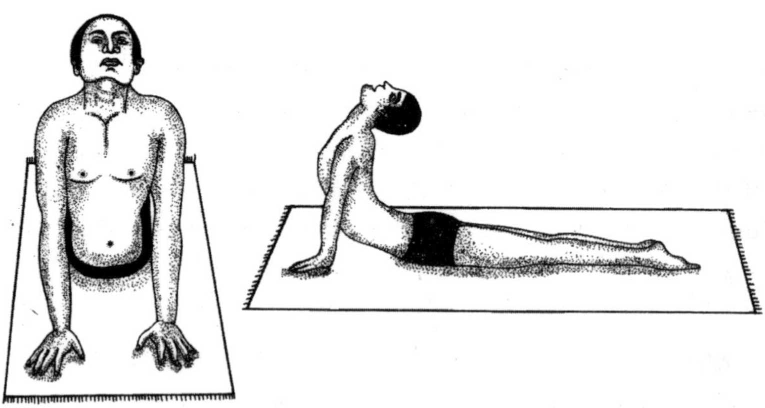

fig. **2.51 *Sūrya-namaskāra* : *bhujaṅgāsana* (the cobra pose).**

Posture 8 : Parvatāsana (the mountain pose)

It has already been described in posture 5. Assume the mountain pose from the stage of *bhujaṅgāsana* (posture 7). Exhale while you raise the buttocks. Do *dhāraṇā* on the *viśuddhi cakra*.

Mantra : *o'ṁ marīcaye namaḥ* (Salutations to the Lord of the dawn).

Alternative *bīja mantra* (seed syllable): *o'ṁ hrīṁ*.

Posture 9 : Aśva Sañcālanāsana (the equestrian pose)

It has already been described in posture 4. Starting from posture 8 (*parvatāsana*), assume this posture by bending the left leg and bringing the left foot forward to a position near the hands. Simultaneously lower the right knee to touch the floor. Inhale while assuming this posture and do *dhāraṇā* on the *ājñā cakra*.

Mantra : *o'ṁ ādityāya namaḥ* (Salutations to the son of Mother Aditi, the infinite Cosmic Nature).

Alternative *bīja mantra* (seed syllable): *o'ṁ hrūṁ*.

Posture 10 : Padahastāsana (the hand to foot pose)

It has already been described in posture 3. Assume the pose from posture 9. Place the right foot by the side of the left foot. Straighten both the legs. Bring the forehead close to the knees, without bending the legs. Do not strain if your forehead does not touch the knees. Exhale while performing the movements. During the pose, do *dhāraṇā* on the *svādhiṣṭhāna cakra*.

Mantra : *o'ṁ savitre namaḥ* (Salutations to the one who is the generator).

Alternative *bīja mantra* (seed syllable): *o'ṁ hraiṁ*.

Posture 11 : Hasta Uttānāsana (the raised arms pose)

It has already been described in posture 2. Assume this pose from posture 10. Straighten the whole body. Raise the arms above the head and keep them separated by one shoulder's width. Slightly bend the head and the arms backwards. Inhale as you straighten the body. While you are in the posture, do *dhāraṇā* on the *viśuddhi cakra*.

Mantra : *o'ṁ arkāya namaḥ* (Salutations to the one who is adorable).

Alternative *bīja mantra* (seed syllable) : *o'ṁ hrauṁ*.

Posture 12 : Praṇāmāsana (the prayer pose)

It is the final pose that has already been described in posture 1. From posture 11, bring the hands to the front of the chest, place the palms together in *namo-mudrā* and stand in an erect position. Relax the whole body. Exhale as you assume the final pose. While you are in the final pose, do *dhāraṇā* on the *anāhata cakra*.

Mantra : *o'ṁ bhāskarāya namaḥ* (Salutations to the one who enlightens).

Alternative *bīja mantra* (seed syllable): *o'ṁ hraḥ*.

Full Round of Sūrya Namaskāra

Postures 1 to 12 constitute half a round of *sūrya namaskāra*. To complete the full round, postures 1 to 12 are to be repeated a second time. In the second half round, the following minor changes are recommended.

1. In posture 4 (*aśva sañcālanāsana*), stretch the left leg backward insted of the right leg.
2. In posture 9 (*aśva sañcālanāsana*), bend the right leg and bring the right foot near the hands.

PRECAUTIONS

1. Ladies should avoid the practice of the following postures during the menstrual period or after the third month of pregnancy.

(a) *sūrya namaskāra*

(b) *bhujaṅgāsana*

(c) *sarvāṅgāsana*

(d) *halāsana*

(e) *śalabhāsana*

(f) *matsyāsana.*

2. Conditions in which some *āsana*s are proscribed are listed below.

(a) *Padmāsana* and *siddhāsana*: sciatica, sacral infections.

(b) *Bhujaṅgāsana*: peptic ulcer, hernia, intestinal tuberculosis, hyperthyroidism.

(c) *Śalabhāsana*: peptic ulcer, hernia, intestinal tuberculosis, weak heart and other cardiac ailments.

(d) *Sarvāṅgāsana*: Enlarged thyroid, enlarged liver, enlarged spleen, hypertension, cardiac ailments.

(e) *Halāsana*: Senility, infirmity, sciatica, back ailments, hypertension.

(f) *Paścimottānāsana*: Slipped disc, sciatica, chronic arthritis, sacral infections.

THE PRACTICE OF *ĀSANAS* IN ORDER OF PREFERENCE

As it has been clarified, *yoga-nidrā* can be practised in *śavāsana* without the prior practice of any other *āsana*. However, for the relaxation of the body and the mind which is conducive to the receptivity of the *saṅkalpa*, the prior practice of some *āsana*s is recommended. The following is the schedule in order of preference.

Preference I

1. *Prāṇa-sañcālana kriyā*
2. *Sarvāṅgāsana*
3. *Halāsana*
4. *Matsyāsana*
5. *Paścimottānāsana*
6. *Bhujaṅgāsana*
7. *Śalabhāsana*
8. *Makarāsana*
9. *Vajrāsana* and *ujjayī prāṇāyāma*
10. *Śavāsana* with breath awareness, or with mental *oṅkāra japa* in synchronization with inhalation and exhalation, or with *ajapā japa*
11. *Yoga-nidrā.*

Preference II

1. *Sūrya-namaskāra* (six to twelve rounds)
2. *Prāṇāyāma* : *nāḍī-śodhana* with or without retention or *ujjayī*
3. *Śavāsana* and mental *oṅkāra japa* in synchronization with inhalation and exhalation
4. *Yoga-nidrā.*

Preference III

1. *Prāṇa-sañcālana kriyā*
2. *Naukāsana*
3. *Śavāsana* and *so'haṁ prāṇāyāma*
4. *Yoga-nidrā.*

Preference IV

1. *Śavāsana* and mental *oṅkāra japa* in synchronization with inhalation and exhalation
2. *Yoga-nidrā*.

Relaxation (*śithilīkaraṇa*) is an indispensable prerequisite to *yoga-nidrā*. Hence, the minimum relaxation technique recommended is *śavāsana* with *oṅkāra japa* or *ajapā japa* in synchornization with respiration. With *oṅkāra japa*, *o'ṁ* is mentally uttered while inhaling and the same *o'ṁ* is repeated while exhaling. With *ajapā japa*, *so* (the *sandhi* form from *saḥ*) is mentally uttered while inhaling and *haṁ* (the *sandhi* form from *aham*) while exhaling.

PRĀṆĀYĀMA

Prāṇāyāma is practised at least 15 minutes after mild *āsana*s and one hour after a long practice of rigorous *āsana*s. For better advantage, it precedes any session of meditation or *yoga-nidrā*. *Āsana*s, however, should not be practised after *prāṇāyāma*, at least within one hour after *prāṇāyāma*. If a full meal is eaten, three hours must be elapsed after the meal and before the *prāṇāyāma*. A light snack half an hour before *prāṇāyāma* is permissible. A cup of milk, fruit juice, tea or coffee may be taken, if felt necessary, any time before doing *prāṇāyāma*. All these restrictions are not applicable, however, to *vajrāsana* and *ujjayī prāṇāyāma*.

For the purpose of *yoga-nidrā*, any one of two *prāṇāyāma*s, namely, *nāḍī-śodhana* and *ujjayī*, has been recommended. *Nāḍī-śodhana* has two varieties — without retention of breath (*kumbhaka-rahita*) and with retention of breath (*kumbhaka-sahita*). The yogic breathing, during *prāṇāyāma*, uses the abdomen, chest and clavicles for each respiration; but air enters into the lungs only, not into the abdomen.

Āsanas for Prāṇāyāma

Siddhāsana and *padmāsana* are ideal *āsana*s for *nāḍī-śodhana prāṇāyāma*. *Svastikāsana* may be used for this *prāṇāyāma* if retention (*kumbhaka*) is excluded. We have already described the techniques of these *āsana*s in this book. *Ujjayī prāṇāyāma* may be practised in any of these *āsanas*, in *vajrāsana*, in *śavāsana*, or in none of these *āsanas*. For *ujjayī*, a posture with sitting on a floor, sitting on a hard chair, standing, walking or lying down is good enough. As *vajrāsana* can be practised at any time of the day in full or empty stomach, so is *ujjayī prāṇāyāma* without retention of breath. Any *prāṇāyāma*, with retention of breath (*kumbhaka*), must be done with empty stomach. Excepting *vajrāsana* and *ujjayī prāṇāyāma*, it is generally recommended that *āsana*s and *prāṇāyama*s should be practised three hours after eating a full meal.

Mudrās for Prāṇāyāma

The vital sheath (*prāṇamaya kośa*) is to be switched on through the *mudrā*s. The *mudrā*s redirect *prāṇa* by linking up certain circuits in the *prāṇamaya kośa*. Those *mudrā*s which are relevant to the practice of *prāṇāyāma* are given here.

When alternate nostril breathing is done in a kind of *prāṇāyāma* such as *nāḍī-śodhana*, only the *nāsikāgra-mudrā* is practised. In *prāṇāyāma*s in which the control of the nostrils is not necessary, the other *mudrā*s mentioned below may be used, depending upon the necessity and suitability.

NĀSIKĀGRA OR NĀSĀGRA-MUDRĀ (NOSE-TIP MUDRĀ)

This *mudrā* is used to control the flow of the breath in one or the other of the two nostrils. The right hand is used for this purpose.

Technique. Place the tip of the right thumb by the side (the soft, cartilaginous part) of the right nostril and tips of the right little and ring fingers by the side of the left nostril. Only the tip of the right ring finger may be placed on the left nostril, with the right little finger remaining idle by the side. Maintain the right index and middle fingers in an erect position so that their tips are close to the eyebrow centre. Both these fingers should be relaxed. The right nostril is closed by pressing the right thumb and opened by releasing the pressure. Similarly, the left nostril is closed by pressing the tips of the right little and ring fingers and opened by releasing the pressure. Exert just enough pressure on the sides of the nostrils so that the nasal septum dividing the two nostrils is not distorted to one or the other side. Keep the right arm out of contact with the chest, the right elbow pointing downwards and the arms and shoulders relaxed. This *mudrā* has been illustrated in *fig*. 2.52.

CIN-MUDRĀ (PSYCHIC GESTURE OF CONSCIOUSNESS)

This *mudrā* is practised while sitting in any of the meditational *āsanas*. Both the hands are used. The tips of the index finger

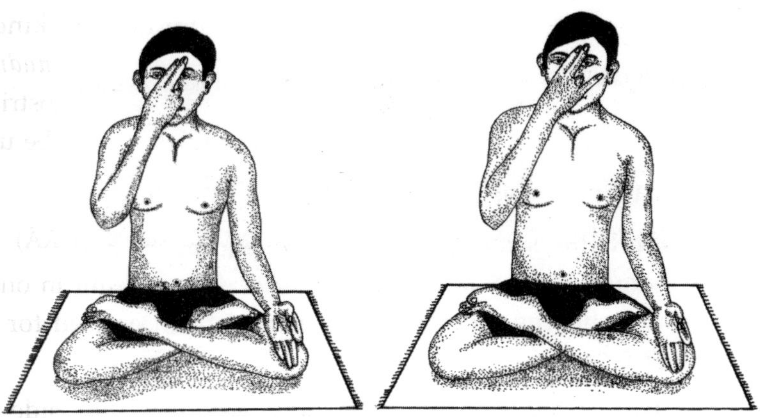

***fig*. 2.52 *Nāsikāgra* or *nāsāgra mudrā* (the nose-tip seal).**

and thumb of each hand touch each other (*fig*. 2.53a). The index finger and the thumb may make a circle, or they may form an acute angle. The hands are placed on the respective knees, with the palms facing upwards. The other three fingers should be straight, but relaxed.

In a variation of the *cin-mudrā*, the tip of the index finger is placed at the root of the thumb (*fig*. 2.53b), the ventral part of the thumb pressing the dorsal part of the index finger.

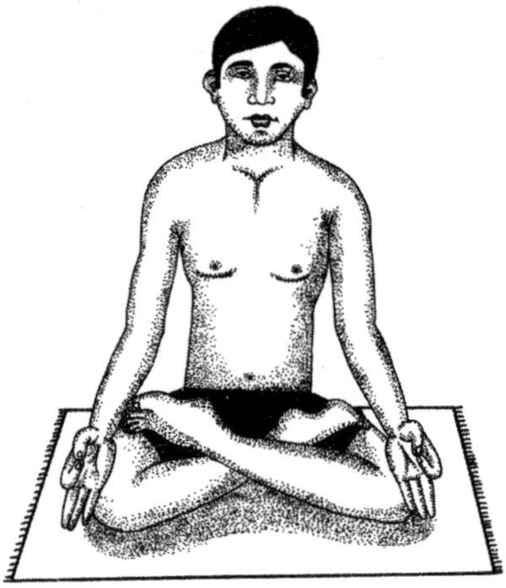

***fig*. 2.53 (a)**

***fig*. 2.53 (b)**

***fig*. 2.53 (a&b) *Cin-mudrā* (the psychic gesture of consciousness).**

JÑĀNA-MUDRĀ (PSYCHIC GESTURE OF KNOWLEDGE)

This *mudrā* is the same as the *cin-mudrā* except the placement of the hands on the knees. In *cin-mudrā*, the palms face upwards, whereas in the *jñāna-mudrā*, the palms face downwards.

The two varieties of the *jñāna-mudrā* are illustrated in *fig*. 2.54a & b.

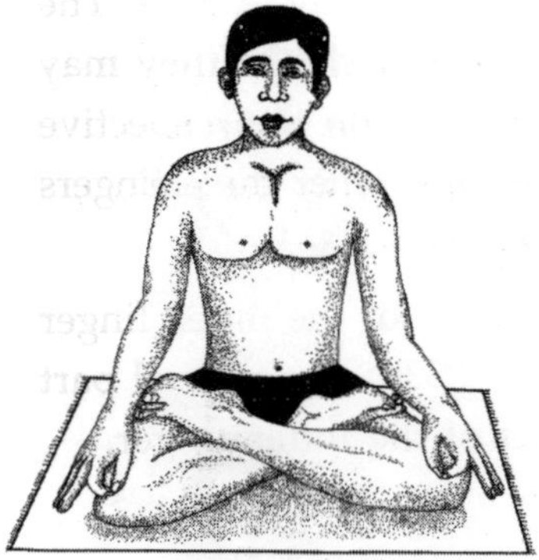

fig. **2.54 (a)**

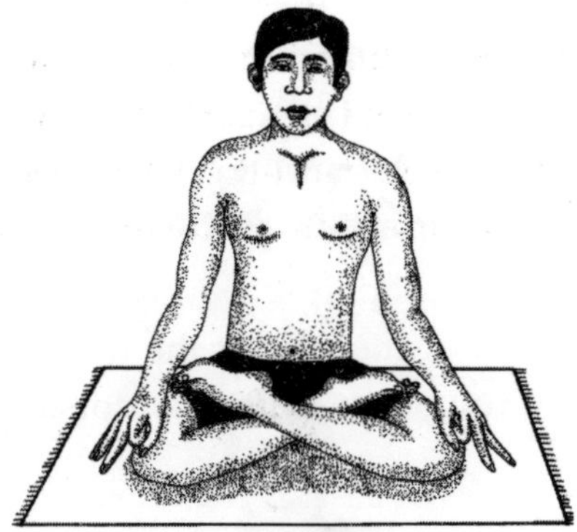

fig. **2.54 (b)**

fig. **2.54 (a&b)** ***Jñāna-mudrā*** **(the psychic gesture of knowledge).**

CINMAYA-MUDRĀ
(PSYCHIC GESTURE OF PERVADING CONSCIOUSNESS)

Fold the index finger to touch the tip or the root of the thumb. Fold the other three fingers so that their tips touch the palm or point towards the palm. Place the hands on their respective knees with the palms facing either upwards or downwards (*fig.* 2.55 a & b).

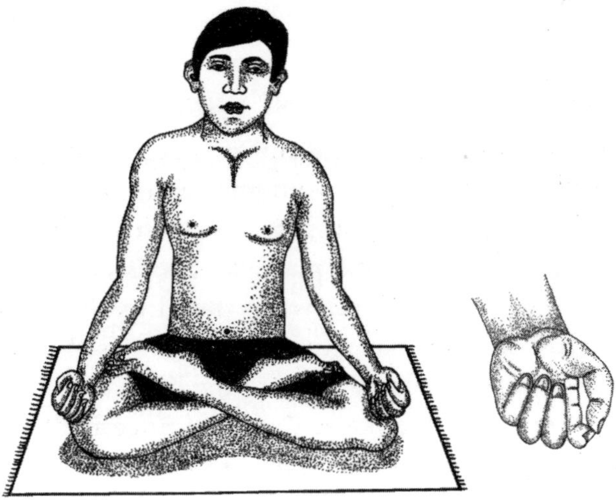

fig. **2.55 a&b:** ***Cinmaya-mudrā***
(the psychic gesture of prevading consciousness).

ĀDI-MUDRĀ (PRIMAL GESTURE)

Fold the thumb into the palm of each hand. Then make a fist of each hand by curling the fingers over the respective thumb. Place each hand on the respective knee with the palm facing either upwards or downwards (*fig.* 2.56 a & b).

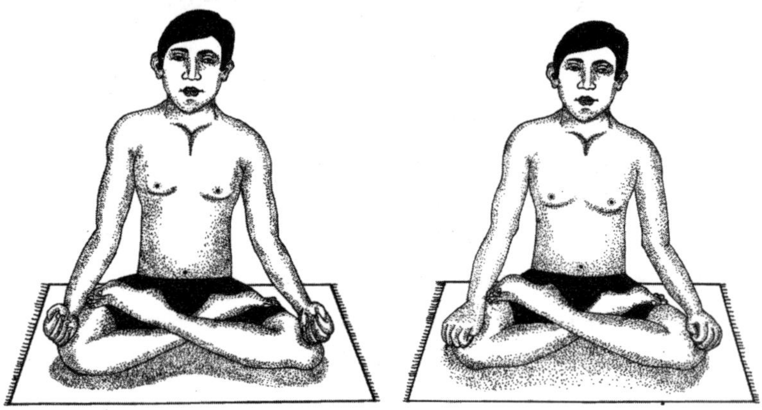

***fig.* 2.56 (a&b) *Ādi-mudrā* (the primal gesture).**

BRAHMA-MUDRĀ
(PSYCHIC GESTURE OF ALL-PERVADING CONSCIOUSNESS)

Turn the thumb of each hand inwards across the palm. Fold the fingers over the respective thumb. Bring the knuckles (the knuckles adjoining the palms, the proximal phalanges) of the fingers to be juxtaposed and place the hands on the lap at the level of the pelvic bone, with the dorsal sides facing downwards and the clasped ventral sides facing upwards. The little fingers should be close to the body and the inserted thumbs away from the body. Keep the fingernails visible by the contact of the finger tips with the rear parts of the palms rather than the palmar middle depression (*fig.* 2.57).

fig.* 2.57 *Brahma-mudrā
(the psychic gesture of all-pervading consciousness).

BHAIRAVA AND BHAIRAVĪ-MUDRĀ (TERRIFYING GESTURES)

Lord Śiva, in his terrifying form, is Bhairava. His Consort (*Śakti*), in her terrifying form, is Bhairavī.

For the *bhairava-mudrā*, place the right hand on the left, both palms facing upwards (*fig.* 2.58 a).

For the *bhairavī-mudrā*, place the left hand on the right, both palms facing upwards (*fig.* 2.58 b).

PRĀṆA-VĀYU-MUDRĀS (VITAL GESTURES)

The main *Prāṇa* has five components, namely, *prāṇa, apāna, vyāna, udāna* and *samāna*. These five *mudrās* are performed by touching the tips of the thumb and the fingers in the following combinations:

(a) (b)

fig. **2.58 The terrifying gesture:**
(a) ***Bhairava-mudrā.*** **(b)** ***Bhairavī-mudrā.***

Prāṇa-mudrā : little finger + ring finger + thumb.

Apāna-mudrā : ring finger + middle finger + thumb.

Vyāna-mudrā : middle finger + index finger + thumb.

Udāna-mudrā : ring finger + middle finger + index finger + thumb.

Samāna-mudrā : little finger + ring finger + middle finger + index finger + thumb.

The respective *mantras* are :

Prāṇa : *o'ṁ prāṇāya svāhā.*

Apāna : *o'ṁ apānāya svāhā.*

Vyāna : *o'ṁ vyānāya svāhā.*

Udāna : *o'ṁ udānāya svāhā.*

Samāna : *o'ṁ samānāya svāhā.*

All the the five *prāṇa-mudrā*s have been illustrated in *figs.* 2.59 to 2.63.

Different scriptures have described these five *mudrā*s in different ways. We have, however, adopted these *mudrā*s as described in the foregoing paragraphs.

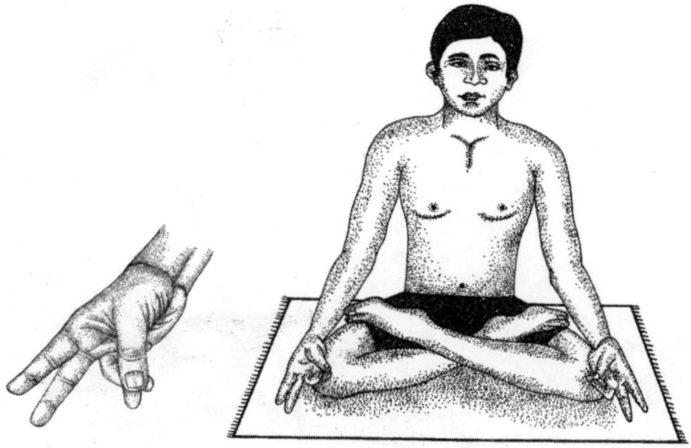

fig. **2.59** ***Prāṇa-mudrā.***

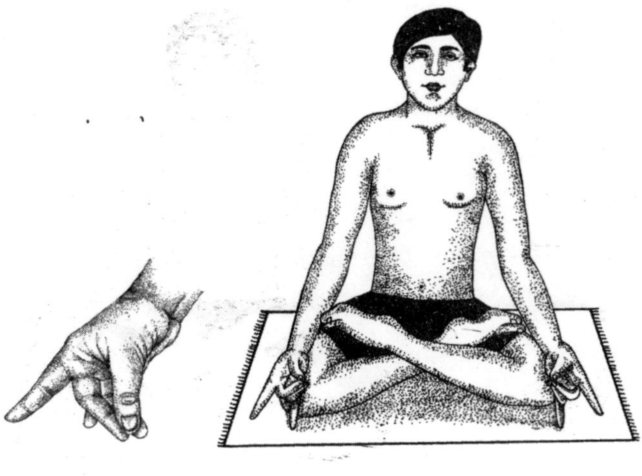

fig. **2.60** ***Apāna-mudrā.***

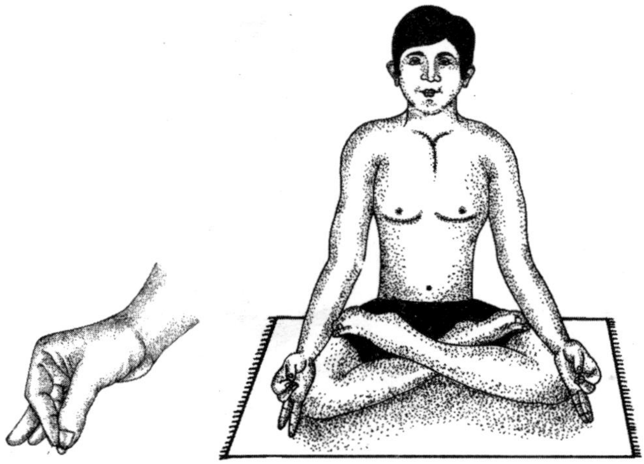

fig. **2.61** ***Vyāna-mudrā.***

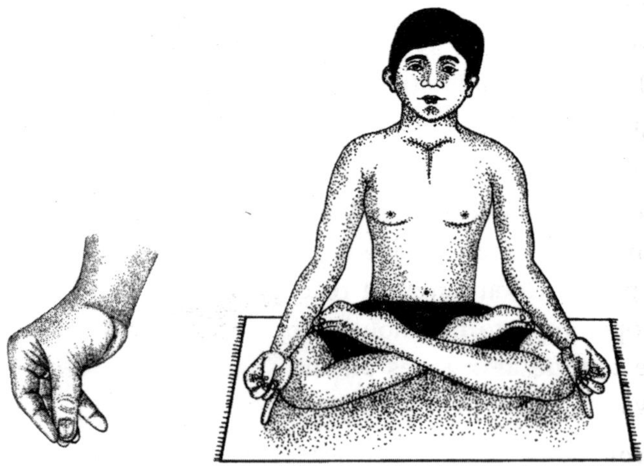

fig. **2.62** ***Udāna-mudrā.***

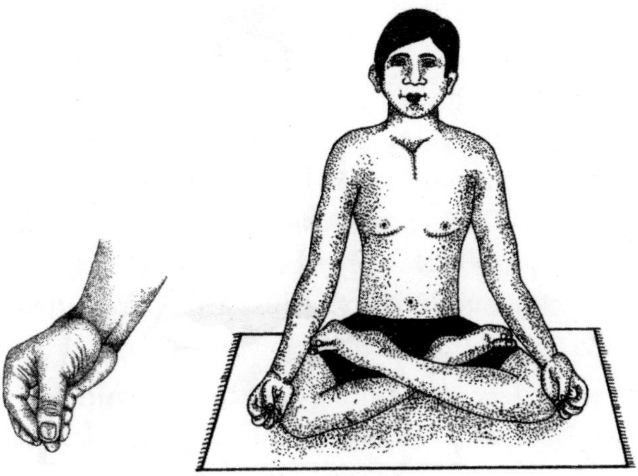

fig. **2.63** ***Samāna-mudrā.***

KHECARĪ OR NABHO-MUDRĀ (TONGUE LOCK)

Sit in any meditational *āsana*. Roll the tongue back. In this rolling process, the lower surface of the toungue touches the upper palate. Close the mouth.

Without straining, try to bring the tongue tip backwards and upwards as far as possible to touch the roof of the pharynx.

Perform this *mudrā* as long as you feel comfortable. You may feel discomfortable after a short time. In that case, relax the tongue for a few seconds and then repeat the *mudrā*.

The word *khecarī* literally means 'roaming through space'. Adept *yogī*s cut the lower tendon of the tongue and thereby they turn the lengthened tongue up and back so as to touch the soft palate, till at length it reaches the inner holes of the nostrils opening into the mouth. The *yogī* closes these holes with the tongue and gazes on the space between the two eyebrows.

Precaution: *Khecarī-mudrā* is not practised in lying down position.

Bandhas for Prāṇāyāma

The word *bandha* means 'blocking', 'putting an obstruction to', 'locking' or 'holding'. *Bandhas* block the flow of *prāṇa* in certain areas of the body and thereby store the *prāṇa* in the concerned area, force it to flow to other areas or to accumulate in certain areas. Through the *bandhas*, certain parts of the gross body are contracted. This physical action influences the *kośas* (sheaths) of the subtle body. Thus, a physical effect brings about a corresponding mental effect.

We will describe four *bandhas* in connection with *prāṇāyāma*. These are : the *jālandhara bandha*, the *uḍḍīyāna bandha*, the *mūla bandha* and the *mahābandha* or otherwise known as the *bandha-traya* (*mūla* + *uḍḍīyāna* + *jālandhara*). When the first three *bandhas* are performed simultaneously, the combination is known as *mahābandha*. The *jālandhara*, the *uḍḍīyāna* and the *mūla bandhas* contract the regions of the throat, upper abdomen and pelvic floor, respectively. They also remove the blockages of the three *granthis* (knots), the *rudra granthi*, the *viṣṇu granthi* and the *brahma granthi*, respectively, of the subtle body.

The *brahma granthi* is located in the *mūlādhāra cakra*. It induces attachment to the material world, sensual, especially sexual gratification and self-centredness.

The *viṣṇu granthi* is located in the *anāhata cakra*. It induces emotions, sentiments, delusion (*moha*), love, affection and attachment to personal relationship. It also creates emotional psychic experiences.

The *rudra granti* is located in the *ājñā cakra*. It creates obstacles generated by intellectual ambitions and thirst, yearning for *siddhis* (miraculous powers) and intellectual psychic experiences.

The *bandhas*, already mentioned, open up these *granthis* and, thus, remove the obstacles created by these *granthis*.

JĀLANDHARA BANDHA (THE THROAT-LOCK OR THE CHIN-LOCK)

Sit in *padmāsana* or *siddhāsana* with head, neck and torso perpendicularly straight and the knees in contact with the floor. Place the palms of the hands on the knees. Close the eyes and relax the body.

Inhale slowly and deeply. Hold the breath inside the chest. In this state of *antara kumbhaka* (internal breath-retention) immediately after the full inhalation (*pūraka*), bend the head forward and press the chin firmly into the notch between the collar-bones on the top of the breast bone (sternum). Then straighten the arms and press the knees down with the hands, simultaneously hunching the shoulders upward and forward (*fig.* 2.64). Remain in this *bandha* as long as the breath can be comfortably retained without straining.

To release the *bandha*, relax the shoulders, bend the

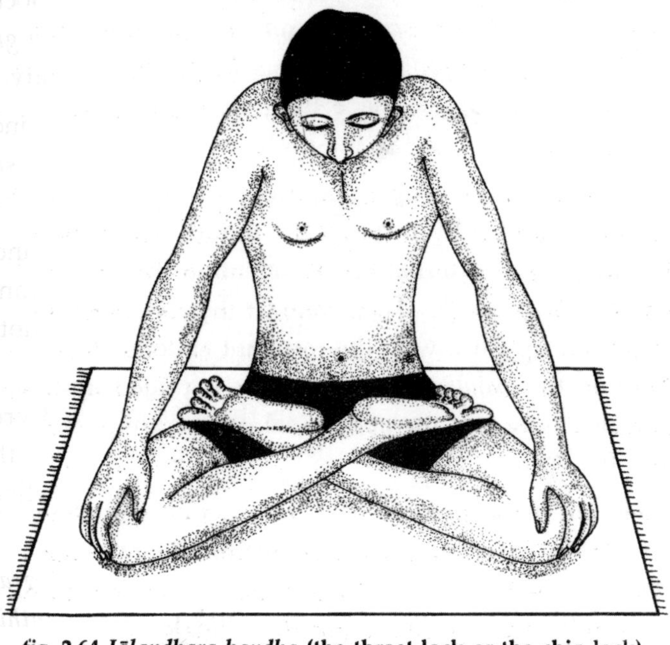

***fig.* 2.64 *Jālandhara bandha* (the throat-lock or the chin-lock).**

elbows, slowly release the chin lock, raise the head and then exhale. The procedure may be repeated.

The *jālandhara bandha* is practised during internal breath retention (*antara kumbhaka*) and external breath retention (*bāhya kumbhaka*) only. Both the *jālandhara* and the *uḍḍīyāna bandha*s are simultaneously performed in *bāhya kumbhaka* only, but not in *antara kumbhaka*, for which *uḍḍīyāna* is contraindicated. During *antara kumbhaka*, both the *jālandhara* and the *mūla bandha*s are combined. Inhalation (*pūraka*) and exhalation (*recaka*) are not done while one is in the chin-lock position.

Contraindications: *Jālandhara bandha* is contraindicated in pathological conditions of cervical spondylitis, intracranial pressure, hypertension, cardiac ailments and vertigo.

UḌḌĪYĀNA BANDHA (THE ABDOMINAL RETRACTION LOCK)

See that *uḍḍīyāna* is practised with an empty stomach and after the evacuation of the bowels and the bladder. Sit in a meditational pose like *padmāsana* or *siddhāsana* that enables the knees to touch the floor. Place the palms on the respective knees. Close the eyes. Relax the body.

Take a slow and deep inhalation through the nostrils. Exhale slowly and fully through the mouth. Hold the breath out. In this state of external breath retention (*bāhya kumbhaka*), perform *jālandhara bandha*. Then contract the abdominal muscles backward and upward, with the resultant abdominal concavity (*fig*. 2.65). In this *bandha*, the diaphragm is pulled up towards the thoracic cavity and the abdominal organs are pushed back towards the spine.

Remain in the *uḍḍīyāna bandha* for a period that allows you a comfortable external breath retention. Then release the *uḍḍīyāna* and the *jālandhara* in sequential succession. Raise the head to a fully erect position and then inhale.

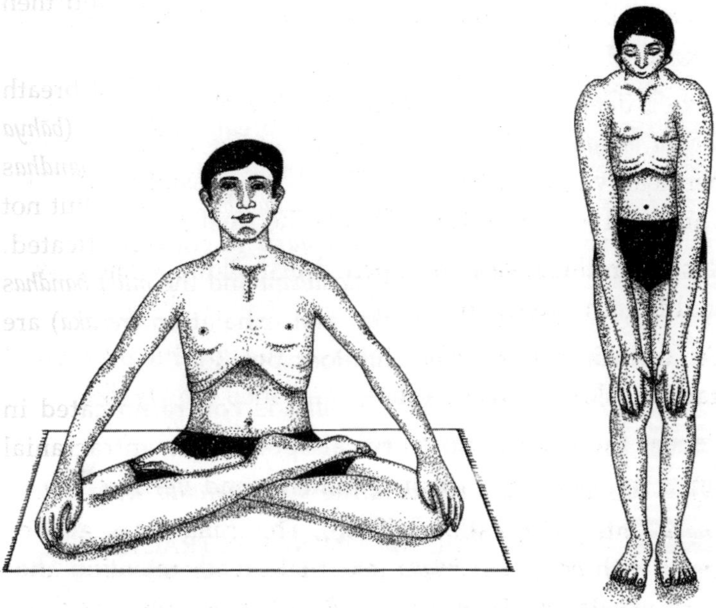

fig. **2.65 *Uḍḍīyāna bandha* (the abdominal retraction lock).**

Repeat the *bandha* after the normalisation of breath.

Special note: *Uḍḍīyāna bandha* should be performed only during *bāhya kumbhaka* following *recaka* (during the interval between complete exhalation and the subsequent inhalation when breathing is fully suspended). It should never be attempted during *antara kumbhaka* (during the interval between complete inhalation and the start of the subsequent exhalation when the breath is retained inside).

Contraindications: *Uḍḍīyāna bandha* is contraindicated for a person suffering from cardiac ailments, peptic ulcer, colitis and hernia. It should also be avoided during pregnancy.

MŪLA BANDHA (THE PERINEUM RETRACTION LOCK)

Sit in any meditational *āsana* with knees firmly fixed to the ground. The best *āsana*, for this purpose, is *siddhāsana/siddha-*

yoni-āsana. Place the palms on the respective knees. Close the eyes. Relax the body.

Take a deep inhalation. Retain the breath inside. Perform *jālandhara bandha*. Without putting excessive strain, contract the perineal/vaginal muscles as tightly as possible and draw them upward and backward. This is the final pose.

Remain in this *bandha* for a period that allows a comfortable internal breath retention.

To unlock the *bandha,* release the perineal/vaginal contraction, slowly raise the head and then slowly exhale.

Repeat the procedure.

What has been described is the *mūla bandha* with *antara kumbhaka* (internal breath retention). This *bandha* can also be practised with *bāhya kumbhaka* (external breath retention after an initial exhalation) *Jālandhara bandha* is necessarily associated with both *antara* and *bāhya kumbhaka*. However, *mūla bandha* can also be practised with normal breathing without internal or external breath retention and without the *jālandhara bandha.* In that case, the *bandha* can be retained for a long period.

In the *mūla bandha,* the region of the lower abdomen between the navel and the anus is contracted towards the spine and pulled up towards the diaphragm. In contrast, in the *uḍḍīyāna bandha,* the entire region from the anus to the diaphragm (up to the sternum) is pulled back towards the spine and lifted up towards the chest.

MAHĀ-BANDHA OR BANDHA-TRAYA (THE TRIPLE LOCK)

The *mahābandha* is a simultaneous combination of the three *bandhas, jālandhara, uḍḍīyāna* and *mūla,* performed during *bāhya kumbhaka* (external breath retention).

Sit in any one of the meditative poses, in which both the knees can touch the ground. The best *āsana,* for this purpose, is *siddhāsana* or *siddha-yoni-āsana*. Sit with knees resting on the floor, spine erect and head straight. Keep the palms on the respective knees. Close the eyes and relax the body.

Take a deep nasal inhalation (*pūraka*). Slowly make a complete exhalation (*recaka*) through the mouth. Retain the breath outside (*bāhya kumbhaka*). Sequentially, perform *jālandhara, uḍḍīyāna* and *mūla bandha*. Maintain this triple lock for a comfortable period without straining.

While you retain this *mahābandha*, rotate your awareness in the sequence : *mūlādhāra* *maṇipūra* *viśuddhi*. Fix your awareness on each *cakra* for a few seconds and then shift to the next. After you complete these three *cakra*s, come back to the *mūlādhāra* and again ascend in the process of the shifting of awareness. Repeat the process until you can comfortably hold your *bāhya kumbhaka*.

To unlock the *bandha*, release *mūla, uḍḍīyāna* and *jālandhara* in the order which is reverse to the starting sequence. Inhale slowly only when the head is upright. This makes one round. Before you commence the next round, allow breath to be normal.

All the three locks of the *mahābandha*, performed together, cannot be illustrated since the *mūla bandha* is concealed. *Fig* 2.66 illustrates the *mahābandha* in which the *jālandhara bandha* and the *uḍḍīyāna bandha* have been shown and the locations of the *mūlādhāra, maṇipūra* and *viśuddhi cakra*s have been indicated.

Nāḍī-Śodhana Prāṇāyāma

Nāḍī means 'a tubular structure with a hollow inside in the network of the psychic channels through which *prāṇa* flows'. Since this *prāṇāyāma* purifies the *nāḍī*s of the body, it is called *nāḍī-śodhana, śodhana* meaning 'purification'.

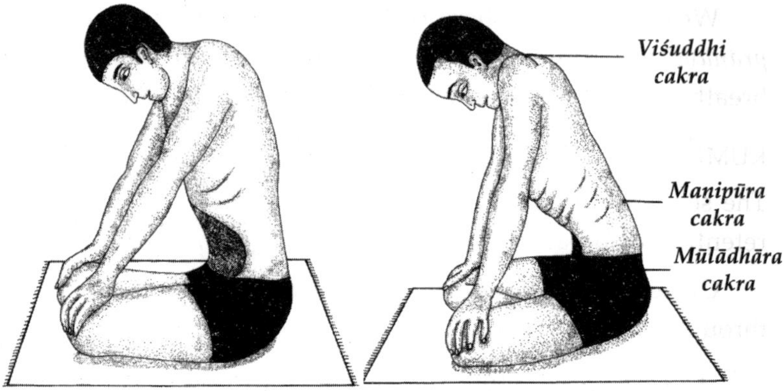

***fig.* 2.66 *Mahā bandha* with the illustration of the *jālandhara bandha* and the *uḍḍīyāna bandha* and the locations of the *mūlādhāra, maṇipūra* and *viśuddhi* (the *mūla-bandha* is concealed).**

Sit in any one of the meditative poses (*padmāsana* and *siddhāsana* are the best ones). Avoid *vajrāsana* for *nāḍī-śodhana*. Keep the left palm on the left knee in *cin-mudrā* or *jñāna-mudrā*. Sit in an erect position with the torso, the neck and head on a vertical line perpendicular to the ground level. Look at the front, Close the eyes. Relax the body.

Fold the right hand at the elbow. Keep it in *nāsikāgra-mudrā* that has already been described. The right thumb-tip on the lateral side of the right nostril controls the flow of air through the right nostril. It closes the right nostril by pressure; it opens it by releasing the pressure. Similar is the control of the left nostril by the tips of the right ring and little fingers or the tip of the right ring finger only. It is important that the nasal septum dividing the two nostrils should not be distorted to one side or the other by the thumb-tip or the finger-tip pressure. The right middle and index fingers should be erect, pointing towards the eyebow centre (*bhrūmadhya sthāna*) throughout the whole practice.

We will describe here two main varieties of *nāḍī-śodhana prāṇāyāma,* namely, *kumbhaka-rahita* (without retention of breath) and *kumbhaka-sahita* (with retention of breath).

KUMBHAKA-RAHITA VARIETY

The sequence of one round of *nāḍī-śodhana prāṇāyāma* without retention of breath (*kumbhaka-rahita*) is given below.

Close the right nostril. Do *recaka* (complete exhalation) through the left nostril. After this, the *prāṇāyāma* round begins.

1. Do *pūraka* (slow, steady and deep inhalation) through the left nostril.
2. Close the left nostril and open the right nostril. Do *recaka* (slow, steady and full exhalation) through the right nostril.
3. Do *pūraka* through the right nostril.
4. Do *recaka* through the left nostril.

This completes one round of the *prāṇāyāma.* Repeat a second round as follows :

1. *Pūraka* through the left nostril.
2. *Recaka* through the right nostril.
3. *Pūraka* through the right nostril.
4. *recaka* through the left nostril.

This is the pattern of the alternate nostril breathing.

One should aim at repeating the rounds of the *prāṇāyāma* for 15 minutes. A five-minutes' period is a good one for the average practitioner.

The period of *pūraka* and that of *recaka* should be ideally equal. We should recommend an approximately equal period. The guide to the practitioner to fix up the length of the period is his comfortableness. The deeper the *pūraka,* the better the effect.

Some *yoga gurus* prescribe counting numbers or counting *praṇava-japa* (repetition of *oṁ*), or even *gāyatrī japa* during inhalation and exhalation. We do not recommend such a practice. In the counting process, attention is focused on the mechanics of counting rather than on the flow of *prāṇa*. But the awareness of the flow of *prāṇa* is more important in the collection, distribution and storage of *prāṇa* in the body.

KUMBHAKA-SAHITA VARIETY

In this variety of *nāḍī-śodhana prāṇāyāma*, the inhaled air is retained in the lungs for some suitable period. This variety has two sub-varieties, namely, with *antara kumbhaka* (internal retention) and with *antara* and *bāhya kumbhaka* (internal and external retentions).

NĀḌĪ-ŚODHANA PRĀṆĀYĀMA WITH ANTARA KUMBHAKA

Close the right nostril. Exhale through the left nostril. Now the round of *prāṇāyāma* begins.

1. Slowly, steadily and deeply do *pūraka* (inhalation) through the left nostril.
2. At the end of the deep inhalation, close both the nostrils and do *antara kumbhaka* (internal retention of breath).
3. Do *recaka* (full exhalation) through the right nostril, while closing the left nostril.
4. Do *pūraka* (full exhalation) through the right nostril, the left nostril remaining closed.
5. Close both the nostrils and do *antara kumbhaka*.
6. Open the left nostril, keeping the right nostril closed. Do *recaka* (exhalation) through the left nostril.

This completes one round. Repeat the process about 25 rounds or more.

The periods of *pūraka, kumbhaka* and *recaka* should ideally be in the proportion of 1: 4: 2. Some *gurus* prescribe the counting of numbers, or counting *praṇava-japa*, or counting *gāyatrī-japa* to strictly control the proportion of the periods. We are, however, not in favour of counting. There is no harm if the proportions are approximate (at best, the benefits may be reduced). There is, however, serious health hazard if the brain is permanently damaged due to anoxia, resulting from the non-availability of oxygen to the brain-cells for a period exceeding three to four minutes. The *prāṇāyāma*-practitioner should decide how long he can comfortably maintain the three processes of *pūraka, kumbhaka* and *recaka* without straining and discomfort. Of course, he should keep in mind the prescribed standard and he approximately attains the standard through continued practice.

There would be a tendency for spurts or gushes of the exhaled air during *recaka* following *kumbhaka*. This should be prevented by voluntary control. The speed of the *recaka* should be slow and steady.

NĀḌĪ-ŚODHANA PRĀṆĀYĀMA WITH ANTARA AND BĀHYA KUMBHAKAS

This *Prāṇāyāma* constitutes the following steps:

1. *Pūraka* through the left nostril.
2. *Antara kumbhaka* (internal breath-retention).
3. *Recaka* through the right nostril.
4. *Bāhya kumbhaka* (suspension of breath after full exhalation when the lungs are completely empty).
5. *Pūraka* through the right nostril.
6. *Antara kumbhaka* (internal breath-retention).
7. *Recaka* through the left nostril.
8. *Bāhya kumbhaka*.

With these eight steps, one round of the *prāṇāyāma* is completed. A repetition of 15 rounds or more is recommended.

The recommended ideal proportion of the duration of inhalation: internal retention: exhalation: external retention is 1 : 4 : 2 : 2. Here also we lay stress on the comfortableness and not on the strict adherence of timing by counting.

During *antara kumbhaka* (internal retention after inhalation), practise *jālandhara bandha* and *mūla bandha*. During *bāhya kumbhaka* (suspension of breath after exhalation or external retention), practise *jālandhara bandha, uḍḍīyāna bandha* and *mūla bandha*. While doing *prāṇāyāma, uḍḍīyāna bandha* is practised during *bāhya kumbhaka* only.

Notes: Introduce *antara kumbhaka* only after gaining mastery over approximately equal *pūraka* and *recaka* in *nāḍī-śodhana prāṇāyāma* without retention.

Do not attempt *bāhya kumbhaka* until you have mastered *antara kumbhaka.*

Learn practising *kumbhaka* under the guidance and personal supervision of an experienced *guru*. It involves risk.

Persons suffering from hypertension and heart diseases should not practise any form of *kumbhaka*. They will be benefitted by the practice of *nāḍī-śodhana prāṇāyāma* without *kumbhaka.*

Persons suffering from low blood pressure will derive benefits from the practice of *nāḍī-śodhana prāṇāyāma* with *antara kumbhaka only.*

It may be emphasized that every *prāṇāyāma* starts with *recaka* (exhalation) and ends with *pūraka* (inhalation). Both these steps are not included in the *prāṇāyāma* cycles.

Ujjayī Prāṇāyāma

The word *ujjayī* (*ut* + *jayī*) literally means 'victorious'. Like *vajrāsana*, this *prāṇāyāma* can be done with empty or full stomach (if breath retention is introduced in *ujjayī*, full stomach is contraindicated). This *prāṇāyāma* can be performed while sitting in any meditative *āsana* (including *vajrāsana*), sitting on the floor or on a hard chair, standing, walking or lying in *śavāsana*. If *khecarī-mudrā* is done along with *ujjayī prāṇāyāma*, the lying down posture is contraindicated, since *khecarī-mudrā* should not be performed while lying. The positions of sitting on a hard chair, standing and walking are not suitable for *ujjayī* with *antara* or *bāhya kumbhaka*. A number of varieties of this *prāṇāyāma* are described here.

VARIETY-1 (THE BASIC FORM)

1. Inhale slowly and deeply through both nostrils. The lungs should be full.

   It is a general recommendation for *prāṇāyāma* that all inhalations are made with a sibilant sound 'ssss' and all exhalations with an aspirate sound 'hhhh'. It is particularly applicable to *ujjayī*.

2. Exhale slowly through both nostrils to evacuate the lungs completely.

This completes one cycle. Repeat the cycles for 10 to 15 minutes. See that the *prāṇāyāma* is done through pulmonary breathing and not through abdominal breathing.

While performing the basic form of *ujjayī prāṇāyāma*, fix your awareness on the inhalations and the exhalations. Think that you are imbibing *prāṇa* from the all-pervading universal source, infusing all the cells of the body with it and storing it in the *cakras*. This is important.

VARIETY-2 (WITH AJAPĀ JAPA)

All human beings, from birth to death, are busy in uttering the *mantra so'ham* in the course of their normal respiration. They silently utter *so* during inhalation and *ham* during exhalation. Unconsciously they do it. The sound is clearly audible to the *yogī* in his intense state of *dhyāna* or *samādhi*. This process is known as *ajapā japa*.

To perform variety-2 of *ujjayī prāṇāyāma*, introduce the *ajapā japa* in the basic form of *ujjayī*.

While inhaling, mentally utter (without producing sound) *so* (the *sandhi* form from *saḥ*) and, while exhaling, *ham* (the *sandhi* form from *aham*). In synchronization with uttering the *mantra so*, shift your awareness from the nostrils through your *ājñā cakra* and *sahasrāra* down to the *mulādhāra*, and with uttering the *mantra ham*, shift your awareness from the *mūlādhāra* through the *sahasrāra* and the *ājñā* to the nostrils.

VARIETY-3 (WITH PRAṆAVA JAPA)

It is the same basic form of *ujjayī* with the introduction of the *japa* of *praṇava* (*o'm*). While inhaling, mentally utter *o'ṁ* and while exhaling, also do the same *praṇava japa, o'ṁ* .

Every entity of the universe, living or non-living, and the universe as a whole are constantly busy in the subtle utterance of the *praṇava*. This universal *japa* is unconsciously done. Its sound is clearly audible to a *yogī* in his intense state of *dhyāna* or *samādhi*.

The shifting of awareness during inhalations and exhalations follows the same pattern as in variety-2.

VARIETY-4 (WITH JĀLANDHARA BANDHA)

Sit in *siddhāsana, padmāsana* or *svastikāsana* with *jālandhara bandha* and *cin-mudrā*.

Inhale and exhale as in variety-1. Listen to the sibilant sound (ssss) during inhalation and the aspirate sound (hhhh) during exhalation.

After each inhalation and exhalation, allow a fractional pause. This momentary pause is not the real *kumbhaka*.

Note: *Jālandhara bandha* is usually practised during *antara kumbhaka* and *bāhya kumbhaka*. It is not usually recommended for *pūraka* and *recaka*. The usual recommendation is: 'Do not inhale and exhale while you are in the *jālandhara bandha*'. However, *ujjayī prāṇāyāma* is an exception. *Jālandhara bandha* can be practised during all the three states (*pūraka, kumbhaka* and *recaka*) of *ujjayī*. It may preferably be dispensed with in *ujjayī*, when done in a standing or a lying down posture or in a sitting posture on a hard chair.

VARIETY-5 (WITH KHECARĪ-MUDRĀ AND JĀLANDHARA BANDHA)

This is the same as variety-4 except the following.

Add *khecarī-mudrā* to *jālandhara bandha* and *cin-mudrā*.

Khecarī-mudrā is not practised in a supine posture.

Hence, avoid variety-5 if you are in *śavāsana*.

VARIETY-6 (WITH ANTARA KUMBHAKA AND BĀHYA KUMBHAKA)

Sit in any meditative posture such as *siddhāsana* or *padmāsana,* with *cin-mudrā*.

Inhale (*pūraka*) fully. Hold the breath for two seconds. During this *antara kumbhaka,* do *jālandhara bandha* and *mūla bandha*.

Exhale (*recaka*) fully. Retain your breath outside for two seconds. During this *bāhya kumbhaka,* remain in *jālandhara bandha* and *uḍḍīyāna bandha*.

Release the *bandha*s and inhale fully. Repeat the cycles.

Be aware of the inhalations with the sibilant sound and the exhalations with the aspirate sound.

Gradually increase the period of *antara kumbhaka* up to 10 to 15 seconds or as long as it is comfortable for you.

Gradually increase the period of *bāhya kumbhaka* up to five seconds.

Note 1: *Uḍḍīyāna bandha* is practised during *recaka* and *bāhya kumbhaka* only. It is contraindicated during *pūraka* and *antara kumbhaka.* Its practice would strain the heart, if done simultaneously with inhalation or internal retention.

Note 2: *Mūla bandha* is not contraindicated during any stage of *prāṇāyāma.* However, both *mūla bandha* and *jālandhara bandha* are specifically recommended for *antara kumbhaka.*

Very little risk is involved in *ujjayī prāṇāyāma,* when done without *kumbhaka.* It is comparatively easy for practice. It is recommended for everybody unless someone has any serious health problem such as heart disease, asthma and very serious hypertension.

For *yoga-nidrā,* the basic form of *ujjayī prāṇāyāma* (variety-1), or its conbination with *ajapā japa* (variety-2) or *praṇava japa* (variety-3) is highly recommended.

With this, we complete the steps preparatory to *yoga-nidrā.* Now the techniques of proper *yoga-nidrā* will be described.

YOGA-NIDRĀ

The basic steps in the sequence of the *yoga-nidrā* techniques are mentioned below:

1. Preparation (*prastuti*)
2. Relaxation (*śithilīkaraṇa*)
3. Resolve (*saṅkalpa*)

4. Rapid shifting of consciousness (*cetanā-sañcāraṇa*)
   A. External body
   B. External body
      and
   internal *cakras*
5. Mental *nāḍī-śodhana* through reverse counting
6. Moving visualization of scenarios (*kālpanika caladdṛśya-darśana*)
7. Resolve (*saṅkalpa*)
8. Finish (*samāpti*)

Preparation (Prastuti)

The *āsanas* and *prāṇāyāmas* preparatory to *yoga-nidrā* have already been described. If their practice precedes *yoga-nidrā,* or is done at other convenient time during the day, better relaxation of the body is achieved, the smooth flow of *prāṇa* in the *nāḍīs* is facilitated and thereby the subconscious and the unconscious are rendered more receptive to the *saṅkalpa*. They are, however, dispensable prerequisites to *yoga-nidrā*. What has been called 'preparation' among the eight limbs of *yoga-nidrā* is different. This preliminary limb is not dispensable.

Lie down in *śavāsana*. Be aware of your physical environment — your room, the mat or the folded blanket on which you lie and your gross body. Do not use any pillow under your head.

Fix your consciousness on the objective of your *yoga-nidrā*. In Tantric language, this is *viniyoga*, the preamble with a positive suggestion to yourself.

In this introductory step, you have to serve two admonitions to yourself. They are: 1. 'No parts of my body will move during *yoga-nidrā*', or, in other words, 'I will be motionless'. 2. 'I will not sleep during *yoga-nidrā*'.

In this initial state, remove all worries, tensions and conflicting thoughts (rather all thoughts other than *yoga-nidrā*) from your mind. Let the mind be still.

Relaxation (Śithilīkaraṇa)

Make all parts of your body, from feet to head, relaxed.

While you are in *śavāsana*, with closed eyes and relaxed body, do *ujjayī prāṇāyāma*, variety-1 (the basic form with awareneness on the inhalations and exhalations), or variety-2 (with *ajapā japa*), or variety-3 (with silent *praṇava japa*). In variety 2 or 3, the silent repetition of the *mantra* should be in synchronization with the inhalations and exhalations.

A minimum period of five minutes is recommended for this second limb of *yoga-nidrā*.

Resolve (Saṅkalpa)

Mentally repeat your resolve (*saṅkalpa*) three times.

External shifting of consciousness (Bahirnyāsa)

Shift your awareness from location to location in your external body. This is *kṣipra calad-dhāraṇā* (*kṣipra* meaning 'fast' and *calat* meaning 'moving'). Follow a definite sequence. Rapidly shift. While you *momentarily* fix your awareness on a location, mentally utter the name of that part of your body, and, for a moment, concentrate on that part (not for more than a moment). This is *kṣaṇika dhyāna* (*kṣaṇa* meaning 'moment'). The following sequence is suggested.

Right side: Right thumb tip (*dakṣiṇa aṅguṣṭhāgra*), index finger tip (*tarjanī-aṅgulyagra*), middle finger tip (*madhyamā-aṅgulyagra*), ring finger tip (*anāmikā-aṅgulyagra*), little finger tip (*kaniṣṭhikā-aṅgulyagra*), thumb root (*aṅguṣṭha-mūla*), index finger root (*tarjanī-mūla*), middle finger root (*madhyamā-mūla*), ring finger root (*anāmikā-mūla*), little finger root (*kaniṣṭhikā-mūla*), right palm (*dakṣiṇa karatala*), the back of the right hand (*dakṣiṇa karapṛṣṭha*), right wrist (*dakṣiṇa maṇibandha*), right forearm (*dakṣiṇa agra-bāhu*), right elbow (*dakṣiṇa kūrpara*), right upper arm (*dakṣiṇa ūrdhva-bāhu*), right shoulder joint (*dakṣiṇa bāhumūla*), right side of the chest (*dakṣiṇa uraḥ-pārśva*), right side of the abdomen (*dakṣiṇa udara-pārśva*), right side of the hip (*dakṣiṇa kaṭi-pārśva* or *dakṣiṇa pādamūla*), right thigh (*dakṣina ūru*), right knee (*dakṣina jānu*), right shank (*dakṣiṇa jaṅghā*), right ankle (*dakṣiṇa gulpha*), right heel (*dakṣiṇa pārṣṇi*), right sole (*dakṣiṇa pādatala*), the top of the right foot (*dakṣiṇa pādapṛṣṭha*), the right big toe (*dakṣiṇa pādāṅguli, prathama*), the second toe, the third toe, the fourth toe, the fifth toe.

Left side: Follow the same sequences as in the right side.

Front side: The top of the head (*śikhā or brahmarandhra*), the forehead (*lalāṭa*), the right eye (*dakṣiṇa netra*), the left eye (*vāma netra*), the spot between the two eyebrows (*bhrūmadhya*), the right ear (*dakṣiṇa karṇa*), the left ear (*vāma karṇa*), the right nostril (*dakṣiṇa nāsāpuṭa*), the left nostril (*vāma nāsāpuṭa*), the right cheek (*dakṣiṇa gaṇḍa*), the left cheek (*vāma gaṇḍa*), the upper lip (*ūrdhvoṣṭha*), the lower lip (*adharoṣṭha*), the upper line of teeth (*ūrdhvadantapaṅkti*), the lower line of teeth (*adhodantapaṅkti*), the roof of the mouth (*mūrdhan*), the tip of the tongue (*jihvāgra*), the chin (*civuka*), the front part of the neck or the throat (*kaṇṭha*), the right collar-bone (*dakṣiṇa jatru*), the left collar-bone (*vāma jatru*), the right chest (*dakṣiṇa vakṣas*), the left chest (*vāma-vakṣas*), the middle depressed part of the chest (*madhya vakṣas*), the upper abdomen (*ūrdhvodara*), the navel (*nābhi*), the lower abdomen (*adhovasti*), the right groin (*dakṣiṇa ūrusandhi*), the left groin (*vāma ūrusandhi*), the genital (*upastha*).

The back side: The occipital (extreme back) head (*paśca-kapāla*), the backside of the neck (*paśca-grīvā*), the right shoulder (*dakṣa-skandha*), the left shoulder (*vāma-skandha*), the right shoulder-blade (*dakṣāṁśa-phalaka*), the left shoulder-blade (*vāmāṁśa-phalaka*), the hump region between the two shoulders (*kakut*), the upper back (*ūrdhva-pṛṣṭha*), the middle back (*madhya-pṛṣṭha*), the lower back (*adhaḥ-pṛṣṭha*), the right buttock (*dakṣiṇa nitamba*), the left buttock (*vāma nitamba*), the anus (*guda* or *pāyu*).

Beginners may omit the *antarnyāsa* (the internal rotation of consciousness). Anyone who wants to do *antarnyāsa* should be acquainted with the anatomy of the lower six *cakras* that have already been described.

Internal Rotation of Consciousness (Antarnyāsa)

VIŚUDDHI CAKRA

It is located at the level of the throat. It has sixteen petals of smoky purple colour. Its *maṇḍala* is a circle containing a white inverted triangle which, in turn, contains a *candra-maṇḍala* (lunar circle). This *maṇḍala* is white in colour. The *bīja* (seed syllable) of this *cakra* is *HAṀ*.

Visualize this *cakra* with its shape, colours, petals, *mātṛkās* (syllables representing the one and the only one Divine Mother) on the petals and the *bīja* (seed syllable).

Mentally utter the *mātṛkās*, arranged clockwise on a horizontal plane around the vertical spinal axis (starting from 1 of the clock-dial) in the following sequence, rapidly shifting your awareness from petal to petal : *AṀ, ĀṀ, IṀ, ĪṀ, UṀ, ŪṀ, ṚṀ, ṜṀ, LṚṀ LṜṀ, EṀ, AIṀ, OṀ, AUṀ, AṀ, Ṁ* (*anusvāra*), *AḤ*.

ANĀHATA CAKRA

The *anāhata cakra* is located behind the breastbone at the level of the heart. It has 12 petals which are crimson-red in colour. Its *maṇḍala* is a hexagon (two interlacing triangles) which contains an inverted triangle in its middle. This *maṇḍala* is smoky in colour. The *bīja* (seed syllable) of this *cakra* is *YAṀ*.

Visualize this *cakra* with its shape, colours, petals, *mātṛkās* on the petals and the *bīja*.

Mantally utter the *mātṛkās*, arranged clockwise on a horizontal plane around the vertical axis of the spine, in the following sequence, rapidly shifting your awareness from petal to petal : *KAṀ, KHAṀ, GAṀ, GHAṀ, ṄAṀ, CAṀ, CHAṀ, JAṀ, JHAṀ, ÑAṀ, ṬAṀ, ṬHAṀ.*

MAṆIPŪRA CAKRA

The *maṇipūra cakra* is located at the level of the navel. It has ten petals which are blue (like heavy rain-clouds) in colour. Its *maṇḍala* is an inverted red triangle with three *svastika* marks. The *bīja* (seed syllable) of this *cakra* is *RAṀ*.

Visualize this *cakra* with its shape, colours, petals, *mātṛkās* on the petals and the *bīja*.

Mentally utter the *mātṛkās*, arranged clockwise on a horizontal plane around the vertical axis of the spine, in the following sequence, rapidly shifting your awareness from petal to petal : ***ḌAṀ, ḌHAṀ, ṆAṀ, TAṀ, THAṀ, DAṀ, DHAṀ, NAṀ, PAṀ, PHAṀ.***

SVĀDHIṢṬHĀNA CAKRA

The *svādhiṣṭhāna cakra* is located at the level of the root of the genital organ. It has six petals of vermilion-red colour. Its *maṇḍala* is a crescent moon, white in colour. The *bīja* (seed syllable) of this *cakra* is *VAṀ*.

Visualize this *cakra,* in your mind's eye, with its shape, colours, petals, *mātṛkās* on the petals and the *bīja*.

Mantally utter the *mātṛkās*, arranged clockwise on a horizontal plane around the vertical axis of the spine, in the following sequence, rapidly shifting your awareness from petal to petal : *BAṀ*, ***BHAṀ***, *MAṀ*, ***YAṀ***, ***RAṀ***, ***LAṀ***.

MŪLĀDHĀRA CAKRA

The *mūlādhāra cakra* is located at the base of the spine, two fingers above the anus and two fingers below the root of the genital. It has four petals. crimson-red in colour. Its *maṇḍala* is a square with eight spears on its four sides and four angles and an inverted red triangle within the square below the *bīja*. This *maṇḍala* is yellow in colour. The *bīja* of this *cakra* is *LAṀ*.

Visualize this *cakra*, in your mind's eye, with its shape, colours, petals, *mātṛkās* on the petals, and the *bīja*.

Mentally utter the *mātṛkās*, arranged clockwise horizontally around the vertical axis of the spine, in the following sequence, rapidly shifting your awareness from petal to petal : *VAṀ*, *ŚAṀ*, *ṢAṀ*, *SAṀ*.

ĀJÑĀ CAKRA

The *ājñā cakra* is located behind the spot between the two eyebrows. It has two petals, white in colour. Its *maṇḍala* is a circle with an inverted triangle within it. This *maṇḍala* is moon-white or silver-white in colour. The *bīja* of this *cakra* is *O'Ṁ*.

Visualize this *cakra*, in your mind's eye, with its shape, colour, petals, *mātṛkās* on the petals and the *bīja*.

Mentally utter the *mātṛkās*, arranged laterally on either side of the *maṇḍala*, in the following sequence, rapidly shifting your awareness from one petal to the second one : *HAṀ*, *KṢAṀ*.

This completes the *cakra* visualization. Now rapidly shift your awareness in the vertical axis of your spine, first downwards and then upwards, with the simultaneous mental utterance of the *bījas* of the *cakras*, as and when your mind reaches the concerned *cakra*. The downward sojourn from the *ājñā* to the *mūlādhāra* is the descent (*avarohaṇa*) of consciousness. The upward sojourn from the *mūlādhāra* to the *ājñā* is the ascent (*ārohaṇa*) of consciousness. The sequence of the *bījas* is as follows :

Descent : *O'Ṁ, HAṀ, YAṀ, RAṀ, VAṀ, LAṀ.*

Ascent : *LAṀ, VAṀ, RAṀ, YAṀ, HAṀ, O'Ṁ.*

Repeat the ascent and the descent cycle three to five times.

The *bahirnyāsa* is an indispensable component of the *yoga-nidrā* for everybody. The *antarnyāsa* is dispensable, however. Advanced *yoga*-practitioners are advised to do both *bahirnyāsa* and *antarnyāsa* for getting better effects.

Mental Channel-Purification through Reverse Counting (Saviloma-Gaṇanā Mānasika Nāḍī-Śodhana)

This is the *nāḍi-śodhana prāṇāyāma,* done mentally, without the nostril control and without the actual alternate flow of the inhaling or the exhaling air through one or the other nostril. It is *imagined* that breathing is done through alternate nostrils : inhalation through the left nostril (*iḍā pūraka*) exhalation through the right nostril (*piṅgalā recaka*) inhalation through the right nostril (*piṅgalā pūraka*) exhalation through the left nostril (*iḍā recaka)* . . . . While doing the reverse counting, one number is counted twice for *pūraka* and for *recaka* (combinedly for one breath). The total number of breaths to be counted may be 108 or 54 or 27, depending upon the time one can afford to spare.

Follow the procedure outlined.

Focus your attention on your natural and quiet breath through both nostrils. Let your breath be spontaneous. After a while, imagine that you are breathing through alternate nostrils. Maintain your awareness and start counting each inhalation and exhalation. Count in the reverse order. Say, you decide to count 27 times. Count as follows : Left inhalation (*iḍā pūraka*) 27, right exhalation (*piṅgalā recaka*) 27, right inhalation (*piṅgalā pūraka*) 26, left exhalation (*iḍā recaka*) 26, left inhalation (*iḍā pūraka*) 25, right exhalation (*piṅgalā recaka*) 25, and so on up to one. After you finish counting, remain aware of your natural and spontaneous breathing through both nostrils.

This completes your mental channel-purification (*mānasika nāḍī-śodhana*). Next, you may go for rotating visualization.

Moving Visualization of Scenarios (Kālpanika Caladdṛśya-Darśana)

Visualize scenes and scenarios in your mind. Rapidly shift your awareness from one scene to the other in succession.

IMAGES OF FAITH, REVERENCE AND LOVE

1. The *praṇava* symbol, the *svastika* symbol, the *triśūla* symbol, the cross, the half-moon with stars, or any other symbol that can invoke pious feeling in you.
2. Lord Viṣṇu or Lord Kṛṣṇa or Lord Śiva or Lord Buddha or Lord Mahāvīra or Lord Jesus or all of them one after another.
3. Mother Durgā or Kālī or Lakṣmī or Mary or all of them one after another.
4. Mahātmā Gandhi or any other social or historical figure of importance.
5. Your mother and your father.

FAMILIAR TREES

1. Banyan tree
2. Pipal tree
3. Neem tree

4. Mango tree
5. Jackfruit tree

You may adopt trees of your locality and familiarity.

FAMILIAR FLOWERS

1. White lotus
2. Red lily
3. Blue *aparājitā* (*Clitoria ternatia*)
4. Yellow sunflower
5. Black rose

You may adopt flowers of your locality and familiarity.

FAMILIAR ANIMALS

1. Deer
2. Elephant
3. Tiger
4. Lion
5. Camel

You may adopt animals of your locality and familiarity.

FAMILIAR BIRDS

1. Peacock
2. Parrot
3. Crane
4. pigeon
5. Vulture

DAY AND NIGHT SCENARIO

1. Sunrise
2. Midday

3. Sunset
4. Full-Moon night
5. Dark night sky studded with twinkling stars

SEASONAL SCENARIO

1. Torrential rain
2. Cyclone
3. River in spate
4. Winter snow-fall; snow-covered mountain
5. Summer heat; dry landscape : desert sands

AQUATIC SCENARIO

1. Oceanic waves
2. A large lake with swimming birds
3. A pond with lilies
4. A water fall
5. A hilly rivulet

GREEN SCENARIO

1. Mountains on three sides; valley expanding to one side
2. A vast, dense, green forest
3. Autumnal green crop field spreading all around; here and there scattered patches of *kāśataṇḍī* (*Sachharum spontaneum*) flower
4. A green park
5. A cactus garden

WORSHIP AND DEATH

1. A temple and deity-worship
2. A church and prayer inside

3. Mass-prayer in a mosque
4. A dead body being carried
5. Funeral or burial

Resolve (*Saṅkalpa*)

Repeat your resolve three times.

Finish (Samāpti)

Relax and maintain your awareness of your natural breathing.

Visualize your surroundings — the room in which you lie and its setting, the physical existence of your body lying on the floor. Become aware of the fact that you were practising *yoga-nidrā*. Keep on closing your eyes for some more time. See that your consciousness is now externalized.

You may now move your limbs and stretch yourself. When you are fully awake, sit up slowly and open your eyes.

The practice of *yoga-nidrā* is now complete.

3

Applications of Yoga-Nidrā

YOGA-NIDRĀ is a technique which may be applied for diverse purposes. It is a self-therapy. No second person is involved in it. Unlike hypnosis, another person does not suggest to do this or not to do that.

The technique for the various applications of *yoga-nidrā* is the same. The resolves (*saṅkalpas*) are different, however. All the diverse applications may be grouped into a few number of categories. These categories are outlined here.

APPLICATIONS OF YOGA-NIDRĀ CATEGORIZED

The broad outlines for which *yoga-nidrā* may be applied are given below :

1. ***Stamping a positive thought.*** A positive thought, good for the body and the mind, can be stamped on the subconscious or the unconscious. It stays there, influences the physical life, the mental life and the spiritual life. Any desirable trait can be acquired by the practice of *yoga-nidrā*. Any good habit that is longed for can be adopted by the practice of this technique.
2. ***The negative of a negative thought.*** Sometimes an individual is inflicted with negative thoughts. Sometimes he develops bad habits and becomes a victim to his habits. Through *yoga-nidrā*, he can get rid of his negative thoughts and bad habits. He develops

distaste for the negative. He starts liking the positive. In this total process, the negative idea or the bad habit is to be erased or expelled, and a positive idea or a good habit is to be imprinted in the subconscious or the unconscious mind as a substitute for the formerly printed thought.

3. ***Annihilating the pernicious undercurrent.*** A number of diseases are psychosomatic or psychovisceral. Their root is in the psyche and branches, with leaves, flowers and fruits, in the physique. The root may be in the subconscious, or it may still be deeper, lying in the unconscious. The Freudian psychoanalysis tries to render the unconscious idea conscious. The person who suffers from the psychosomatic disorder or disease is made conscious of the dormant, sleeping idea which bubbles up from the bottom and stealthily pinches the conscious and affects some body organs without the knowledge of the person who suffers. The *yoga-nidrā* technique erases the imprinted idea from the subconscious and the unconscious. The patient does not need the services of a psychoanalyst or psychotherapist. He does it himself. Without recognizing the nature of the root, he burns it or erases it. When the root is destroyed, the psychosomatic disorder is cured.

4. ***Normalizing the body functions.*** Sometimes the physiological functions of the body organs and tissues are altered. The body organ or tissue may be hypo-active or hyper-active. There may be hormonal imbalance. For all such physiological disorders, *Yoga-nidrā* may be a potent tool to correct the defect.

5. ***Normalizing the biochemical activities of the body.*** The body is a huge biochemical workshop. A large

number of biochemicals are synthesized in the body. Sometimes, some biochemical is not synthesized at all, or, if synthesized, is excessively produced or produced at a rate below the normal level. Some other times, the utilization and the degradation of a biochemical are not normal. Many physical and mental diseases are brought about due to the malfunctioning of the biochemical machinery. *Yoga-nidrā* has the potential ability to cure such malfunctioning.

6. ***Correcting and potentiating the immune system.*** The immune system of the body is its defence department. On the failure of the immune system, no doctor can help and no medicine can work. It is impossible to live in a situation of the total failure of the immune system. Sometimes, the immune system works; but its working is inefficient. In the former situation, *yoga-nidrā* brings the immune system back to a functional state. In the latter situation, *yoga-nidrā* strengthens the activity of the immune system. Antibiotics and chemotherapeutic agents can fight against microbial infection if and when the immune system functions efficiently. Without the help of the immune system, therapy by any good drugs is bound to fail.

7. ***Spiritual attainment.*** *Yoga-nidrā* can be a means to spiritual attainment and to the final end of liberation (*mokṣa*). All the recordings in the *karmāśaya* of the unconscious located in the causal body (*kāraṇa-śarīra*) can be erased. With the total erasure, the *karmāśaya* vanishes, and the remainder is the 'individual self'. As a matter of fact, the self is no longer individual since it is not bound (*baddha*) at this state. The self, without the *karmāśaya*, is the same as the Universal (Great) Self or the *Paramātmā*. Nevertheless, the 'self'

has been qualified here as 'individual' since it is still in a body, although not bound by the latter. This is the *jīvanmukta* state — free although still living.

It would not be practicable to present an exhaustive list of all the applications of *yoga-nidrā.* A few typical cases, out of the many, from each of the seven categories will be briefly described in this concluding chapter of this book.

CATEGORY-1

Early Getting Up from the Bed

It may be necessary for you to change an old habit and acquire a new one. You are a late riser. Your service schedule demands that you are to get up early. You may be a writer. Your busy day schedule does not give you much time for writing. You wish to rise at 4.00 a.m. You have some health problem. You have been instructed to do *yoga* early in the morning. In such situations, you do *yoga-nidrā* with the following *saṅkalpa.*

"I will get up early, at 4.00 a.m."

Loving Your Wife

Your wife is not very beautiful although she is not ugly. Your religion, your family conditions and your social status do not allow you to go for a divorce. Moverover, your wife is a lovable person; she loves you; she has many virtues; you have no moral justification to divorce her. Whenever you see a beautiful woman, you are attracted towards her and your feeling towards your wife becomes estranged. You want to love your wife, but you are unable to do. Practise *yoga-nidrā* with the following *saṅkalpa* :

"I love my wife, love her intensely."

To Build Up Courage during the Period of Bad Days

You have lost your job. You have been ruined in business. Somebody, very near and dear, has expired. You are about to collapse in anxiety and sorrows. You want to live. You want to build up courage to get over the bad days. Do *yoga-nidrā* with the following *saṅkalpa* :

> "I must build up courage to fight the darkness of the night, to see the morning."

To Develop Satisfaction (*Santoṣa*) in the Availing Conditions

You had an ambition to become an administrative officer, a doctor, an engineer, a successful politician or an industrialist. Your ambition could not be fulfilled in spite of your sincere efforts. You are dissatisfied and frustrated. In the mental state of despair and frustration, you live an agonising life. To get rid of your mental agony, practise *yoga-nidrā* with the following *saṅkalpa* :

> "I have the capacity to live a meaningful life with full satisfaction."

To Surrender to God

Ignore it if you are an atheist.

You are feeling insecure. You are afraid of probable accidents, calamities, dangers from enemies and criminals, fatal diseases such as heart attack and cancer and death. You are apprehensive of property-loss, business-failure or political downfall. Your mind is constantly agitated with conflicts and apprehensions. You long for peace and tranquillity of mind. You yearn for solace. Practise *yoga-nidrā* with the following *saṅkalpa.*

> "I surrender to God. He takes care of me."

To Develop Will Power

You have immense potentialities. You are not conscious of your intrinsic abilities. You feel yourself diffident and helpless. You have developed an inferiority complex. You do not have self-confidence. You have a feeling that nothing can be done by you. You believe that others can beat you and that you cannot compete with them. You have a false notion that you are useless and incapable for doing anything. Practise *yoga-nidrā* to develop your will power.

A *saṅkalpa* in confirmity with Advaita Vedānta is as follows:

"I am *Brahman*, the omnipotent one. I can do everything good, nothing bad."

Alternative *saṅkalpa*s are given below :

"I can do anything that can be done by others."

"I have the will, the power, the competence to get success."

"My will-power is improving to reach the summit."

If you lose the confidence to speak in a public meeting or to act in a drama due to stage fright, you may be specific in phrasing your *saṅkalpa* which may be as follows :

"I can speak fearlessly and confidently with success."

"I can act fearlessly and confidently with success."

If you are a sales promotion executive and have diffidence in conversation, you may adopt the following *saṅkalpa* :

"I can speak fluently in favour of my products to fully influence my customers".

To Improve One's Vitality

You may be lacking in vitality (*prāṇa-śakti*). You may be debilitated. You may lack in physical and mental strength. After a prolonged illness, you may be convalescing. You are to collect *prāṇa* from the cosmic source of *prāṇa* and store in the *cakra*s of your subtle body, your storage batteries. To improve your vitality, practice *yoga-nidrā*, using the following *saṅkalpa* :

> "I am collecting *prāṇa*, storing it in my body. I am becoming vitally stronger."

CATEGORY-2

Giving Up Addictions

You may be addicted to drugs. You may be an alcoholic. You may be a chain-smoker, with chronic throat problems. If you want to get rid of such bad habits, practise *yoga-nidrā* with any of the following *saṅkalpa*s as per suitability in your case.

> "I hate drugs. I must stop taking them".

> "Alcoholism is harmful. I must stop drinking."

> "Smoking is injurious to health. I must not smoke".

To Abstain from Extra-Marital Sex Relation

If you have indulgence in extra-marital sex, if your indulgence is giving trouble to you and if the indulgence mars your family conjugal life, you should opt for abstaining from it. It may seem impossible for you to stop your indulgence. You may psychologically be upset while thinking of the discontinuance of your habit. Still you want to get rid of the entanglement for your total well-being. To do that, practise *yoga-nidrā* with the following *saṅkalpa.*

> "I hate sex with women other than my wife. I must refrain from it."

To Switch Over from Non-Vegetarianism to Vegetarianism

You may be a non-vegetarian, a voracious eater of meat, fish and eggs. You may have a strong taste for such food. The doctor predicts that you are prone to heart attack and advises you to become a vegetarian. It seems impossible for you to give up meat, fish and eggs. Still, for your good health, you cannot afford to ignore your doctor's advice. To get over the dilemma, practise *yoga-nidrā* with the following *saṅkalpa* :

> "Non-vegetarian food is bad for health. I must be a vegetarian."

Obsessive-Compulsive Disorder (OCD)

Obsessive-Compulsive Disorder (OCD) is a type of anxiety disorder. It is the experience of prolonged, excessive worry about circumstances in one's present life or past life (lives). This syndrome is characterized by distressing, repetitive thoughts, impulses or images that are intense, frightening, absurd, or unusual. These inner feelings are externally exhibited by ritualized actions that are usually bizarre and irrational. Such actions reduce anxiety caused by the individual's obsessive thoughts. For our discussion, one example may be taken. You might have developed a habit of washing your hands frequently. The same thing may be true with your feet, floor, bathroom, etc. When some outsider comes to your house, you may feel that he has made your house dirty and immediately you may develop the urge to wash your floor, furniture and utensils. You may be conscious of the fact that your actions are not correct. In spite of that, you helplessly and irregistibly continue to do the same thing to satisfy your inner, unconscious urge. You want to get rid of this mania. You have no remedial measure. In such a situation, practise *yoga-nidrā* with the following *saṅkalpa*:

"I wash without any purpose and necessity. I must give it up."

To Control Anger and Short-Temperedness

At the slightest provocation, you may be losing your temper. You may not be able to tolerate dissent and criticism. You may be very fond of your own ideas and may have hatred towards others' ideas hostile or disagreeable to yours. In meetings and personal discussions, you may immediately become wild with others when they express their ideas or arguments contrary to yours. You may be losing your temper very shortly and calming down after a moment. You may be very good in your heart. You may repent for your fault immediately after the angry moment. You may be ready for apologising after the angry moment is over. But everything might have been spoilt irreparably by that time. What has been damaged in a moment can hardly be repaired in a life's time. Unnecessary enemies may be created. Home as well as public life may be marred. If you are a victim of your own ill temper, practise *yoga-nidrā* with any one of the following *saṅkalpa*s:

"I must give up anger. I will be calm, quiet and tolerant."

"It is bad to be short-tempered. I must not be".

To Give Up Cruelty and Violence

Anger is associated with cruelty and violence; but it is not always the sole causative factor of the latter. Some persons are cruel and violent by nature. They might have stored bad *saṁskāra*s from their previous lives. Some genes may be responsible for such undesirable traits. A bad nurture at home, a bad social environment, a bad indoctrination, a bad company and lack of good and liberal education might be conducive to the development of cruel and violent behaviour. Sometimes, the person concerned with cruelty and violence is repentent too at later moments. Such individuals may immensely be benefitted in getting rid of these bad traits if they practise *yoga-nidrā.* The following *saṅkalpa* may be used:

> "Cruelty and violence are inhuman. I must be kind and non-violent."

Not to Hate a Person

You may be hating a person because he is inimical to you or his actions give you pain. You may be very much revengeful towards him. You may be mentally allergic when you remember his name. You may be a good man and he may be a bad man. It is your duty to save you from his attack. But you harm yourself by your mental reactions and pass through sleepless nights. Maintain mental calmness and avoid mental agitation. Do not allow the feeling of hatred to be nested in your mind. To become revengeful is not a good quality. Do not enterain revenge in your mind. In spite of taking all physical measures to protect yourself from your enemy, on a psychological level, love your enemy, avoid bad will (*dveṣa*) towards him, do not hate him, hate his actions and ignore (*upekṣā*) his faulty personality. For achieving such a mental status, practise *yoga-nidrā* with the following *saṅkalpa*:

> "I love X. I ignore his/her faults."

Not to Covet

Avarice is one of the major enemies of a person. Covetousness is a bad trait engendered by bad *saṁskāras* through past lives and the present life. It leads to exploitation of others and accumulation (*parigraha*) of wealth. Such a person, through accumulation, may become the richest person in the world, but at the mental level, he still remains the poorest and miserly (*kṛpaṇa*). As he gets more and more, his thirst for wealth, without being quenched, is more intensified. Being mentally impoverished, he develops anxiety neurosis for more and more acquisition and for the so-called precarious protection of his accumulated wealth. His acquisitive tendency increases. He is covetous of everything of the world. He desires to devour everything and thereby to bloat himself. He becomes apprehensive of the safe custody of his accumulated wealth. He becomes a neurotic patient. Avarice is a potent malady of modern civilization. It must be cured in order to get peace. You need wealth for your living and your family. To earn wealth in an ethical way is your duty. But accumulation is a social evil and personal problem. Why should you earn more than your basic requirements? Why should you deprive others of their fundamental rights of basic living? For a purposeful living, you are to take care of your belly, your head, your heart and your spirit. Don't be fully engaged with the three lowest *cakra*s of your body — the *mūlādhāra*, the *svādhiṣṭhāna* and the *maṇipūra*, the centres of activities of eating, excreting, sex and procreation and material attachment. To conquer greed and avarice, practise *yoga-nidrā* with the following *saṅkalpa*:

> "I live for simple living and high thinking. I am free from avarice."

To Shun Jealousy

Jealousy or envy (*asūyā* or *mātsarya*) is a fire that burns the person who indulges in it. A jealous person does not take a broad view of the full height of the ladder. He stands on one rung of the ladder, higher than which there are some and lower than which there are many. He takes pity on himself, because he looks upward to see people standing on higher rungs. He does not bother to look downward and see multitudinous mass suffering and agonising. He has no sympathy for them because he rarely thinks of them. He invites physical and mental illness by his jealous behaviour. Peace and contentment are alien to him because of this envy. If you are a victim of your envy, practise *yoga-nidrā* with the following *saṅkalpa*:

> "I am happy with others' happiness. I don't envy anybody.

CATEGORY-3

In this category, a few typical psychosomatic diseases will be discussed. It is not claimed that *yoga-nidrā* is sure to cure all psychosomatic diseases. Some of them are very complicated. Take, for example, asthma. It has a hereditary susceptibility. A genetic genesis of this disease cannot be ruled out. Physical allergens flare up the symptoms. Adverse environmental conditions are aggravating factors. That mental allergy plays havoc in this disease is not very often appreciated. *Yoga-nidrā* may be a therapy supplementary to the medical therapy by expert doctors. *Yoga* is not contradictory to medical or surgical therapy. One is to take note of this fact and use the technique of *yoga-nidrā* for one's self-therapy in the treatment of one's physical, mental and spiritual ailments.

Peptic Ulcer

Peptic ulcer is the term used for both gastric ulcer and duodenal ulcer. Ulceration is the sequel to the prolonged action of an excess of pepsin-hydrochloric acid on the mucous membrane on which the mucous coat is poorly protective. Duodenal ulcer is more common in males whereas gastric ulcer occurs with equal frequency in males and females. In duodenal ulcer, the clinical symptoms of pain are felt when the stomach is empty. In gastric ulcer, the pain is felt when the stomach is full and it may be accompanied by vomiting. Hyperacidity is associated more commonly with duodenal ulcer, but less commonly or not at all with gastric ulcer. Untreated chronic gastric ulcer may be complicated with cancer; it is not generally the case with duodenal ulcer.

Fig. 3.1 illustrates the points at which peptic ulcers frequently occur. The pyloric region of the duodenum is the most frequent site of peptic ulcers. The second site of importance is the mucous membrane of the lesser curvature of the stomach. More rarely, the lower end of the oesophagus is ulcerated, following reflux of gastric juice. A type of peptic ulcer called a marginal ulcer has the site in the jejunum immediately distal to the anastomosis after gastrojejunostomy and partial gastrectomy.

Hereditary factor. Peptic ulcer frequently occurs in several members of a family in one or more generations. A genetic predisposition of this disease is strongly evident. The mechanism of the genetic action has not yet been clear,

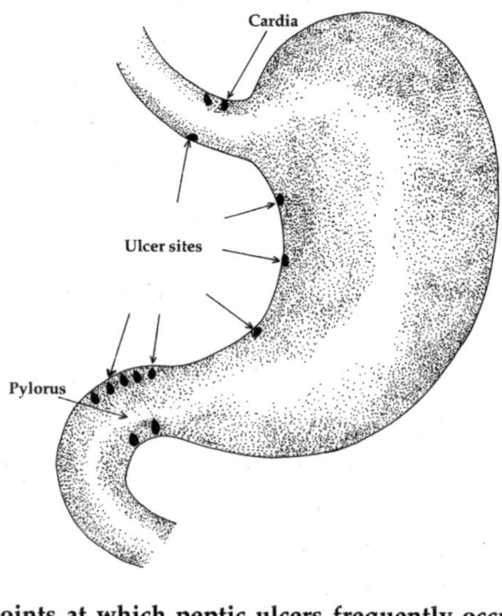

***fig.* 3.1 The points at which peptic ulcers frequently occur.**

however. The synthesis and secretion of mucus may be less efficient in some families. The mass of HCl-secreting cells in the stomach mucosa may be more in some families. The turnover of enzymes responsible for the synthesis of HCl may be greater in these families. The limbic system may be anatomically greater developed, or physiologically hypersensitive, or biochemically hyperactive. The pair of the vagus nerve (10th cranial nerve), which contains both afferent and efferent fibres, arises from the nerve cells of the medulla oblongata and other nuclei of the brain. The pharynx, larynx, trachea, heart, oesophagus, stomach, intestines, pancreas, gall bladder, bile ducts, spleen, kidneys, ureter and blood vessels in the thoracic and abdominal cavities are innervated by the vagus nerves. The nuclei of the origin of the vagus nerves may be more in number in some families. They may be more irritable and hyper-sensitive. They may be excessively stimulated by the limbic system. Lastly, some families may be having hyper-functioning of the sympathetic nervous system, the adrenal medulla, the adrenal cortex and the histamine-liberating cellular components.

Stress. Any sort of hostile environment becomes a potent source of stress to an individual person. If he is genetically predisposed, it may be difficult for him to withstand the psychic stress. The personality type is also a contributory factor. An ambitious personality is more susceptible. The cerebrum, in a stressful situation, excessively stimulates the dorsal motor nucleus of the vagus. Impulses reach from the vagal centre to the stomach wall where the parasympathetic nerve endings release an excessive quantity of acetylcholine, finally leading to the hypersecretion of acid gastric juice. This is the parasympathetic pathway through which the gastric glands are over-stimulated to secrete more acid gastric juice, finally leading to ulceration in the stomach or the duodenum.

Psychic stress affects the prefrontal area of the cerebral cortex. Impulses pass from the prefrontal area to the hypothalamus via the limbic system. The hypothalamus overstimulates the sympathetic nervous system and the adrenal medulla to secrete more adrenaline and noradrenaline. The two hormones cause constriction of the blood vessels supplying the alimentary tract. Excessive cigarette smoking also causes the same thing. Ischaemia, followed by multiple foci of necrosis, becomes the cause of peptic ulcer. This is the sympathetic pathway through which psychic stress can produce peptic ulcer. In the opinion of Dr. Udupa, the sympathetic division remains dormant and the parasympathetic division becomes overactive in the causation of peptic ulcer.[1]

The hypothalamus, being stimulated by the prefrontal area of the frontal lobe, secretes corticotrophin releasing hormone (CRH) that reaches the anterior pituitary through the bloodstream (through the pituitary portal system). The anterior pituitary secretes adrenocorticotrophic hormone (ACTH) that is transported to the adrenal cortex by blood. Finally, the adrenal cortex secretes more of corticosteroids. Steroids reduce the replacement of the epithelial cells of the mucous membrane of the stomach and the duodenum. They reduce the secretion of mucus. They cause excess of acid gastric secretion. They are anti-inflammatory and immunosuppressive. Any substance that is anti-inflammatory reduces the secretion of mucus. Thus, it has been well established that stress can cause ulceration in the stomach and duodenum through the action of corticosteroids.

Histamine. The blood of patients suffering from chronic peptic ulcer shows higher concentration of histamine. Hisamine causes vasodilatation, increases capillary permeability and

1. K.N. Udupa, 1985, p. 262.

increases acid gastric secretion. It is always associated with tissue damage and an inflammatory process. The mast cells in the tissues and basophils in blood release histamine which is contained in their granules. Histamine has been experimentally used for the artificial production of peptic ulcer.

Infection. In patients suffering from peptic ulcer, the alimentary tract is commonly colonized by the bacterium, ***Helicobacter pylori***. This organism was discovered by Barry Marshall and Robin Warren of Australia in 1983. The majority of persons infected by it remain asymptomatic. The manifestation of the peptic ulcer disease is most likely modulated by host genetics and a hostile environment.

Complicating factors. The excessive consumption of alcohol, smoking, excessive intake of caffeine through tea and coffee and consumption of hot, irritant and spicy foods increase acid gastric secretion. Spices may not directly stimulate the glands for the secretion of the acid. But they have decidedly an indirect effect. Hyperacidity is induced by irregular intake of food and long hours of keeping the stomach empty.

Serotonin. Serotonin is 5-hydoxytryptamine. It causes vasoconstriction whereas histamine causes vasodilatation. It inhibits acid gastric secretion whereas histamine promotes it.

The Ayurvedic system of medicine uses two herbal products (the fruits of *āmalaka, Emblica officinalis*, and banana powder) for the successful treatment of peptic ulcer. The former is rich in vitamin C. Both contain 5-hydroxytryptamine that inhibits acid secretion and heals the peptic ulcer.

Yoga-Therapy for the Treatment of Peptic Ulcer. Meditation does not allow the cerebrum to release excess of acetylcholine and it establishes an equipoise between the parasympathetic and the sympathetic nervous divisions. The practice of *āsanas*, *bandhas*, *mudrās* and *prāṇāyāma* produces synergistic effects to be added to the benefit of meditation. Here the scope is limited to elaborate details.

Yoga-nidrā for the treatment of peptic ulcer. If you suffer from peptic ulcer, practise *yoga-nidrā* in addition to other yogic practices. Avoid hot and spicy diet. Take small quantity of food at frequent intervals. Take the help of your doctor for medicinal treatment. *Yoga* and medical treatments are not incompatible. The following *saṅkalpa* is suggested for *yoga-nidrā*.

> "I am worry-free, tension-free. No hyperacidity and enough secretion of mucus. My peptic ulcer is healed up."

Chronic Colitis

The colon is part of the large intestine which comprises three components, namely, caecum, colon and rectum. The ileum of the small intestine joins the large intestine in a kind of pouch called the caecum which is the first part of the large intestine. The vermiform appendix is a small organ jutting out from the beginning of the large intestine. Thus, the caecum is a blind pouch or cul-de-sac, the dilated intestinal pouch into which open the ileum, the colon and the appendix vermiformis. The colon is the middle part of the large intestine, extending from the caecum to the rectum. The rectum is straight and the lowest part of the large intestine, extending from the last curve of the colon to the anus.

The colon has been illustrated in *fig.* 3.2. The ascending colon is the portion of the colon which passes cephalad between the caecum and the right colic flexure. The transverse colon is the portion of the colon that runs transversely across the upper part of the abdomen, from the right to the left colic flexure. The descending colon is the portion of the colon which passes

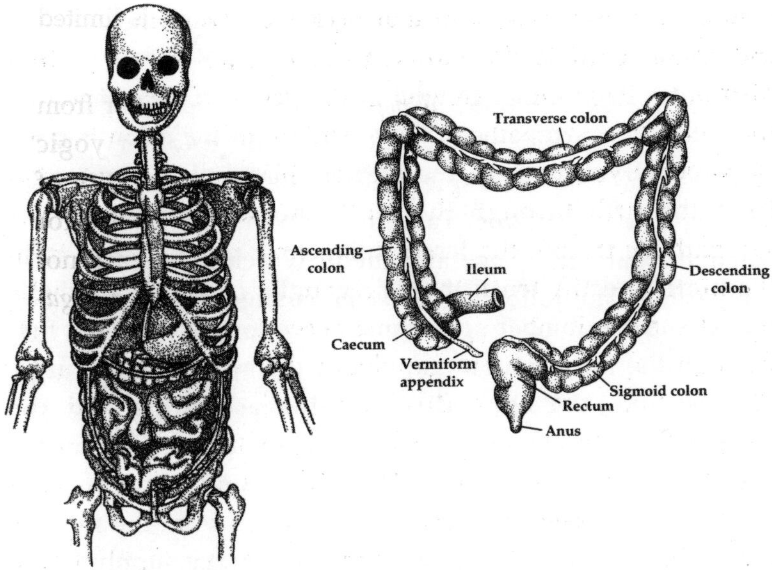

fig. **3.2 The different parts of the colon.**

caudad between the left colic flexure and the sigmoid colon. The sigmoid colon is the part of the colon in the pelvis that extends from the descending colon to the rectum.

The colon is not the site for the digestion of nutrients. Solid, undigested waste is accumulated in it and prepared for elimination from the body in the form of faeces. Thus, it is the site for the storage of faecal matter until it can be expelled. The colon has a second function. Water and electrolytes from the chyme are absorbed into the bloodstream across its mucous membrane. The proximal half of the colon is concerned principally with absorption and the distal half with storage.

The colon is innervated by both the parasympathetic and the sympathetic nerves. The parasympathetic supply is done through the vagus (the tenth cranial nerve) and the pelvic nerve. The former supplies to the proximal portion of the colon and the latter to its distal portion. The pelvic splanchnic nerve (called also *nervi erigentes*) that originates from the S2-S4 of the spinal cord is the parasympathetic pelvic nerve that distributes its terminal ganglia in the pelvic viscera including the colon. The sympathetic nerve supply to the colon is done by three nerves, namely, the greater splanchnic nerve (origin from the fifth through the tenth thoracic ganglia of the sympathetic trunk), the lesser splanchnic nerve (origin from the ninth and the tenth thoracic ganglia of the sympathetic trunk) and the lumbar splanchnic nerve (origin from the first through the third lumbar ganglia of the sympathetic trunk). The caecum, the appendix, and the ascending and the transverse colon are supplied by nerves which arise from the superior mesenteric plexus. The descending colon and the rectum are supplied by nerves which arise from the inferior mesenteric plexus. *Fig.* 3.3 illustratus the nerve supply to the colon.

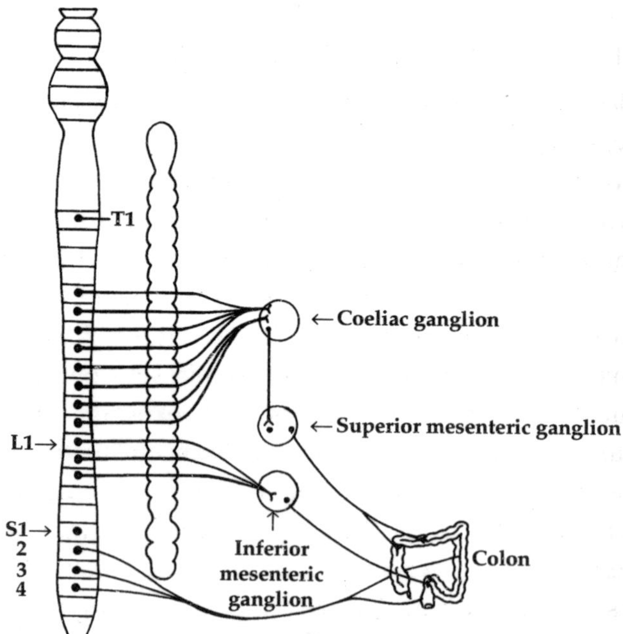

fig. **3.3 The nerve supply to the colon.**

Ulcerative colitis is a disease of the colon with ulcer and inflammation of part or all of the colon. The clinical symptoms are: rectal discharge of blood, mucus and pus, fever, secondary anaemia, dehydration, prostration and loss of weight.

The chief pathological lesion in ulcerative colitis is ulceration in the mucosa of the colon. The other layers of the colon do not ulcerate; they may hypertrophy and become thickened and rigid. The vascularity of the colon is increased. It becomes oedematous. But there is little fibrosis. The disease most often begins as procto-colitis, the lesions starting in the rectum and sigmoid, and, in due course, spreads to the whole colon.

In the differential diagnosis of the disease, amoebic dysentery by the invasion of *Entamoeba histolytica* must be ruled out.

If the disease persists for a decade or longer, carcinoma may develop in the ulcerated bowel.

Ulcerative colitis is caused by intense psychological trauma. The type of personality is a factor that cannot cope with the emotional conflict. The person who is more susceptible to ulcerative colitis due to personality type may be outwardly calm and superficially peaceful. But, beneath the calm surface, there are severe under-currents characterized by intense hostility, resentment and guilt. An individual of this personality type feels helpless, he lacks in self-confidence and becomes dependent on others. He exhibits obsessive-compulsive behaviour. He involves himself in too much of neatness, purity and precision. He is indecisive in temperament. He is rigid in his standards of morality. He engages himself in over-intellectualization. A stressful situation creates anxiety in him. Ulcertive colitis is a psychosomatic disease. It is primarily caused by mental stress, intense anxiety and tension.

In the stressful situation, the cerebral cortex pours out acetylcholine. This is followed by the sympathetic response, leading to hyper-secretion of catecholamines, namely, adrenaline and noradrenaline. Higher concentrations of catecholamines produce microcirculatory changes in the mucosa of the colon. Vaso-constriction takes place at the arteriolar and venous blood vessels. These sites of the mucosa are devitalized. The mucosa may slough off, resulting in the formation of stress ulcers. These local reactions lead to excessive liberation of histamine which causes severe inflammation and ulceration. Haemorrhagic and mucous discharges from the ulcerated colonic mucosa take place. The sloughed off mucosal cellular material is absorbed into the lymphatic vessels. Such material acts as antigen to trigger the production of antibodies in the regional mesenteric lymph nodes. The released antibodies reach the colonic mucosa via the bloodstream. The result is an antigen-antibody reaction of the autoimmune type in the colonic mucosa, with chronic inflammation and marked lymphocytic infiltration.

If you suffer from ulcerative colitis, get yourself treated by a doctor who can belp you by his medical treatment, but cannot remove the root of your disease which is in your mind. You can cure yourself by meditation and especially by *yoga-nidrā*. Use the following *saṅkalpa*:

> "No anxiety, no tension, no worrry. My colon does not react. I can live with my persisting problem."

Pychosomatic Skin Disorders

All diseases of the skin are not of psychosomatic origin. Dermatitis may be due to infection by bacteria, viruses, fungi, and other parasites; it may be due to some allergen, some physical irritant or some chemical irritant; and it may be due to many other causes. All those will not be discussed here.

There are a number of skin disorders that have their roots in mental stress. Emotional disturbances produce pathological changes in the skin. Some such diseases are : neurodermatitis, eczematous dermatitis, hyperhydrosis, psoriasis.

When a person is emotionally disturbed, his autonomic nervous system affects the skin. It may be mentioned here that the nervous system and the skin are embryologically ectodermal in origin. The skin and its appendages like the sweat glands are richly supplied by the sympathetic nerves. The sympathetic nerve endings, through their secretion of catecholamines, bring about changes in the microcirculation of the skin. Catecholamines produce excessive and prolonged vasoconstrictive effects. Excessive vasoconstriction, persisting for a prolonged period, causes the necrosis of the local tissue. The necrosed material is absorbed into the venous and the lymphatic circulation and acts as auto-antigen. As a response, the immune system produces antibodies, resulting in an antigen-antibody reaction of the autoimmune type. Histamine is closely associated with catecholamines, in an antagonistic way, of course. It has a vasodilating effect, the opposite of that of catecholamines. Its production is increased in all allergic conditions.

Neurodermatitis. This is a psychosomatic disease, involving extensive areas of the skin, with pruriginous eruptions. The patient has the problem of maladjustment to the environment, especially in situations of deprivation of occupational activities, bereavement, sexual frustration and a feeling of unwantedness.

Eczematous dermatitis. This is a type of dermatitis of psychosomatic origin, with oozing skin. The term, 'eczema' implies a 'boiling over' of the skin. The skin is inflamed with itching and discharge from blisters. In this condition, spontaneous eruptions, characterized clinically by papulovesiculation and microscopically by spongiosis, occur. Strong emotions, deeply buried in the subconscious or the unconscious, provoke the skin to react and weep.

Hyperhydrosis. Hyperidrosis or hyperhydrosis is a pathological condition of the skin, in which excessive sweating is the symptom. Adolescents and young adults are affected more often than children or older people.

Over-stimulation of the parasympathetic system or the cerebral cortex, leading to hyper-secretion of the neurohumour, acetylcholine, causes excessive sweating. The generalized form of hyperidrosis has generally a systemic cause. Its localized form, however, is psychosomatic in origin. It is very often associated with anxiety or guilt.

In the localized hyperidrosis, the sites most commonly affected are the palms and soles, the axillae, the anogenital region or the centre of the face. The palms and soles have sometimes a tendency to perniosis. Sweaty feet are often ideal for the growth of saprophytic organisms and fungi. The pH of sweat, when secreted, is acidic. It becomes alkaline due to subsequent decomposition. An alkaline pH of the sweat is conducive to the growth of bacteria and fungi. Bacterial decomposition of the sweat, especially in axillary hyperidrosis, produces offensive odour (bromidrosis). Chromidrosis, due to the proliferation of chromogenic bacteria, becomes also a problem. It causes discolouration and rotting of fabrics.

Psoriasis. Psoriasis is a skin disease marked by red scaly patches. The reddened areas of the skin are sharply marginated with abnormal scaling.

Hereditary predisposition has been found in the causation of psoriasis. The fundamental aetiology is a biochemical fault in the formation of the epidermal cells, resulting in abnormal horn cells. Trauma to the skin, infections and emotional conflict are the other precipitating causal factors.

Emotional conflict may be a precipitating factor in the causation of psoriasis. For this reason, this desease has been considered as psychosomatic.

The Yoga-Nidrā Treatment of Psychosomatic Skin Disorders. A number of *saṅkalpa*s are suggested here for the treatment of skin disorders of psychosomatic origin.

Neurodermatitis — "No anxiety, no emotional conflict. My skin must not react. I can cope with my problem."

Eczematous Dermatitis — "No anxiety, no tension. My skin must not react. My sympathetic nerve-endings must not over-act."

Hyperidrosis — "No tension, no worries. My brain, my parasympathetic system must not over-act. My sweat-glands must not react."

Psoriasis — "No emotional conflict. I am happy. My skin must behave normally."

Asthma

Spasmodic bronchial asthma, or loosely speaking asthma, is a chronic disease of the respiratory system. It manifests itself in attacks of severe expiratory dyspnoea, occurring in paroxysms due to bronchospasm.

Asthma generally runs in families. This heredity is not always direct, however. In other generations, the manifestation may be in the form of migraine, epilepsy or hysteria. Perhaps an unduly irritable bronchomotor centre in the medulla oblongata of the brain is the factor transmitted by heredity.

A group of patients suffer from allergic asthma. The allergen may be a physical agent such as dust. It may be the pollen of some particular flowers. It may be some chemical substance emanated from the body or the excreta of some animals or insects such as horses, cats, dogs, cockroaches, etc. At least 50 per cent of asthmatics show hypersensitiveness to various protein antigens obtained from animals, birds, fishes, shrimps, foods of animal and plant origin, drugs, etc.

'Mental allergen' is one of the many aetiological factors of asthma. This is the reason of including asthma as one of the psychosomatic diseases. Some mental impression, deeply rooted in the Subconscious or the Unconscious, stealthily comes to the surface of the mind and provokes the symptoms of asthma.

Any mental trauma imprinted in the depth of the mind comes to the surface and stimulates the cerebral cortex. The parasympathetic division of the autonomic nervous system is over-activated by the cerebral cortex, resulting in the hyper-secretion of acetylcholine. As a result, the tracheobronchial tree becomes the target of various physiopathological changes. In the initial stage, the concentration of acetylcholine rises, without the concurrent rise of catecholamines (adrenaline and noradrenaline), resulting in a spasmatic contraction of the smooth muscles of the bronchi. This leads to constriction of the bronchi and bronchioles. Especially bronchiolar constriction causes constriction of the respiratory airway. A diagramatic picture of the tracheobronchial tree is presented in *fig*. 3.4.

The bronchial mucous membrane becomes congested and swollen, resulting in an excessive secretion of mucus. This mucus accumulates in the tracheobronchial tree. In this condition, bacterial infection sets in. This complicates the physiopathology of the respiratory tract. The bronchial spasm, accompanied by the collection of mucus in the tracheobronchial

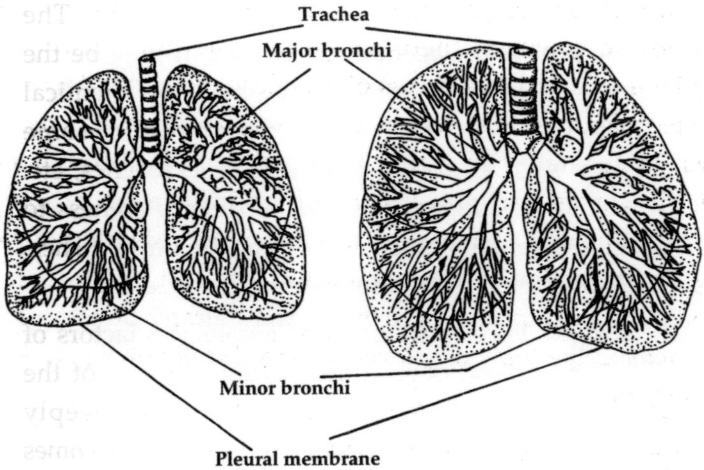

fig. **3.4 A diagramatic picture of the tracheobronchial tree.**

tree is the cause of the expiratory wheezing.

Allergic phenomena are added to the complication. The allergen may be exogenic. It may also be endogenic as in the autoimmune reaction. In all allergic conditions, tissue damage leads to more of histamine secretion. Histamine causes vasodilation.

Thus, in the aetiology of bronchial asthma, a hereditary predisposition, psychological stress, adverse environmental conditions (physical stress like cold weather) and allergens synergistically complicate the disease.

In the acute condition of bronchial asthma, medical treatment which is symptomatic becomes unavoidable. The doctor may prescribe bronchodilators such as isoprenaline inhalation or adrenaline injection. He may prescribe corticosteroids, antibiotics and expectorants. The elimination of allergens, if practicable, is also indicated. Psychotherapy may be useful. *Yoga*-therapy may be complementary to medical treatment.

All methods of *yoga*-therapy for the treatment of asthma will not be discussed here. However, one important point may be mentioned. An excess of acetylcholine and a deficiency of catecholamines is observed in asthma. This can be reversed towards normalcy by *Haṭha Yoga* practices including some specific *āsanas* and *prāṇāyāma*, which induce reduction of acetylcholine and increase of catecholamines. Meditative *yoga* only, without *Haṭha Yoga* practices, may not be enough to alleviate the symptoms of asthma. Self-therapy of asthma by *yoga-nidrā* is the topic of relevance here. The following *saṅkalpa* is suggested.

> "I am free from worries. I order my respiratory centre in my brain to function normally. I order my respiratory system in my chest not to be over-sensitive."

Thyrotoxicosis

Before we present 'thyrotoxicosis', a disease condition of the thyroid gland, we would like to describe the position of the gland itself. The thyroid gland is situated in the neck in front of the larynx and trachea. Its level corresponds to that of the 5th, 6th and 7th cervical and 1st thoracic vertebrae. It has two lobes, jointed by a narrow isthmus, lying in front of the trachea. The positions of the thyroid gland and its associated structures have been diagramatically illustrated in *fig*. 3.5.

The thyroid gland secretes its hormones thyroxine (T_4) and triiodothyroxine (T_3). The cerebral cortex regulates the hypothalamus that secretes thyroid releasing hormone (TRH) which stimulates the secretion of thyroid stimulating hormone (TSH) by the anterior pituitary. The levels of T_3 and T_4 in plasma have a feedback effect on the secretion of TSH by the anterior pituitary. Thus, increased levels of T_3 and T_4 decrease TSH secretion and vice versa.

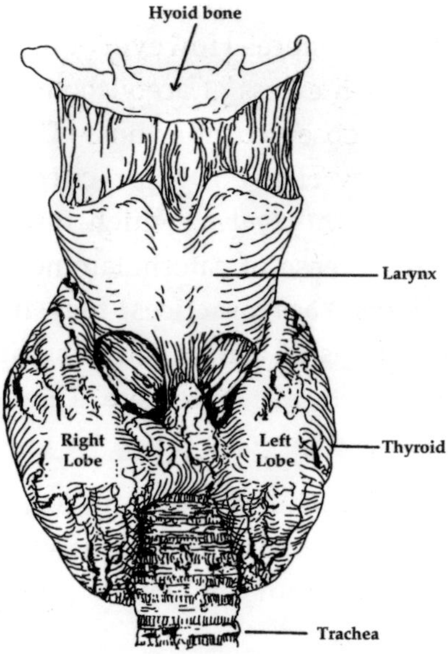

fig. **3.5 The position of the thyroid gland and its associated structures.**

Iodine is a constituent of both T_3 and T_4, one molecule of the former having three atoms of iodine and the latter four atoms. The thyroid hormones influence the basal metabolic rate in a positive way. Similar is their action on carbohydrate, protein and lipid metabolism. They are essential for physical growth and mental development.

The enlargement of the thyroid gland is known as goitre. If it is simple goitre, there is deficient secretion of T_3 and T_4 in spite of excess TRH and TSH. Dietary deficiency of iodine, presistent for a prolonged period, is one of the causes of simple goitre. Genetic abnormality may be the aetiological factor. The intake of antithyroidal chemicals and drugs (goitrogens) may interfere with the synthesis of T_3 and T_4 and thus may be the cause of simple goitre. The picture of an enlarged thyrcid gland has been presented in *fig*. 3.6. The chances of geting a cure of the simple goitre by *yoga-nidrā* are bleak. Medical treatment is necessary for this disease condition.

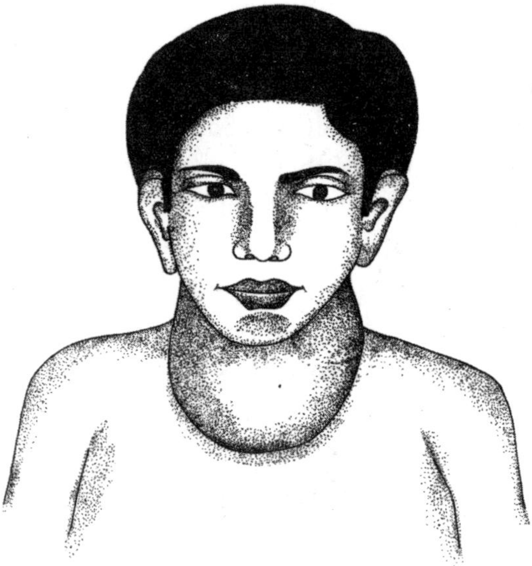

fig. **3.6 An enlarged thyroid gland.**

Thyrotoxicosis is another disease condition of the thyroid gland. It is a syndrome of hyperthyroidism in which the levels of T_3 and T_4 are excessive in the body. It is not due to iodine deficiency in the diet and it is opposite of hypothyroidism.

The main effects of hyperthyroidism are due to increased metabolic rate. The gland enlarges. The hyperplasia may be nodular or diffuse. The extra cells so produced secrete the hormones T_3 and T_4. The metabolic rate is raised. Heat production is excessive. There is increased gluconeogenesis from body proteins, causing loss of weight. The patient has physical restlessness and mental excitability. Cardiac arrhythmias are the invariable symptoms of this disease.

The first idea that comes to the mind about the aetiology of thyrotoxicosis is the hypersecretion of the thyroid stimulating hormone (TSH) by the anterior pituitary. However, contrary is the experimental finding. The quantity of TSH in the blood of thyrotoxic patients is much less than in that of normal persons.

Thyrotoxicosis is a psychosomatic disease along with some hereditary predisposition. Some type of psychic trauma precedes the onset of this disease. The disease may manifest immediately after the psychic trauma or after a variabale length of interval.

Due to psychic trauma, all the centres of the cerebral cortex and especially the psychic centre in the frontal lobe are hyperactivated. Information reaches the posterior hypothalamus via the limbic system from the prefrontal area of the cerebral cortex. The hypothalamus, in turn, activates the autonomic nervous system. In the first phase, the parasympathetic nerve endings throughout the body liberate excess of acetylcholine, which is associated with symptoms of neurosis. Subsequently, the adrenal medulla and the sympathetic nerve endings secrete excessive quantity of catecholamines (adrenaline and noradrenaline).

The vagus nerve (the tenth cranial nerve) which is parasympathetic innervates the thyroid gland. The sympathetic supply is through nerves of the sympathetic ganglia originated from the T_1- T_4 locations of the spinal cord. Many other organs are innervated by these nerves. Why is the thyroid so over-sensitive to the psychic trauma ? Almost all persons happen to experience psychic trauma in life some time or other. Why do some individuals succumb and not others ? Some genetic explanation may answer this question. Enzymes that neutralize the neurohumors (acetylcholine, catecholamines, histamine) such as cholinesterase, monoamino-oxidase and histaminase may be deficient in the thyroid gland of the patients, and this deficiency may be genetic in origin.

We have not yet given the full picture of the neurohumoral

secretions. Vasoconstriction at the arteriolar level in the thyroid gland for a prolonged period due to sustained, higher concentration of catecholamines leads to necrosis in some foci of the organ. Some of this necrosed material is absorbed into the venous and lymphatic circulation and acts as auto-antigen. The immune system develops antibodies against this antigen. The antibodies come in contact with the necrosed areas of the thyroid gland and evoke antigen-antibody response. As a result of this autoimmune response, there is a marked cellular infiltration of lymphocytes and plasma cells in the tyroid gland. The plasma cells are derived from B-lymphocytes. They produce specific antibodies in response to the antigen. Basophil leucocytes in blood and mast cells in loose connective tissues produce cytoplasmic granules containing histamine (both basophils and mast cells are similar) which is released when the cells are damaged. Histamine causes vasodilatation and increases the permeability of small blood vessel walls; it assists the movement of phagocytes and antibodies into the tissue spaces; it is involved in local and general inflammatory reactions; it is associated with the development of allergies and hypersensitivity.

The neurohumors, in thyrotoxicosis, are secreted in three phases. Acetylcholine, catecholamines and histamine are sequentially secreted in phase one, two and three, respectively. The third phase is the late phase in which autoimmune response is manifested. In this late phase, the autoimmune response leads to the liberation of long-acting thyroid stimulator (LATS)[2,3]. This substance is not secreted by the pituitary gland. In chemical composition, it is different from TSH. It is an antibody of IgG in nature. It is possibly a product of

---

2. Adams, *et al.*, 1969.
3. J.M. Mckenzie, 1968.

lymphocytes. Both TSH and LATS have stimulating effects on the thyroid; but the latter has its greater duration of action. In thyrotoxicosis, the secretion of TSH by the anterior pituitary is reduced since its function is taken over by LATS. This explains the lower concentration of TSH in the plasma of thyrotoxic patients.

The psychosomatic and neurohumoral explanation provided by us in the genesis of thyrotoxicosis has been based on the research work done by Dr. K.N. Udupa[4] at Banaras Hindu University.

If you are suffering from thyrotoxicosis, get yourself treated by a doctor. Simultaneously, practise *yoga-nidrā* with the following *saṅkalpa* :

"I can cope with my problems. I am free from worries. My thyroid becomes normal."

Stress-Induced Organic Heart Diseases

Heart diseases are many in types. Some are congenital, with defects in the anatomy of the heart. Some are due to disorders of the heart valves. Rheumatic heart disease is an autoimmune disease, occurring 2 to 4 weeks after a throat infection, caused by *Streptococcus pyogenes*. There are many other types too. All types of heart diseases will not be discussed here.

Consumption of nicotine (through smoking or otherwise), alcoholism and obesity are direct or predisposing causes of many heart diseases.

Some individual persons are prone to be obsese due to genetic reasons. But, even without any hereditary predisposition, obesity can be developed due to excessive intake of calories, lack of physical exercises and execessive

4. K.N. Udupa, 1985, pp. 278-304.

intake of saturated fats (fats of animal origin, hydrogenated vegetable fats and oils containing less quantity of unsaturated fatty acids, especially polyunsaturated fatty acids).

Cholesterol is one type of lipid with multiple rings and a side-chain in its molecular structure. It is present in the animal kingdom and absent in the plant kingdom. Some foods of animal origin such as shrimps, egg-yolk, butter, meat and fish are rich in cholesterol. The body can synthesize cholesterol out of acetate (acetyl-coenzyme A) which is ubiquitous in the body. It is a common product of carbohydrate, fat and protein metabolism. It is useful for the body, especially for the structure and functions of the central nervous system and as a precursor of hormones such as sex hormones and steroid hormones. The normal level of total cholesterol in the serum is 170-265 mg/dl and 175-280 mg/dl for the age group of 50-65 years and over 65 years, respectively. The desirable level of the total cholesterol in serum is less than 200 mg/dl. A level between 200 and 240 mg/dl is considered to be border line. When the level is greater than 250 mg/dl, the person is at definite high risk for cardiovascular diseases.

Cholesterol is one out of the many types of lipids. Lipids are transported in the blood as lipoproteins — complex molecules consisting of triglycerides, cholesterol, phospholipids and proteins. With the fractionation of lipoproteins and cholesterol, the LDL cholesterol (LDL = low-density lipoprotein) and the HDL cholesterol (HDL = high-density lipoprotein) in the serum can be determined. These values would be a more reliable guide for assessing the risk or no risk for cardiovascular diseases. The reference values for serum LDL-cholesterol are 105-190 and 105-200 mg/dl for the age group of 50 to 65 years and over 65 years, respectively. These values for serum HDL-cholesterol are 34-70 and 35-75 mg/dl for the corresponding age groups, respectively.

Individuals with LDL-cholesterol levels greater than 160 mg/dl are considered to be at high risk. Individuals at or above 70 mg/dl for HDL-cholesterol have half the average risk, while those at or near 35 mg/dl have two, three, or more times the average risk. From these figures, it is evident that the LDL-cholesterol is more harmful than the HDL-cholesterol. In the case of the HDL-cholesterol, the serum level and the risk involved are inversely correlated, whereas, for the LDL-cholesterol, the correlation is direct rather than inverse.

How does cholesterol pose a problem for cardiovascular health ? An excess of serum cholesterol is associated with the formation of atheromatous plaques in the tunica intima of large and medium-sized arteries. Most commonly involved arteries are those in the heart, brain, kidneys, small intestine and lower limbs. The plaques consist of cholesterol, other lipid compounds, smooth muscle and fibroelastic cells. They grow in size and form swellings that protrude into the arterial lumen. Arteries may be partially or completely blocked by atheromatous plaques alone or by plaques combined with a thrombus. This reduces the blood-supply to the tissue distal to it. Depending on the site and the size of the artery affected and the extent of collateral circulation, the seriousness of the pathological condition varies.

Due to the narrowing of the coronary artery that supplies blood to the heart muscles, the tissues distal to the narrow point become ischaemic. When the heart muscle activity is increased, acute cramp-like pain is felt. Such ischaemic pain in the heart is known as *angina pectoris*.

When the coronary artery is completely occluded, the cardiac tissues it supplies rapidly undergo degeneration and die from ischaemia. This leads to myocardial *infarction* (the term *infarction* meaning 'an area of dead tissue').

The role of a higher concentration of cholesterol in blood in the genesis of atheroma has already been discussed. The predisposing factors of atheroma include : heredity, advanced age, male sex hormone, hypertension, diabetes mellitus, cigarette smoking, faulty diet (high intake of animal fat/ cholesterol/refined carbohydrates), obesity, sedentary lifestyle, excessive alcohol consumption and emotional stress. The last-mentioned factor, that is, emotional stress, is last but not the least. In order of importance, it is of very serious nature. Because of its importance, we have included heart diseases in the category of psychosomatic diseases.

Emotional stress first affects the cerebral cortex and especially the prefrontal area of the frontal lobe. The prefrontal area stimulates the limbic system which, in turn, stimulates the hypothalamus. In the present context, the hypothalamus functions through two channels. The first pathway of action is the autonomic one. It stimulates the sympathetic subdivision of the autonomic nervous system. The adrenal medulla is also stimulated by its extensive sympathetic nerve supply. As a result, excessive amount of catecholamines (adrenaline and noradrenaline) is secreted by the sympathetic nerve endings and the adrenal medulla. The second pathway of action of the hypothalamus is the secretion of releasing hormones that are carried by the portal circulation to the pituitary gland. Among other releasing hormones, CRH (corticotrophin releasing hormone) is secreted by the hypothalamus. It stimulates the anterior pituitary to secrete more of ACTH (adrenocorticotrophic hormone) that induces the adrenal cortex to secrete more corticoid (steroid) hormones. Both cateholamines and cortisol cause inreased glycogenolysis and gluconeogenesis. Excessive output of cholesterol is an outcome of this altered biochemistry. Normally, an excess of cateholamines is antagonised by acetylcholine, the neurohumor of the parasympathetic system, and degraded by the enzyme MAO (monoamine oxidase). In extreme stressful situations, the levels of acetylcholine and MAO do not proportionately rise in comparison with that of catecholamines. An excessive amount of catecholamines accelerates the rate and force of heart beat and increases blood pressure for a prolonged period throughout the long duration of the emotional stress. The enhancement of the activity of the heart, without the corresponding increase in the oxygen supply to the myocardium and with the insufficiency of coronary circulation, leads to the manifestation of *angina pectoris*.

In addition to the physiopathology brought about by the neurohumors of the sympatho-adrenal system, pathological lesions are created in the two (right and left) coronary vessels and the heart musculature by the excessive secretion of catecholamines. Epidemiological studies have clearly indicated that atheromatous plaques are formed in the tunica intima of the coronary arteries and their branches due to prolonged hypersecretion of catecholamines. The mechanism of action is, however, not clear.

Higher concentration of catecholamines in blood causes vasodilatation in the coronary arteries in contrast to vasoconstriction in the arteries of many other organs. Hence the concept of microcirculation causing necrosis of tissues cannot explain the occurrence of myocardial infarction.

It is a fact that sympathetic stimulation, due to prolonged emotional stress, favours blood coagulation by increasing the viscosity of blood and decreasing the coagulation time. How it does is not known. If the endothelium lying over an atheromatous plaque breaks down, platelets (thrombocytes) are stimulated by the damaged cells. They clump to each other. Their surface becomes sticky and they adhere to the damaged wall of the coronary artery. They then release serotonin (5-hydroxytryptamine), which constricts the blood vessel. Thus, the blood supply to the tissues supplied by the vessel is reduced.

A platelet plug is formed at the damaged site by the arrival of more and more platelets which stick together to form a temporary seal at the site of the vascular damage.

The next process is the formation of a blood clot (thrombus) which is much stronger than the rapidly formed platelet plug. The thrombus may block the artery and cause ischaemia and infarction. Since catecholamines increase the coagulability of the blood, they thereby enhance the chances of ischaemic heart disease and infarction of the myocardium. A thrombus is an intravascular blood clot. The occlusion (partial or complete) of an artery or a vein is called thrombosis.

An embolus is a material mass carried in the bloodstream. Most emboli consist of fragments of thrombi. One such embolus may lodge in and block a smaller vessel in the myocardium. As a result, the tissue supplied by the vessel becomes ischaemic and dies; this is myocardial infarction.

Stress-Induced Functional Cardiac Disorders

About 50 per cent of the heart patients do not have organic cardiac diseases. They usually suffer from cardioneurosis, otherwise known as neuro-circulatory asthenia. Due to excessive psychological and emotional disturbances, their autonomic nervous system is adversely affected. Some dysfunctions of the cardiovascular system are mentioned as follows.

Cardiac arrhythmia. A cardiac arrhythmia is any disorder of the heart rate or rhythm. It is due to abnormal generation or conduction of impulses. The measurement of the pulse indicates the heart rate. An electrocardiogram (ECG) is required to determine the rhythm. The heart rate is initiated by intrinsic impulses generated in the SA node. The route of impulse transmission through the conducting system determines the rhythm. So far was cardiac arrhythmia considered to be due to some organic changes in the cardiac musculature or in the coronary vessels. It has recently been realized that excessive psychic trauma disturbs the autonomic nervous system and thereby may cause cardiac arrhythmia as a functional disorder rather than an organic disorder. The different types of cardiac arrhythmias are the following: (1) Sinus tachycardia, (2) Sinus bradycardia, (3) Sinus arrhythmia, (4) Extra systole, (5) Paroxysmal tachycardia and (6) Pseudo-angina.

Sinus tachycardia is sinus rhythm above 100 beats per minute when the person is at rest. It occurs as a result of physical excercise, increased metabolism, or rise in temperature. An increased stimulation of the sympathetic nervous system is generally involved in sinus tachycardia. For this reason, anxiety or emotional excitement is accompanied with sinus tachycardia. Tachycardia is considered pathological when the accelerations of the heart rate is too great or too prolonged.

Sinus bradycardia is sinus rhythm below 60 beats per minute. This is very often due to psychic stress or hyperactivity of the brain which produces an increased activity of the parasympathetic nervous system rather than the sympathetic nervous system. Giddiness and fainting for a variable period are the usual symptoms.

Sinus arrhythmia occurs in severe emotional stress which alternately stimulates both the parasympathetic and the sympathetic nerves of the autonomic nervous system. Persons most susceptible to this disease are often creative and highly emotional; their autonomic nervous system is genetically reactive; from their birth, they are hyper-sensitive to slightest provocation. The prefrontal area (the psychic centre of the brain) is easily disturbed, and it disturbs the hypothalamus. The heart exhibits irregular symptoms of tachycardia and bradycardia, when the patient goes into a state of psychic excitement. When the excitement subsides, the irregularities of the heart-beat stops.

Extra systoles may be due to organic lesions in the myocardium or due to emotional tension, psychic stress or malfunction of the autonomic nervous system. The second category of symptoms is psychic in origin, with no pathology in the cardiac organ itself.

Paroxysmal tachycardia is a functional cardiac disorder in which attacks of tachycardia occur all of a sudden. It is usually preceded by anxiety and severely emotional mental state, sometimes by the spontaneous emergence of hurt sentiments from the Unconscious. As the state of anxiety subsides, the cardiac function returns to its normal state.

Pseudo-angina is a functional disorder of the heart, with angina-like symptoms without any pathology of the true angina in the heart. The patient feels a dull pressure over the pericardium for some time, followed by an attack of sharp pain in the region of the heart. Pseudo-angina occurs all of a sudden, not necessarily after an exertion, whereas true angina often follows physical exertion, sexual intercourse, cold stress or heavy meals. Further, pseudo-angina often exhibits additional respiratory symptoms such as the sensation of strangulation of the upper respiratory tract, a feeling of suffocation, laboured breathing, dyspnoea, etc. The symptoms of pseudo-angina are exhibited by the heart whereas the root of the disease lies in the psychic centre of the brain.

***Treatment* by *yoga-nidrā*.** If you suffer from any type of heart disease for which anxiety and emotional stress are directly or indirectly the incriminating factors or are the complicating factors contributing to some other aetiology, practise *yoga-nidrā* with the following *saṅkalpa*:

"I can cope with my problems. I am worry-free. My heart is healthy."

Medical and surgical treatments of heart diseases are not antagonistic to *yoga-nidrā* therapy or any other method of *yoga* therapy. Hence the treatment by the doctor and self-therapy through *yoga* may be done concurrently. Even if a by-pass surgery or any other surgery has been done, post-surgical therapy may include *yoga-nidrā* and other *yoga* techniques to prevent any probability of recurrence.

Hypertension

Hypertension is a condition of raised blood pressure, sustained at a level higher than the normal for a particular age group.

Before we discuss hypertension, we would like to introduce some concepts and preliminary information on blood pressure.

Blood pressure. It is the pressure which the blood exerts on the walls of the blood vessels. The systemic arterial blood pressure is the result of the discharge of blood from the left ventricle of the heart. The systolic blood pressure is due to the contraction of the left ventricle which pushes blood into the aorta. The pressure so produced within the arterial system is called the systolic blood pressure. The diastolic blood pressure, on the other hand, is the pressure within the arteries at the time of the complete cardiac diastole, following the ejection of blood.

***The cardiovascular centre*.** The cardiovascular centre (CVC) is located in the medulla oblongata and pons of the brain. It is a collection of interconnected neurons. The CVC receives inputs from the baroreceptors (special nerve endings, sensitive to pressure changes; they are present in the arch of the aorta and the carotid sinuses), the chemoreceptors (special nerve endings, sensitive to changes in the levels of carbon dioxide, oxygen and the acidity of the blood; they are present in the carotid and aortic bodies) and higher centres in the brain. This cardiovascular centre plays an important role in the genesis of essential hypertension to be described later. This centre mediates emotional states such as fear, anxiety, agony and anger and all such influences of the prefrontal area, the limbic system and the hypothalamus in the genesis of essential hypertension. Any type of *yoga*-therapy in the control of hypertension has relation with the working of this centre.

The output of the CVC is through the autonomic nervous system (both sympathetic and parasympathetic). It sends sympathetic and parasympathetic nerves to the heart and blood vessels. Of course, there is little parasympathetic innervation to most blood vessels. The CVC controls blood pressure by slowing down or speeding up the heart rate and by dilating or constricting the blood vessels. Sympathetic stimulation accelerates the heart rate and increases the strength of cardiac contraction and thereby raises the blood pressure. It causes vasoconstriction in most blood vessels (the blood vessels of the heart, brain and skeletal muscles dilate), resulting in the increase in blood pressure. The vasoconstriction of the blood vessels of the skin by sympathetic stimulation is worth mentioning here in this context. The cardiac response to the parasympathetic stimulation is just the reverse and hence the blood pressure is decreased.

The vasomotor centre. There is a vasomotor centre in the medulla oblongata. It sends sympathetic nerve fibres to all blood vessels. Blood vessels except capillaries have smooth muscle fibres in their tunica media. These muscle fibres are innervated by the sympathetic nerves which arise from the vasomotor centre. There is no parasympathetic nerve supply to most blood vessels. Increased sympathetic nerve stimulation causes vasoconstriction and hence the blood pressure is increased. Decreased sympathetic nerve stimulation causes relaxation of the smooth muscle and vasodilatation, thus reducing the blood pressure. There is always some nerve input to the vessel walls; this input is sometimes increased and some other times decreased.

Peripheral resistance. Medium-sized and small arteries have more smooth muscle than elastic tissue in the tunica media of their walls. In contrast, in large arteries, such as the aorta, the tunica media is almost entirely elastic tissue. For this reason, the diameter of small arteries and arterioles varies in response to nerve stimulation whereas that of large arteries varies in response to the amount of blood they contain.

The small arterioles are primarily responsible for providing resistance to the blood flow. Arterioles are the resistance vessels because of their peripheral resistance to the flow of blood. Constriction and dilatation of the arterioles are the main determinants of peripheral resistance. Blood pressure rises due to vascoconstriction and falls due to vasodilatation. When the elastic tissue in the tunica media of arterioles is replaced by collagen fibres or white connective tissue (inelastic fibrous tissue), blood pressure rises. This is part of the ageing process.

The renin angiotensin aldosterone system. On the reduction of blood flow to the kidneys or the fall of blood sodium levels, the kidney cells secrete an enzyme known as renin. Angiotensinogen is a plasma protein, produced by the liver. Renin converts angiotensinogen to angiotensin 1. This angiotensin 1 is converted to angiotensin 2 by the enzyme ACE (angiotensin converting enzyme), formed in small quantities in the proximal tubules of the kidneys, lungs and other tissues. Angiotensin 2 directly increases blood pressure by causing vasoconstriction. It stimulates the adrenal cortex to secrete aldosterone, which stimulates the reabsorption of sodium through the renal tubules and the excretion of potassium in the urine. The increased level of sodium in the blood leads to retention of water in the body, resulting in higher blood volume and increased blood pressure.

With these preliminary information on blood pressure, we come back to the original topic of hypertension.

There are two main types of hypertension, namely, essential (primary, idiopathic) and secondary.

ESSENTIAL HYPERTENSION

About 85 to 90 per cent of hypertension patients suffer from this essential type. Conventionally, it is said that the cause of this type is unknown. This statement is partially true and partially untrue for the purpose of *yoga* therapy. Essential hypertension is a psychosomatic disease. The exact psychic condition may not be known. In that sense, the cause of essential hypertension is unknown. But it is mostly due to some psychic trauma which may be manifest or unmanifest. In this second sense, the cause is known.

Some painful experience of recent origin or of remote past is the cause of essential hypertension. Physical or mental adversity, family disaster, economic distress, job adversity, ambitions unfulfilled, frustration and failure, difficulties in interpersonal relationships and such other states of emotional stress are the primary causes of essential hypertension.

Sometimes the patient can narrate his/her painful experiences. Very often he/she is not aware of the root of the agony which is deeply buried in the Subconscious or the Unconscious. The unconscious agony may or may not refer to incidences of the present life and may be traced back to past lives. The patient may not be aware of the gnawing agony emerging from the deep layers of the mind and may be *apparently* happy. Worries, anxiety and tension may not be contemporary with the onset of the hypertensive symptoms. Any situation, provoking the awakening of the dormant *vāsanā* or past and forgotten painful experiences, can shoot up the blood pressure insidiously.

What is the mechanism of action of this type of hypertension ? The mechanism has already been described, partly at least. The mind and the brain are not identical, the latter being the apparatus of the former. Any emotional stress, latent or patent, adversely affects the cerebral cortex, especially its prefrontal area which stimulates the limbic system and the hypothalamus. The limbic system and the hypothalamus stimulate two centres in the medulla oblongata, namely, the cardiovascular centre (CVC) and the vasomotor centre. Autonomic nerve fibres, both parasympathetic and sympathetic, leave the CVC and reach the heart and blood vessels (there is little parasympathetic innervation to the blood vessels). As a result of the sympathetic stimulation, the heart rate is increased and the strength of the heart beat is also increased. This results in the rise of blood pressure. Both the CVC and the vasomotor centre send sympathetic fibers to the arterioles. Excess of sympathetic stimulation causes vascoconstriction and peripheral resistance, and thereby increases the blood pressure.

Hypertension has an inherited tendency. In some families, the genotype may be conducive to the higher development of the right hemisphere of the brain, the limbic system, the hypothalamus or the nuclei of CVC and the vasomotor centre in the medulla. Some of these centres may be genetically hypersensitive. The DNA constitution may be more favourable for the biosynthesis of enzymes concerned with the secretion of adrenaline, noradrenaline, renin, aldosterone or the formation of angiotensinogen. Future research on molecular biology will throw more light on these aspects. However, it may be noted here that hypertension due to hereditary predisposition may not be called a psychosomatic disease, it being somatic in origin.

Obesity predisposes a person to hypertension. Lack of exercise is also another predisposing factor. Both these factors, however, are very much related. Although members of certain families are likely to be obese due to genetic reasons, obesity is not always due to genes. Excessive intake of calorie-rich food and minimum consumption of energy due to lack of excercise may be the cause of obesity. The excess energy is stored in the form of fat.

The level of triglycerides in the plasma increases in obesity. The level of serum cholesterol also increases in this condition. This leads to atherosclerosis and finally to hypertension. This type of hypertension is not psychosomatic in origin. It is somatic rather than psychosomatic.

Exercise has definitely some beneficial effect in relieving hypertension. It reduces fat in the body and relieves the symptoms of atherosclerosis. But, according to yoga and tantra, this is not the only mode of action. Exercises in general and some special types of exercises in particular facilitate the free flow of *prāṇa* in the *nāḍīs*. If there is obstruction to the free flow of *prāṇa* somewhere in the body, the blood pressure rises. Thus, in addition to the reduction of adiposity due to physical exercises, the free flow of *prāṇa,* consequent on doing exercises, has some relieving effect on hypertension.

Excessive alcohol intake and cigarette smoking are very much conducive to hypertension. Here also, the hypertension is somatic in origin rather than psychosomatic. Alcoholism and cigarette smoking produce lesions in some tissues and organs. Thus, the pathogenesis, in these cases, leads to hypertension.

SECONDARY HYPERTENSION

When hypertension results from other diseases, it is known as secondary hypertension. About 10 to 15 per cent of all cases of hypertension are secondary.

When the kidneys are diseased, blood pressure rises. This is due to the vasoconstriction brought about by the renin angiotensin aldosterone system, already described. This is one of the known causes. There may be others, however, as yet unknown.

Secondary hypertension may result from endocrine disorders. The disorder may be in the adrenal cortex or the adrenal medulla.

Oversecretion of aldosterone and cortisol from the adrenal cortex causes retention of excess sodium and water by the kidneys, leading to raising the blood volume and consequently blood pressure. A hormone-secreting tumour may be the cause. An excess of adrenocorticotrophic (ACTH) hormone secreted by the anterior pituitary may overstimulate the adrenal cortex for the oversecretion of cortisol.

There may be a hormone-secreting tumour in the adrenal medulla which may secrete excess adrenaline and noradrenaline.

Hypertension may be due to a stricture in the aorta. In this case, hypertension develops in branching arteries proximal to the site of stricture.

Treatment by some drugs such as corticosteriods, non-steroidal anti-inflammatory drugs and oral contraceptives may produce hypertension as complications.

Yoga-nidrā therapy is not very promising for the treatment of secondary hypertension and also for that of any other type of hypertension which is not psychosomatic in origin. It is not said here that *yoga-nidrā* is totally useless for any type of somatic hypertension. But the results are not expected to be spectacular.

AGEING, ARTERIOSCLEROSIS AND HYPERTENSION

Arteriosclerosis is a progressive degeneration of arterial walls.

In the large medium arteries, the tunica media is infiltrated with fibrous tissue (collagen fibres) and calcium. The vessels lose their elasticity, resulting in hypertension.

In small arteries and arterioles, hyaline thickening of the tunica media and tunica intima occurs. The lumen of these small blood vessels becomes narrower. As a result, peripheral resistance is increased, finally leading to hypertension. Arteriosclerosis is associated with ageing and accompanied by hypertension.

Senile arteriosclerosis. Elderly people are affected by this condition. The loss of elasticity in the blood vessels, especially the small arteries and arterioles, is progressive. This leads to reduced arterial lumen, and finally to cerebral ischaemia and loss of mental function. It may or may not be accompanied by hypertension.

Yoga-nidrā and other methods of *yoga* are preventive to arteriosclerosis and senile arteriosclerosis. Especially the relaxation type of *yoga* is both preventive and curative. *Yoga-nidrā* can retard the onset and progress of arteriosclerosis and senile arteriosclerosis. But, with advanced pathology, the prospect of cure by *yoga-nidrā* is bleak.

Arteriosclerosis is a disease of organic degeneration. It is mainly somatic in nature, although involvement of psychic factors is not altogther ruled out.

Any hypertension which is psychosomatic has a better chance of being cured by *yoga-nidrā*.

Treatment by yoga-nidrā. What is essential or primary hypertension is our psychosomatic hypertension. *Āsanas*, *prāṇāyāmas*, *mudrās*, *prāṇa-sañcālana kriyā*, meditational techniques and relaxation techniques are very useful for the treatment of hypertension. All these things will not be discussed here. Only a typical *saṅkalpa* of *yoga-nidrā*, applicable to the treatment of psychosomatic hypertension, is prescribed here.

> "I am worry-free. I can cope with my problems. My blood pressure is normal."

Stress-Induced Cancer

All cancers are not stress-induced. In most cases, carcinogenesis may be of genetic and/or environmental origin.

The environmental, predisposing factors of carcinogenesis are:

Chemical carcinogens. Some examples of chemical carcinogens are: aniline dyes, vinyl chloride, some fuel oils, cigarette smoking, asbestos, benzene derivatives, arsenic compounds, nickel compounds.

Radiation carcinogens. Malignant growths can be caused by exposure to ionising radiation including X-rays, gamma rays, radioactive isotopes, ultraviolet rays in sunlight and enviornmental radiations.

Constant irritation. Any source of constant irritation may be carcinogenic. It may be pressure and frictional irritation, thermal irritation, or ulcerative irritation as in the case of untreated gastric ulcer.

Hormonal imbalance. Some types of malignant neoplasms may be due to hormonal imbalance or precipitated by hormonal imbalance. Uterine cancer, breast cancer and prostate cancer belong to this category.

Oncogenic viruses. Some viruses, consisting of DNA and RNA, have been known to cause malignancy in animals. On the entry of viruses into the host cell, the additional DNA or RNA in the nucleus of the host cell undergoes mutation. The mutant cells, thus produced, may be malignant. What has been proved for animals may be true for human beings. There may be oncognic viruses for human beings too.

Tension and anxiety. This last causative agent for carcinogenesis has been detected by medical specialists; but it has not yet been highlighted in textbooks. This will be our focus for this discussion.

It is a fact that prolonged psychic trauma is carcinogenic. How do we explain this fact? How is the pathogenesis brought about.

If psychic stress is sustained for a prolonged period, cancer may develop in some organ which is otherwise weak and susceptible. The cerebral cortex and especially the prefrontal area are first of all affected. Next, the limbic system and the hypothalamus are stimulated by the prefrontal area. The hypothalamus responds in two ways. It stimulates the sympathetic division of the autonomic nervous system. It also sends releasing factors through the portal circulation to the anterior pituitary which secretes more of adrenocorticotrophic hormone (ACTH).

The adrenal cortex secretes excess of corticosteroids. The adrenal medulla secretes excess of catecholamines (adrenaline and noradrenaline).

Excessive secretion of corticosteriods causes immuno-suppression, leading to the proliferation of mutant cells which would otherwise have been phagocytized or destroyed through other means. These mutant cells are the source of cancer.

An excess of catecholamines causes vasoconstriction. Prolonged vasoconstriction is the cause of anoxia to the cells and tissues of an organ. If such a state persists, a devitalized organ develops cancer.

Treatment by yoga-nidrā. *Yoga-nidrā* can be practised to prevent stress-induced cancer and retard the growth and proliferation of any type of malignancy. It can also be practised for the successful treatment of cancers. The following *saṅkalpa* is prescribed.

> "I am free from tensions and anxiety. I can cope with my problems. My cancer cells, regress and die, regress and die, regress and die."

Chronic Arthritis

Three diseases fall in the category of chronic arthritis. They are: gout, osteoarthritis and rheumatoid arthritis. These diseases are more common in the Western countries than in the tropical ones. Gout and osteoarthritis are commonly seen in late middle age or old age. Rheumatoid arthritis affects people of all ages, and occasionally children.

There is a familial tendency in all these three diseases. But the details of the genetics are yet to be known.

Gout is caused by the deposition of sodium urate crystals in joints and tendons. This provokes an acute inflammatory condition. Uric acid is a catabolic product of DNA and RNA. Persons who suffer from gout have abnormally high levels of uric acid in blood. This is due to either overproduction of uric acid or defective excretion by the kidneys.

Osteoarthritis (or the more appropriate name — osteoarthrosis) is a degenerative, non-inflammatory disease, resulting in pain and restricted movement of the affected joints. In this disease, the articular cartilage gradually becomes thinner since its renewal is comparatively less than its breakdown. Eventually the bony articular surfaces come in contact and they start degenerating. The repair of bones in the joints becomes abnormal, with the result that the articular surfaces become misshapen. Now chronic inflammation develops, but this becomes secondary to the primary lesions. Sometimes osteophytes are formed as a result of abnormal outgrowth of cartilages and subsequent ossification at the edges of bones.

Osteoarthrosis may be complicated with osteoporosis which may sometimes be primary to the former. The doctor may prescribe extra intake of calcium with vitamin D_3 daily throughout the life of an aged person in order to alleviate the pathology of osteoporosis. He may also prescribe drugs containing dietary nutraceutical supplements such as chondroitin sulphate, glucosamine hydrochloride, vitamins, minerals and others for the regeneration of the articular cartilage that degenerates in osteoarthrosis. Medical treatment by an expert doctor is advisable, in addition to *yoga-nidrā* therapy, for getting partial or complete relief from osteoarthrosis.

Rheumatoid arthritis is a chronic, progressive, inflammatory, autoimmune disease. It is more common in females than in males. It affects people of all ages, including children, although the commonly susceptible age is between 35 and 55 years.

Rheumatoid arthritis is a systemic disorder. The inflammatory changes, in this disease, not only affect synovial joints but also many other sites such as the heart, blood vessels and skin.

The comparative features of osteoarthritis and rheumatoid

arthritis may briefly be mentioned here. The former is degenerative whereas the latter is inflammatory and autoimmune. The tissue affected in the former is the articular cartilage; that in the latter is the synovial membrane. The joints affected in osteoarthritis are the weight-bearing ones, namely, the hip or the knee (often only a single one). The small joints of the hands and feet are affected in rheumatoid arthritis and often multiple joints are involved.

The Role of Psychic Stress in Rheumatoid Arthritis. For this topic, reference may be made to Udupa's book *Stress and Its Management by Yoga*.[5] With excessive psychic stress, the psychic centre in the prefrontal area of the cerebral cortex of persons, with certain personality traits, becomes chronically excited. The excited psychic centre recurrently stimulates the limbic area which, in turn, stimulates the hypothalamus. The hypothalamic stimulation induces the sympathetic nervous system for the outpouring of catecholamines — adrenaline and noradrenaline. Catecholamines cause severe vasoconstriction in some specially susceptible sites. These sites are around small joints — carpal, metacarpal, tarsal, metatarsal and phalanges.

Prolonged and repeated vasoconstriction leads initially to ischaemia and finally to necrosis of the cells of the synovial membrane. The necrosed microsomal antigenic fractions of the synovial cells are absorbed into the lymph stream and reach the lymph nodes where antibodies are produced. These autoimmune bodies are carried back to the damaged synovial membrane where an antigen-antibody reaction is evoked with severe inflammatory response.

As a result of the autoimmune response, there is a marked cellular infiltration of lymphocytes and plasma cells in the

5. K.N. Udupa, pp. 321-25.

affected joint. Basophil leucocytes in blood and mast cells in loose connective tissues also infiltrate the area. They produce cytoplasmic granules containing histamine. When these cells are damaged, histamine is released to cause vasodilatation. Histamine increases the permeability of the walls of small blood vessels and accentuates the inflammatory reactions.

At a later state, the inflamed synovial membrane creeps into the joint, leading to the involvement of the articular cartilage in the inflammatory process. Finally the cartilage is destroyed and the bones of the joint too. The entire joint becomes a mass of granulation tissue with variable amount of scar tissue. Such an affected joint loses the ability of movement.

Treatment of Rheumatoid Arthritis by Yoga. Some *āsanas*, if regularly practised, can fully cure or relieve rheumatoid arthritis. It may be painful for a patient to do *āsana*s if the disease has progressed too much. Hence, it is advisable to start *yoga* treatment at an early state.

The following yogic postures and *prāṇāyāma*s are recommended:

A. *Prāṇa-sañcālana kriyā, dhanurāsana, cakrāsana, bhujaṅgāsana, śalabhāsana, trikoṇāsana, supta vajrāsana.*

B. *Naḍī-śodhana prāṇāyāma* without retention, *ujjayī prāṇāyāma* with concentration on the nosetip, while sitting on *vajrāsana*.

How do *āsana*s help in the treatment of rheumatoid arthritis ? They help in two ways.

The regular practice of yogic *āsana*s increases the acetylcholine content of the cerebral cortex. This produces tranquillity of the psychic centre of the brain. As a result, the limbic system, the hypothalamus and sympathetic nervous system are not overstimulated. Thus, the outpouring of catecholamines is prevented.

The second line of action is through the regulated secretion of corticosteroids. Steroid-therapy is done for the treatment of rheumatoid arthritis. It is suppressive by virtue of its being anti-inflammatory; but it is not curative. Its dose is gradually increased in the course of treatment. Higher doses create a number of problems. Yogic postures, however, regulate the secretion of the right quantity of corticosteroids as and when needed by the body.

A second question pops up. How does *prāṇāyāma* help the treatment of rheumatoid arthritis ?

In our opinion, any obstruction to the flow of *prāṇa-vāyu* in the small joints of the limbs is the fundamental cause of rheumatoid arthritis. Agonising and prolonged psychic stress is an aggravating factor only; it is not the primary cause. Similarly genetic inheritance is a predisposing factor only; it is not the primary cause. *Prāṇāyāma* ensures the free flow of *prāṇa* through the *suṣumṇā*, the *iḍā*, the *piṅgalā* and the branching channels. *Prāṇa-sañcālana kriyā* also facilitates the free flow of *prāṇa*. If *prāṇa* is not obstructed and if it flows freely, there is no occasion for rheumatoid arthritis to occur.

Treatment by yoga-nidrā. If you suffer from any of the three joint diseases, get it properly diagnosed by the doctor. You may undergo medical treatment and simultaneously treat yourself with *yoga*. Some specific *āsanas*, *mudrās*, *kriyās* and *prāṇāyāmas* are definitely beneficial. Continue the *yoga*-practices even if you are cured. This would prevent the recurrence of the disease. Practise *yoga-nidrā* with dfferent types of *saṅkalpas* for each type of the three joint diseases. The following *saṅkalpas* are recommended.

> *For gout* : "My body cells, retard the catabolism of DNA and RNA to form uric acid. No deposition of sodium urate in my joints."

For osteoarthrosis: "My knee joint/my hip joint, be healthy. Let the degeneration of the joint cartilage be retarted. Let the regeneration of the joint cartilage be accelerated."

For rheumatoid arthritis : "I am free from worries. No autoimmune response in my joints. I order my adrenal cortex to secrete enough cortisone."

Tension Headache

Migraine is a recurrent throbbing headache that usually affects one side of the head, often accompanied by nausea and disturbance of vision. Psychic stress is an important cause of this tension headache, otherwise known as migraine.

The migraine patients have some common psychic features which can be grouped to designate a psychic personality. Such persons are perfectionists, orderly, rigid, ambitious, competitive and unwilling to delegate responsibilities. Their ideals are generally unrealistic. Frustration results from the non-attainment of the ideals. A feeling of anxiety, an inner feeling of nervous tension, some sort of suppressed anger and emotions repressed in the Unconscious are common features that predispose persons to tension headache. Such persons are highly emotional from their birth. They are also allergic to some food items.

Psychic stress over-stimulates the prefrontal area (psychic centre) of the cerebral cortex. The limbic system gets information from the psychic centre and stimulates the hypothalamus. The hypothalamus excites the sympathetic nervous division of the autonomic nervous system. Catecholamines (noradrenaline and adrenaline) are secreted by the sympathetic nerve-endings. This leads to vasoconstriction. This is followed by the local liberation of histamine which causes abnormal vasodilatation. A prolonged vasodilatation causes severe pain in the region of the head.

Very often, additional constitutional symptoms accompany an attack of migraine. These are: vomiting, visual abnormality, biliary colic, angina pectoris, paroxysmal tachycardia, urinary frequency. All these symptoms are due to psychogenic stress too. Migraine usually starts with unilateral involvement; but later on it may affect both sides of the body. The pain reaches its peak within one to two hours and then gradually subsides within four to five hours.

Yoga in the treatment of migraine. Any yogic practice that induces physical as well as mental relaxation is effective in the treatment of migraine. *Āsanas*, in general, stimulate the secretion of acetylcholine in the cerebral cortex and the parasympathetic nerve endings. They bring about mental tranquillity. *Śavāsana* and the *prāṇa-sañcālana kriyā* are the ideal *yoga* techniques for producing relaxation. *Nāḍī-śodhana prāṇāyāma* without retention, *ujjayī prāṇāyāma* with *khecarī-mudrā* and *ujjayī prāṇāyāma* on *vajrāsana* with *ajapā japa* may be practised to induce relaxation and reduce mental tension. Some *mudrās* are definitely helpful. In addition, *yoga-nidrā* is to be practised.

Yoga-nidrā for the treatment of migraine. The following *saṅkalpa* is recommended :

"I am free from tension. I am relaxed. My migraine is cured."

Mental Conflict

Some persons are wavering and vacillating in nature. In most issues, they are indecisive. When they have to take a decision and they take one, later they become dissatisfied for having taken that decision and for not having taken any other one out of the alternatives. Their oscillating mind broods over the so-called wrong decision taken. Mental conflict arises out of such vacillation or oscillation.

Religious indoctrination, rigid social restrictions, inflexible cultural norms and moral or ethical inelastic standards are stamped on the minds of some persons as sacred and inviolable. It is sacrilegious and profane for them to violate this sacredness. They are puritan and perfectionist. Their parents, elders, the clergy and social neighbourhood have brain-washed them. They are also susceptible subjects to be brain-washed. Willingly and happily they accept these environmental influences and, thus, these impressions become firmly nested in their minds. Their minds become blunt to logical analysis and rationality. They resent ideas alien to their own and revolt against any rational thinking which is considered by them to be profane.

But circumstances sometimes force these persons to act contrary to their imprinted standards. It may so happen that their personal weakness yields to their moral and religious sanctity and impels them to indulge in the so-called profanity and immorality. The breach and violation of their standards, due to any reason, breed emotional conflicts (*dvandva*) in their minds. Finally, they fall victim to their mental conflicts.

A third category of mental conflicts has its origin in the Subconscious or the Unconscious. Some so-called ideals and sacred ethics have already been deeply lodged in their Subconscious or Unconscious. Their storage might have relevance to incidences in the present life or past lives. The person is ignorant of his unconscious ideals and norms. When he commits something in action out of compulsion or due to personal weakness, he is consciously unaffected, but unconsciously agitated due to mental pull and push in an inner tug of war. He falls victim to his mental conflict unawares.

Emotional conflict, especially of the second and the third type described in the foregoing paragraphs, is the causal factor of a variety of psychosomatic diseases. Any system of the body and any organ of any system may be affected. The nature of the conflict, the personality type and the intrinsic devitalization of the tissue decide the site and the pathology.

The *Bhagavadgītā* advises to be free from vacillating doubts (*saṁśaya*)[6] and mental conflicts and contradictions (*dvandva*).[7]

Yoga-nidrā is a potent, effective technique to cure psychosomatic diseases due to emotional conflicts. The following *saṅkalpa* is suggested.

> "I think logically and rationally. I erase the irrational, rigid standards from my Unconscious. I am free from conflicts and contradictions."

It also may be a fact that the person's action is really bad when judged rationally. His action cannot be supported by any good ethical standard. It is bad, ugly, heinous and inhuman. Even in such a situation, the person can disentangle himself from the feeling of guilt and sin and free himself from emotional conflicts. He should genuinely repent for the commission and omission and swear not to repeat the misdeeds in future. With this mental set-up, he can practise *yoga-nidrā* with the following *saṅkalpa*.

> "I am sorry for what I have done. I really repent. I am free from emotional conflicts."

CATEGORY-4

This is the category of physiological malfunctioning. Some organ may be hyperactive, or it may be hypoactive. Some organ

6. *BG*, IV.40.
7. *Ibid.*, II.45; IV.22; V.3; VII.28.

or its tissue may atrophy or degenerate. Some organ may be sluggish in action and may not perform its normal physiological function. We will take a few examples and prescribe the *yoga-nidrā saṅkalpa* for each.

Decreased Secretion of Ovarian Hormones

A young woman has irregular menstrual cycles. Ova in her ovaries are not maturing. The oestrogen content of her blood is very low. She is showing symptoms of sterility.

This is a case of the decreased physiological activity of the ovaries. The ovarian follicle secretes the female hormone 'oestradiol' (oestrogen). For the ovaries to function normally, the anterior pituitary is to secrete FSH (follicle-stimulating hormone). For the anterior pituitary to secrete FSH, the hypothalamus is to secrete GTHRH (gonadotrophic hormone releasing hormone). For the hypothalamus to do its job, the prefrontal area of the frontal lobe of the cerebral cortex is to issue proper directive.

For *yoga-nidrā* to be very effective, the patient should have a clear picture of the anatomy of the female reproductive organs in the pelvis (*fig.* 3.7), the locations of the endocrine glands in the body (*fig.* 3.8) and the pathway of infromation-transmission from the brain to the ovaries (*fig.* 3.9).

Yoga-nidrā for the treatment of ovarian hypo-function. The following *saṅkalpa* is recommended.

> "My psychic centre, hypothalamus, pituitary and ovaries, normally function in perfect coordination."

Decreased secretion of insulin in diabetes mellitus

The pancreas is a dual gland, situated in the abdominal cavity. It consists of a broad head, a body and a narrow tail. The

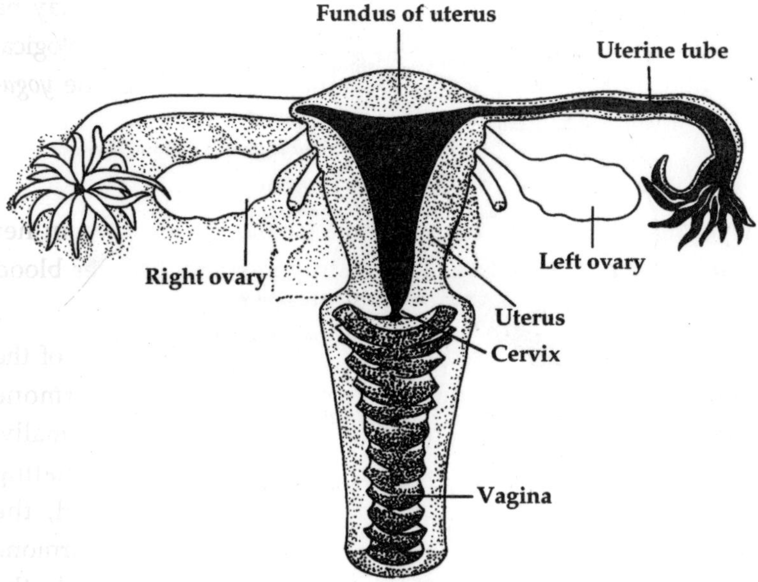

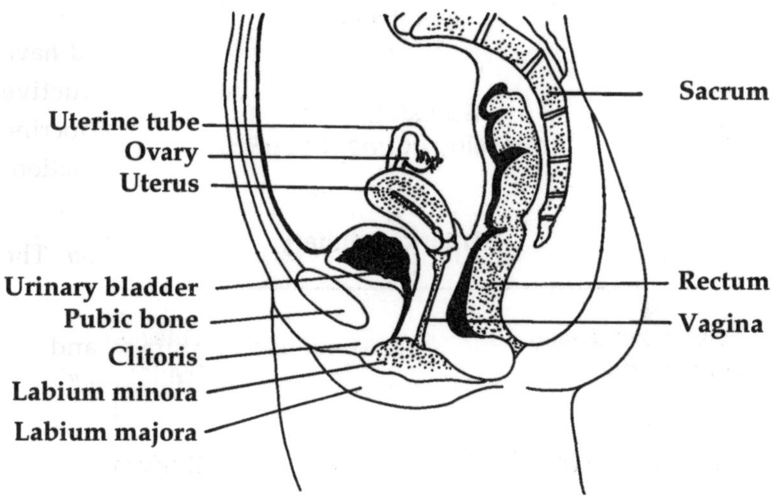

fig. 3.7 (a & b) The anatomy of the female reproductive organs in the pelvis.

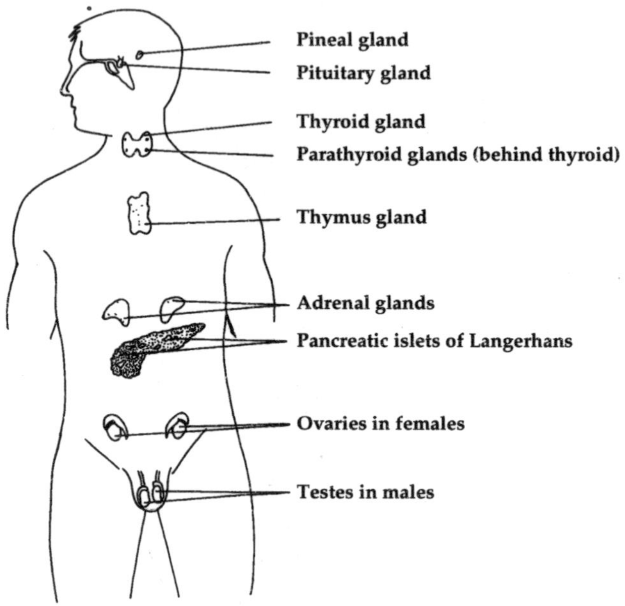

fig. 3.8 The locations of the endocrine glands in the body.

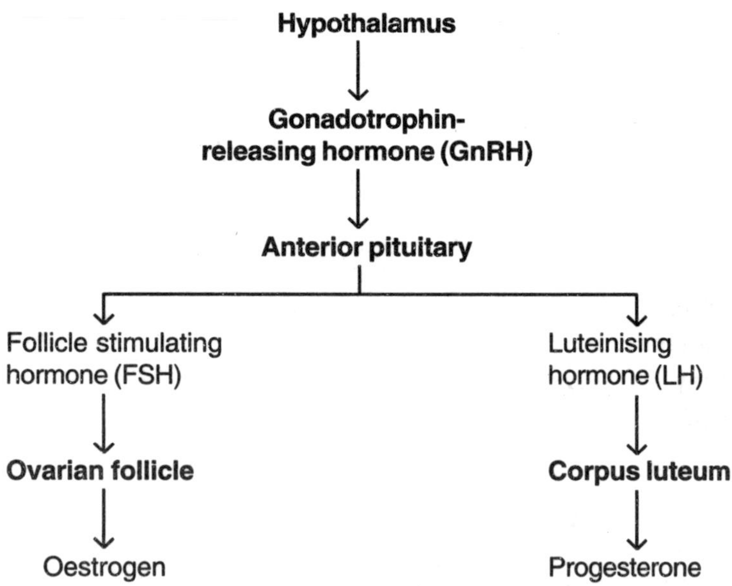

fig. 3.9 The pathway of information-transmission from the brain to the ovaries.

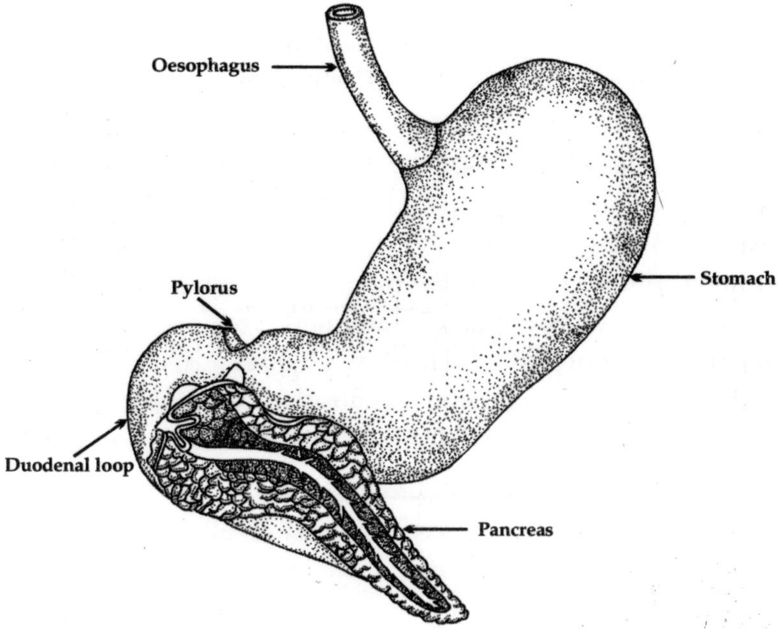

fig. **3.10 The location of the pancreas.**

head lies in the curve of the duodenum and the body behind the stomach (*fig.* 3.10). It is both exocrine (with duct) and endocrine (without duct). The exocrine part secretes digestive juices which are carried through the pancreatic duct into the small intestine.

Distributed throughout the gland are groups of specialized cells like islands. These are the pancreatic islets (of Langerhans). These islets do not have ducts. The hormones they secrete diffuse directly into the blood. All the islets combinedly constitute the endocrine pancreas.

The pancreatic islets contain three main types of cells, namely, alpha cells that secrete glucagon, beta cells that secrete insulin and delta cells that secrete somatostatin. Glucagon increases blood glucose levels and insulin reduces them.

Diabetes mellitus is due to deficiency or absence of insulin or rarely to impairment of insulin activity (insulin resistance). Insulin acts on the cell membranes. It increases the permeability of the cell membrane to glucose.

Yoga-nidrā for the treatment of diabetes. Get yourself treated by the doctor who may decide to prescribe oral drugs or insulin injection. Control your diet. Do exercise regularly. In addition, you may do *yoga* for the treatment of diabetes. *Yoga-nidrā* is one of the many techniques you are to follow. Depending upon the conditions, you may dispense with medicinal treatment or lower the dose, to be decided by your doctor. The following *saṅkalpa* is recommended for *yoga-nidrā.*

> "The islet cells of my pancreas, secrete enough insulin, not more, not less. My cell membranes, allow glucose to pass through."

Osteoporosis

Osteoporosis is a skeletal disease with reduction in mass without change in chemical composition. This happens because bone deposition does not take place to keep pace with the resorption. The bones become porous and fragile. As bone mass decreases, susceptibility to fracture increases.

For the purpose of *yoga-nidrā,* we will confine our discussion to osteoporosis of old people as a senile symptom of ageing. Peak bone mass occurs around 35 years of age and then gradually declines in both sexes. In women, oestrogen favours the deposition of bone salts (calcium phosphate). After the menopause, the bone mass decreases in women and the decrease is relatively more in comparison with men at any comparable age. Osteoporosis is a geriatric problem in old persons, both men and women, and it cannot be altogether prevented.

Oestrogens (female hormones) and androgens (male hormones) are anabolic steroids. They favour bone depositions. Glucocorticoids are antianabolic steroids. Corticosteroids enhance the chances of osteoporosis. Deficiency of androgens in old men and of oestrogens in old women causes loss of bone mass, resulting in osteoporosis. Excess alcohol intake and smoking are contributory factors of osteoporosis. Lack of exercise, immobility and low-calcium diet predispose a person to osteoporosis. Exercise and high-calcium diet in childhood and adolescence can delay the onset of this senile process and alleviate the severity of the disease in old age. A higher daily intake of calcium along with vitamin D_3 in old age is definitely beneficial, but it cannot altogether prevent the disease, since the malfunctioning itself is a normal physiological process of ageing.

The severity of osteoporosis can be minimized by *yoga* and yogic diet. Milk or curd should be a component of the diet of old persons. Milk is rich in calcium and phosphorus. *Āsana*s improve the circulation of blood to the bones. A deficiency of blood circulation in bones is a factor that contributes to osteoporosis. Some strenuous *āsana*s are contraindicated in old age. Most of the items of the *prāṇa-sañcālana kriyā* can be practised by old persons and they definitely improve the blood circulation in most bones of the body. The minimum exercise recommended for old persons is walking.

Regularly practise *makarāsana* (the crocodile pose) with the following minor modification. The palms shall exert pressure on the front and the sides of the neck and the fingers shall support the respective mandibles. The simultaneous practice of *saṁyama* (*dhāraṇā, dhyāna* and *samādhi*) on the parathyroid gland should be done for the normal secretion of the parathyroid hormone. The usual *makarāsana* has been illustrated in *fig*. 2.44.

The practice of *kaṇṭha-mudrā* stimulates the thyroid and the parathyroid glands to secrete more hormones. Parathyroid hormone is necessary for the deposition of calcium in the bones.

The *kaṇṭha-mudrā* has been illustrated in *fig*. 3.11. Sit in any suitable *āsana* (even *sukhāsana* will do), or even on a chair. Keep your head, neck and torso perpendicularly erect. Fold all the fingers of each hand towards the respective palm. Place both the thumbtips on the notch between the collar-bones (clavicles). Place the backs of the fingers distal to the knuckles on the respective side of the front of the neck and exert lateral pressure on the trachea and related structures including the thyroid and the parathyroid glands.

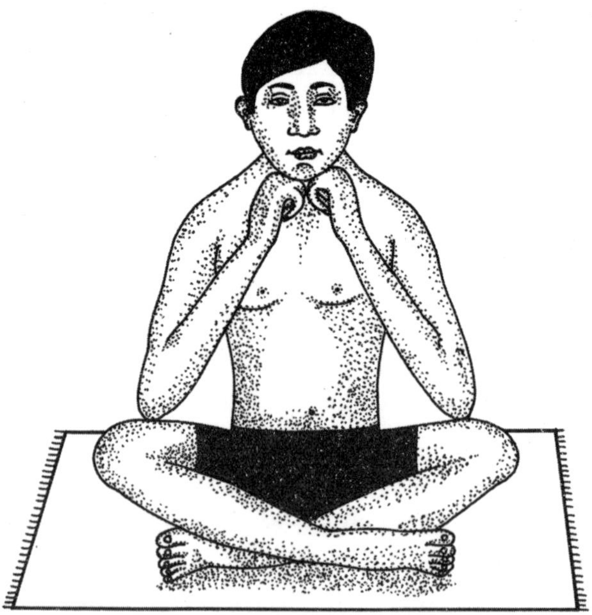

***fig*. 3.11 The *kaṇṭha-mudrā* (the throat seal).**

Jālandhara bandha has been described in chapter 2. If practised, it presses the thyroid and parathyroid glands and thereby stimulates these glands to secrete more hormones. Parathyroid hormone is necessary for better calcium assimilation and deposition in the bones.

If your senile debility has not been too much advanced and you can still practise *sarvāṅgāsana*, you will be able to stimulate your thyroid and parathyroid glands. *Sarvāṅgāsana* has been illustrated in chapter 2.

Old age itself brings worries, tension and painful and agonising experiences. Some individuals brood over death consciousness. Such mental condition is very conducive to excessive secretion of corticosteroids by the adrenal cortex. Corticosteroid hormones are potent substances to cause osteoporosis.

Practise meditation. That will decrease the secretion of corticosteroids by your adrenal cortex. Try to forget and ignore your worries. Create mental happiness for you. If you are a believer in God, do *japa* regularly and surrender to the Almighty.

Yoga-nidrā for the treatment of osteoporosis. The following *saṅkalpa* is recommended.

"My bone formation is keeping pace with its resorption.
My bone mass is maintaining."

Alzheimer's Disease

This condition was previously known as pre-senile dementia. Its present name is Alzheimer's disease. It is named for the German psychiatrist and neurologist Alois Alzheimer who first described it in 1907. One out of 25 cases of senile dementia is Alzheimer's disease. Females are affected twice as often as males. Persons of over 60 years of age are usually affected, the incidence increasing with age. The cerebral cortex is progressively atrophied. The cerebral atrophy is accompanied by loss of memory and deteriorating mental functioning. The aetiology is unknown. Familial susceptibility and, thus, genetic factors may be involved. The patient usually dies two to eight years after the onset of the disease.

Brain cells start dying at the age of 20 years or so. Ordinarily they are not newly formed after the embryogenesis and the formation and development of the brain early in life. Hence the dead nerve cells of the brain are not replaced. Memory and mental ability decline as age advances, especially after the age of 65. However, the brain compensates the loss by increasing the efficiency of the living cells.

In Alzheimer's disease, the quantitative atrophy, degeneration and death of the cerebral cells are hastened at an alarming rate. The usual senile dementia is mainly accounted for by arteriosclerosis (hardening of the arteries) and the slow, but progressive loss of the cerebral cells. By age 80, on an average, 7 per cent of the peak weight of the brain is usually lost. Arteriosclerosis can be minimized by judicious diet, avoidance of tension and yogic practices. But it, being a normal ageing process, cannot be prevented altogether. Multiple small strokes in old age are another cause of progressive mental disability. But none of these factors can be said to directly cause Alzheimer's disease.

In very old age, *śīrṣāsana* is contraindicated. But the *yogī* who had been practising *śīrṣāsana* from his earlier age gets the benefit in the advanced age. Alzheimer's disease is prevented by this *āsana*. *Prāṇāyāma*, especially *nāḍī-śodhana prāṇāyāma*, with or without retention, avoids anoxia to the brain. A *yogī* who practises *prāṇāyāma* regularly prevents the onset of Alzheimer's disease.

The yogic diet contains little fat. It is not supposed to be greasy. It is vegetarian. The *yogī* practises meditation. The concentrations of catecholamines and corticosteroids are not allowed to be high in the *yogī*'s blood. Meditation itself retards the ageing process of the brain. A life, with no tension and anxiety, or with a bare minimum with spiritual ecstasy, ever surrendered to God, drastically retards the ageing process of the brain.

Old persons should avoid disuse atrophy of the brain. They should have some mental hobby. If the brain is not allowed to be non-functional and idle, it is not likely to atrophy due to disuse.

One should make conscious efforts to be happy, even amidst threatening situations of hostility and roughness of life. It is possible for a *yogī* to be detached and to be unaffected with agony and adversity. Detachment is the key to happiness. Such a *yogī* can hardly be a victim to Alzheimer's disease.

Yoga-nidrā for the prevention of Alzheimer's disease. If you get the preliminary symptoms of senile dementia, practise *yoga-nidrā* to prevent the onset of Alzheimer's disease. The following *saṅkalpa* is recommended.

> "No atrophy of my cerebrum. My brain is healthy and active."

Insomnia

Insomnia is habitual sleeplessness. We shall use this word for inability to sleep at night. In contrast, hypersomnia is excessive sleepiness during the day. Some insomnia patients cannot get sleep neither during the day nor at night whereas some others get hypersomnia during the day and insomnia at night. The latter condition is a wrong habit; but the former condition is serious for the health. Insomnia reduces the efficiency of mental activity and makes one susceptible to fatigue, weakness and infection. It suppresses the immune system and increases the blood pressure.

Sleep is our natural condition. In order to be wakeful, we must be stimulated by sensory experiences, muscular activity and chemicals such as caffeine and catecholamines (adrenaline and noradrenaline). Without such stimulation, we stay asleep.

CONTROL OF SLEEP BY THE BRAIN

It may not be exactly correct to say that the brain has some sleep centres. The brain has regions for wakefulness. In order of importance, they are in the brain stem, in the thalamus and in the hypothalamus. Wakefulness results from enhanced activity of these regions, while sleep represents lack of adequate brain excitation.

Reticular formation is a collection of neurons in the core of the brain stem. It is surrounded by neural pathways which conduct ascending and descending nerve impulses between the brain and the spinal cord. Since it is an arousal system, it is known as the reticular activating system (RAS).

The RAS has little intrinsic activity. When one is asleep, one's RAS is almost totally dormant. The RAS must be stimulated to action by input signals from other sources.

The RAS has input signals and output signals. It receives nerve fibres from all parts of the body and the brain. Almost any sensory stimulus from the body can activate it. The cerebral cortex can also stimulate it. The hormone adrenaline increases the activity of the RAS. Caffeine stimulates it. Being stimulated, it transmits signals both upward into the brain and downward into the spinal cord. It is adequately structured to perform the arousal functions.

Three feedback loops operate for the regulation of

wakefulness and sleep. They are : (1) the cerebral cortex and back to the RAS, (2) the peripheral muscles and back, (3) the adrenal medullae and back via the hormone adrenaline.

The mesencephalic portion of the RAS is basically responsible for the normal wakefulness of the brain. It transmits signals to the cerebral cortex through two separate pathways — (a) directly and (b) indirectly through the thalamus.

The thalamus relays signals from the mesencephalic RAS to all parts of the cerebral cortex. The thalamic activating system directly activates the cerebral cortex too. The stimulation of selected points of the thalamus activates specific areas of the cerebral cortex.

The hypothalamus contains a preoptic nucleus that acts as a wakeful centre. The stimulation of this centre excites the RAS of the brain stem.

AETIOLOGY OF INSOMNIA

Loss of sleep is due to a number of causes. Mental overactivity, worries, tension and anxiety and re-emergence of agonising experiences stored and buried in the Subconscious or Unconscious are the major causes of insomnia.

Mental overactivity causes over-secretion of acetylcholine in the cerebral cortex. This neurohumor, in excessive concentration, stimulates the mesencephalic reticular activating system, the thalamus and the hypothalamus. As a result, wakefulness dominates over sleep. This cerebral overactivity does not involve worries and anxiety and the brain-work may be even creative. For this purpose, overactivity means 'cerebral over-straining'.

Emotional stress is a cause of insomnia. Any sort of worries, tension and anxiety can affect the sympathetic nervous system and the adrenal medulla. The hypothalamus is also stimulated via the cerebral cortex and it subsequently stimulates the sympathetic nervous system. The result is the hyper-secretion of catecholamines (adrenaline and noradrenaline). These neurohumors stimulate the reticular activating system of the brain stem. The result is insomnia. In periods of bereavement, grief, loss of job, family problems and any type of intense mental agony and stress, insomnia is caused by excessive secretion of catecholamines.

Sometimes a person suffers from insomnia without cerebral over-work and emotional stress. Many agonising experiences, dreadful and unpleasant, rise to the surface of the mind. They had been stored in the Subconscious or the Unconscious and very often deeply buried. Some current situations and circumstances may provoke the re-emergence of these buried emotions. They stimulate the sympathetic nervous system through the cerebral cortex to secrete an excess of catecholamines that stimulate the reticular activating system of the brain stem. The result is sustained wakefulness and loss of sleep.

The pineal gland is situated inside the brain. It is the biological clock of the body. It regulates the biological rhythms through its hormone 'melatonin'. This hormone-secretion is decreased in old age. Melatonin-deficiency is a potent cause of insomnia.

YOGA THERAPY FOR INSOMNIA

Āsanas have a calming effect on the cerebrum through the optimization of the secretion of acetylcholine. *Naḍī-śodhana prāṇāyāma,* with or without retention of breath, calms the cerebral cortex and balances the parasympathetic and the sympathetic nervous system. Meditation, in any of the meditational yogic postures with *cin-mudrā* or *jñāna-mudrā,* has a great therapeutic value in the treatment of insomnia.

Sitting in *vajrāsana*, with nose-tip-gazing (*nāsikāgra-dṛṣṭi*), is very much helpful in the restoration of sleep. The combination of *vajrāsana*, *khecarī-mudrā* and *ujjayī prāṇāyāma* is beneficial. *Śavāsana* and *ajapā japa*, combinedly done, would definitely give benefits. Any *yoga* technique that induces relaxation is helpful.

One has to avoid over-working the brain and give some rest to it by relaxing in the midst of work. To get rid of worries and anxieties or at least to minimize them, one has to change one's philosophy of life. Try to solve the problems you face. If some problems are unsolved or partly solved, bear with them and do not recognize them as problems. Live a detached and spiritual life. If you are a believer in God, surrender to Him and accept His verdict without grudge and grumblings. Live for some nobler purpose. Do not magnify your suffering and agony and accept them as part of life.

Yoga-nidrā for the treatment of insomnia. *Yoga-nidrā* can cure insomnia due to any of the three major causes. Whereas the other treatments are not very efficacious to cure insomnia due to the re-emergence of agonising subconscious or unconscious impressions, *yoga-nidrā* is the specific treatment for this. The following *saṅkalpa* is suggested.

> "All the agonising *saṁskāra*s are erased from my subconscious and unconscious. I am free from tension, worries and anxieties. My pineal gland is secreting enough melatonin. I will have sound and deep sleep."

CATEGORY-5

This is the category of biochemical abnormality. We will give one common example. The body of an individual patient is synthesizing excessive quantity of cholesterol. He is a vegetarian. His serum cholesterol level is more than 400 mg/dl. He suffers from hypertension. He has undergone bypass heart surgery. For such a patient, we recommend *yoga-nidrā* treatment.

The body cholesterol may be exogenous or endogenous. Foods of animal origin are high in cholesterol. Egg-yolk, prawns, crabs and such other foods are rich sources of cholesterols. Excess of saturated fats in the diet is very conducive to the synthesis of cholesterol in the body. Acetates (acetyl-coenzyme A) are produced in the body as a result of the metabolism of carbohydrates, fats and proteins. Cholesterol is synthesized by the body out of acetates.

It has been firmly established from observations that psychic stress accelerates the biosynthesis of cholesterol. Suppressedly oozing feelings of anxiety, frustration, unfulfilled desires and hurt sentiments, deeply buried in the Subconscious or the Unconscious simmer in the depth and bubble up to the surface of the mind. They might have their origin in the present life or in some former lives. They affect the cerebral cortex. Impulses reach the hypothalamus from the prefrontal area of the frontal lobe. The hypothalamus over-stimulates the sympathetic nerves and the adrenal mudulla to secrete more catecholamines. It stimulates the anterior pituitary through its releasing hormone to secrete more ACTH (adrenocorticotrophic hormone). In the presence of higher concentration of catecholamines and corticosteroids in the blood, the body synthesizes more cholesterol. Introverts are more susceptible to this type of altered biochemistry in comparison with extroverts.

Even after a bypass cardiac surgery, excess of cholesterol synthesized in the body may pose serious cardiac health problem. There may be recurrence of the conditions of ischaemic heart disease. The solution to the problem lies in the retardation of the cholesterol biosynthesis in the body.

Yoga-nidrā for reducing hypercholesterolaemia. We propose the following *saṅkalpa* for *yoga-nidra*.

> "My body, I order you to retard the biosynthesis of cholesterol."

CATEGORY-6

This is the category of strengthening the immune system of the body. Like the defence department of a country, the body has an immune system. The leucocytes (white blood cells) defend the body against microbes and other foreign materials. Without this defence system, it would have been impossible for us to live.

Leucocytes in Blood

There are two main types of leucocytes, namely, granulocytes and agranulocytes. Neutrophils, eosinophils and basophils are the granulocytes. Monocytes and lymphocytes are the agranulocytes. All leucocytes, irrespective of their types and subtypes, are formed in the bone marrow.

Neutrophils protect the body against any foreign material, mainly microbes, and remove waste materials, e.g., cell debris. They rush to the affected area, pass through the capillary walls by amoeboid movement and thereafter engulf and kill the microbes by phagocytosis. The granules they contain are lysosomes that possess enzymes to digest the engulfed microbes.

Eosinophils are capable of phagocytosis. But they play their main role in the elimination of parasites by releasing certain toxic chemicals stored in their granules.

Very often eosinophils are found in large numbers at allergic sites. They promote tissue inflammation in those areas by releasing their toxic chemicals. Sometimes, they also dampen down inflammation by releasing histaminase.

Basophils are closely associated with allergic reactions. Their cytoplasmic granules contain heparin (an anticoagulant) and histamine (an inflammatory agent). When an allergen comes in contact with the basophil membrane, the basophil releases the contents of its granules. Thus, basophils promote inflammation.

The *mast cell,* not different in type from the basophil, is found in the tissues rather than the blood circulation. Heparin, histamine and other inflammatory substances are released from the cytoplasmic granules of mast cells immediately after binding an allergen.

The *monocyte-macrophage system* is sometimes called the *reticuloendothelial system*. Monocytes originate in red bone marrow. They are actively motile and phagocytic. Some of them circulate in the blood. Some others migrate into the tissues where they develop into macrophages. Some macrophages are mobile whereas others are fixed.

Neutrophils, as phagocytic defence cells, have already been described. Monocytes and macrophages, as phagocytes, also play a very important role in the defence system of the body. Phagocytes trap particles either by engulfing them or by extending long pseudopodia towards them. They are non-selective; they bind, engulf and digest all targets that are foreign cells or foreign particles.

Immunity

The lymphocyte which is a type of leucocyte and an agranulocyte is involved in providing immunity to the body. Lymphocytes originate from pluripotent stem cells in red bone marrow. After being released into the blood stream, they are processed either in the bone marrow or in the thymus to develop into activated B-lymphocytes and activated T-lymphocytes, respectively.

T-lymphocytes. The thymus gland lies in the chest cavity between the heart and the sternum. It secretes the hormone, thymosin. Lymphocytes from the bone marrow come to the thymus where they are processed by thymosin to become fully specialized (differentiated), mature, functional T-lymphocytes. They are antigen-specific. A specific type of T-lymphocyte is programmed to recognize only one type of antigen.

B-lymphocytes. Like T-lymphocytes, the B-lymphocytes are produced in the bone marrow. But, unlike the T-lymphocytes which are processed in the thymus, the B-lymphocytes are processed in the bone marrow. All B-lymphocytes produce antibodies which are immunoglobulins. But each B-lymphocyte targets one specific antigen only. The antibody released by each B-lymphocyte is programmed to bind to, and cause the destruction of, an antigen.

The T-lymphocytes provide cell-mediated immunity whereas the B-lymphocytes provide antibody-mediated immunity. The possible antigens to be encountered in a life's time may be millions or billions in type. But, for each type of antigen, there is one corresponding type of T- and B-lymphocyte in the body.

CELL-MEDIATED IMMUNITY

T-lymphocytes, after being activated in the thymus, are released into the circulation. When they encounter their specific antigen, they become sensitized to it. Now the antigen is to be presented to the T-lymphocyte on the surface of an antigen-presenting cell. Among others, macrophages are a type of antigen-presenting cell. They indiscriminately and non-specifically engulf and digest antigens and then display the most antigenic fragment on their surface. They eventually come into contact with the T-lymphocytes which are stimulated to divide and proliferate (clonal expansion). As a result of this clonal expansion, three main types of T-lymphocytes (cytotoxic T-lymphocyte, helper T-lymphocyte and memory T-lymphocyte) are produced. Each of these three types of T-lymphocyte is directed against the original antigen in its own way.

ANTIBODY-MEDIATED (HUMORAL) IMMUNITY

T-lymphocytes are free to circulate around the body whereas B-lymphocytes are fixed in the lymphoid tissue (spleen and lymph nodes). An antigen-presenting cell has to present the antigen to the T-lymphocytes whereas the B-lymphocytes recognize and bind the antigen particles without having to be presented. After the B-lymphocytes detect and bind the antigen, they get the assistance of a helper T-lymphocyte to enlarge and divide (clonal expansion) to produce two functionally distinct types of cells, namely, plasma cells and memory B-cells.

Plasma cells secrete antibodies that are carried throughout the body. These antibodies are gamma-globulins (special proteins) that bind to antigens specifically. Each plasma cell lives no longer than a day and produces only one type of antibody.

Like the memory T-lymphocytes, the memory B-lymphocytes are also long-lived. They possess memory and thereby rapidly respond to subsequent encounters with the same antigen by stimulating the production of antibody-secreting plasma cells.

THE IMMUNE SYSTEM

Here we complete our theoretical discussion on the immunity of the body. This defence system is not localized and not confined to any single organ. All the leucocytes which are the soldiers of the body are manufactured in the bone marrow. The thymus gland in the chest plays an important role in the defence of the body by activating the T-lymphocytes that freely circulate throughout the body. They provide cell-mediated immunity. The B-lymphocytes are activated in the bone marrow and are subsequently fixed in the lymphoid tissue. They provide antibody-mediated immunity. The lymphoid tissue is diffusely distributed in the spleen and lymph nodes. The spleen is the largest lymph organ. It lies in the abdominal cavity between the fundus of the stomach and the diaphragm. It contains T- and B-lymphocytes, which are activated by the presence of antigens. Lymph nodes, usually eight to ten in number, are located along the length of lymph vessels. Lymph is filtered while passing through the lymph nodes. Particulate matter, including microbes, cells from malignant tumours and cell debris, is destroyed in lymph nodes by macrophages and antibodies. Both activated T- and B-lymphocytes multiply in lymph nodes. Sensitized B-lymphocytes produce antibodies in the lymph nodes. These antibodies enter lymph and blood draining the node.

Throughout the body, at strategic locations, are collections of lymphoid tissue, known as mucosa-associated lymphoid tissue (MALT). These are not capsulated unlike the spleen and the thymus. They have no afferent lymphatic vessels, and, hence, they do not filter lylmph unlike the lymph nodes. Systems exposed to the external environment such as the gastrointestinal tract, the respiratory tract and the genitourinary tract do contain MALT. The tonsils, located in the mouth and throat, and the Peyer's patches, found in the wall of the small intestine, are two main groups of MALT. The former destroy swallowed and inhaled antigens and the latter intercept swallowed antigens. B-lymphocytes and T-lymphocytes, migrated from the bone marrow and the thymus, respectively, settle in the MALT, where they detect the invaders early.

YOGA AND IMMUNITY

Yoga can improve the immunity of the body for the purpose of prophylaxis and therapeutics. *Āsanas, bandhas*, *mudrās*, *prāṇāyāma* and meditation can fortify the immune system. The yogic techniques help in the prevention and treatment of cancer. The cancerous cell is a non-self cell and so does it behave like an antigen. Even without the consciousness of the patient who regularly practises *yoga*, the immune system of the body destroys the cancer cell at the very early stage. The individual, with body, mind and self, lives holistically. The bone marrow, the thymus and the whole lymphatic system are triggered to fight infection and cancerous growth.

The defence department of the body lunges a three-pronged attack on the invading microbes. (1) It recruits more soldiers like the neutrophils, the monocytes and the macrophages. (2) It gears up the cell-mediated immunity through the T-lymphocytes. (3) It strengthens the antibody-mediated (humoral) immunity through the B-lymphocytes. For these functions, a huge demand is made on the enhanced supply of protective nutrients such as quality proteins, viamins and minerals. Hence, the yogic diet should be balanced and rich in protective nutrients.

Yoga-nidrā for immunity. You may practise *yoga-nidrā* for the prevention as well as the treatment of infectious diseases, and also for the prevention and treatment of malignant tumours. The following *saṅkalpa* is suggested.

> "My immune system, fight the infection/the cancer, protect the body."

CATEGORY-7

This is the category of spiritual attainment, finally leading to liberation (*mokṣa*).

If you are inclined towards *karmayoga* (the *yoga* of action) practise *yoga-nidrā*, with the following *saṅkalpa*, for the fortification of your efforts.

> "Let me do *karma* without attachment to the fruits thereof. Let me work for the sake of my duty only."

If you are inclined towards *bhaktiyoga* (the *yoga* of devotion), practise *yoga-nidrā* with the folowing *saṅkalpa*.

> "I completely surrender to God, with my mind firmly fixed on Him."

If you are inclined towards *jñānayoga* (the *yoga* of knowledge) practise *yoga-nidrā* with the following *saṅkalpa*.

> "He is I (*so'ham*). I am *Brahman* (*ahaṁ brahmāsmi*). I am Pure Consciousness, Pure Bliss."

By the practice of *yoga*, it is possible for you to be liberated in this life. You can be a *jīvanmukta* (liberated albeit living) through the practice of *yoga*. In that state, your self is in your body, but not bound by the latter; your self is no longer different from the Great Self (*Paramātmā*), except the lack of possession of the power of creation, sustenance and dissolution.

Along with the other techniques of the Pātañjala Yoga, you can practise *yoga-nidrā* for becoming a *jīvanmukta*. Erase your *karmāśaya* lying in your causal body (*kāraṇa śarīra*) with the following *saṅkalpa*.

> "My *karmāśaya* is erased, completely erased. I am *Brahman* (*ahaṁ brahmāsmi*)."

MULTI-DIMENSIONALITY OF YOGA-NIDRĀ

Yoga-nidrā is a technique only. It is a yogic means. It is not an end. The means can be used to achieve many goals. The multi-purpose use of *yoga-nidrā* cannot be exhausted through some pages in a book like this. What has been attempted is aimed at giving a bird's eye-view of the large extensive sphere of the potentiality of *yoga-nidrā*. Some typical examples of the use of *yoga-nidrā* have been presented. Once properly understood, the use can be multiplied and a *saṅkalpa* for each individual case can be appropriately framed. The technique can be made use of for bringing about physical, mental and spiritual improvement in one's life through self-therapy. The technique is simple. But the effect it produces to improve the quality of life is spectacular.

4

Addenda

The Tantric Nyāsa

The shifting of awareness has been given in chapter 2. It is an important technique in *yoga-nidrā*. Through practising it, the mind is brought to a state which is neither awake nor sleeping. In *yoga-nidrā*, the *yogī* stays somewhere between the waking and the sleeping states. This intermediate state is very receptive to the retention of the resolve by the Subconscious and the Unconscious. This basic idea has been borrowed from the Tantra in which *nyāsa* is an unavoidable ritual.

Nyāsa means (1) consigning or intrusting anything to the mind, (2) mental appropriation or assignment of various parts of the body to tutelary deities. In this connection, the word *mātṛkā* has a relevance. It means (1) a mother, figuratively, the source or origin, (2) a divine mother, (3) the names of particular diagrams written in characters to which a magical power is ascribed, (4) the alphabet so employed in (3).

The Tantra has many types of *nyāsa*, two of which will be given here. They are : the external (*bahiḥ*) *mātṛkā nyāsa* and the internal (*antaḥ*) *mātṛkā nyāsa*.

BAHIRMĀTṚKĀ NYĀSA

***Ṛṣyādinyāsaḥ* (*Nyāsa for the seers and others*)**

O'Ṁ AṀ brahmaṇe ṛṣaye (prajāpatirṣaye) namaḥ ĀṀ śirasi.

(*OṀ AṀ* salutation to seer Brahmā *ĀṀ* — on the head.)

O'Ṁ IṀ gāyatrīchandase namaḥ ĪṀ mukhe.
(*O'Ṁ IṀ* salutation to the *gāyatrī* metre *ĪṀ* — on the face.)

O'Ṁ UṀ sarasvatīdevatāyai namaḥ ŪṀ hṛdaye.
(*O'Ṁ UṀ* salutation to the deity Sarasvatī *ŪṀ* — in the heart.)

O'Ṁ EṀ haḷbhyo bījebhyo namaḥ AIṀ guhye.
(*O'Ṁ EṀ* salutation to the consonant seeds *AIṀ* — on the genitals.)

O'Ṁ OṀ svaraśaktibhyo namaḥ AUṀ pādayoḥ.
(*O'Ṁ OṀ* salutation to the vowel powers *AUṀ* — on the feet.)

O'Ṁ AṀ (anusvāra) KṢAṀ kīlakāya namaḥ AḤ sarvāṅgeṣu.
(*O'Ṁ AṀ* (*anusvāra*) *KṢAṀ* salutation to the protecting power of the *mantra AḤ* — on all parts of the body).

Karanyāsaḥ (Nyāsa on the hands)

O'Ṁ AṀ KAṀ KHAṀ GAṀ GHAṀ ṄAṀ ĀṀ aṅguṣṭābhyāṁ namaḥ (salutation to the divine mother on the thumbs).

O'Ṁ IṀ CAṀ CHAṀ JAṀ JHAṀ ÑAṀ ĪṀ tarjanībhyāṁ namaḥ (salutation to the divine mother on the index fingers).

O'Ṁ UṀ ṬAṀ ṬHAṀ ḌAṀ ḌHAṀ ṆAṀ ŪṀ madhyamābhyāṁ namaḥ (salutation to the divine mother on the middle fingers).

O'Ṁ EṀ TAṀ THAṀ DAṀ DHAṀ NAṀ AIṀ anāmikābhyāṁ namaḥ (salutation to the divine mother on the ring fingers).

O'Ṁ OṀ PAṀ PHAṀ BAṀ BHAṀ MAṀ AUṀ kaniṣṭhikābhyāṁ namaḥ (salutation to the divine mother on the little fingers).

O'Ṁ AṀ (anusvāra) YAṀ RAṀ LAṀ VAṀ ŚAṀ ṢAṀ SAṀ HAṀ ḶAṀ KṢAṀ AḤ karatalakarapṛṣṭhābhyāṁ namaḥ (salutation to the divine mother on the palms and the backs of the palms).

Hṛdayādiṣaḍaṅganyāsaḥ (Nyāsa on the Six Organs — Heart, etc).

O'Ṁ AṀ KAṀ KHAṀ GAṀ GHAṀ ṄAṀ ĀṀ hṛadayāya namaḥ

(salutation to the divine mother on the heart).

O'Ṁ IṀ CAṀ CHAṀ JAṀ JHAṀ ÑAṀ ĪṀ śirase svāhā (salutation to the divine mother on the head).

O'Ṁ UṀ ṬAṀ ṬHAṀ ḌAṀ ḌHAṀ ṆAṀ ŪṀ śikhāyai vaṣaṭ (salutation to the divine mother on the crown of the head).

O'Ṁ EṀ TAṀ THAṀ DAṀ DHAṀ NAṀ AIṀ kavacāya huṁ (salutation to the mystical defending jacket).

O'Ṁ OṀ PAṀ PHAṀ BAṀ BHAṀ MAṀ AUṀ netratrayāya vauṣaṭ (salutation to the divine mother on the three eyes).

O'Ṁ AṀ (anusvāra) YAṀ RAṀ LAṀ VAṀ ŚAṀ ṢAṀ SAṀ HAṀ ḶAṀ KṢAṀ AḤ astrāya phaṭ (salutation to the mystical weapon that destroys all evils).

Mātṛkānyāsa

O'Ṁ AṀ namaḥ śirasi (salutation to the *mātṛkā AṀ* — on the head).

O'Ṁ ĀṀ namaḥ mukhe (salutation to the *mātṛkā ĀṀ* — on the face).

O'Ṁ IṀ namaḥ dakṣiṇanetre (salutation to the *mātṛkā IṀ* — on the right eye).

O'Ṁ ĪṀ namaḥ vāmanetre (salutation to the *mātṛkā ĪṀ* — on the left eye).

O'Ṁ UṀ namaḥ dakṣiṇakarṇe (salutation to the *mātṛkā UṀ* — on the right ear).

O'Ṁ ŪṀ namaḥ vāmakarṇe (salutation to the *mātṛkā ŪṀ* — on the left ear).

O'Ṁ ṚṀ namaḥ dakṣiṇanāsāpuṭe (salutation to the *mātṛkā ṚṀ* — on the right nostril).

O'Ṁ ṜṀ namaḥ vāmanāsāpuṭe (salutation to the *mātṛkā ṜṀ* — on the left nostril).

O'Ṁ LḶṀ namaḥ dakṣiṇagaṇḍe (salutation to the *mātṛkā LḶṀ* — on the right cheek).

O'Ṁ LḸṀ namaḥ vāmagaṇḍe (salutation to the *mātṛkā LḸṀ* — on the left cheek).

O'Ṁ EṀ namaḥ ūrdhvoṣṭhe (salutation to the *mātṛkā EṀ* — on the upper lip).

O'Ṁ AIṀ namaḥ adharoṣṭhe (salutation to the *mātṛkā AIṀ* — on the lower lip).

O'Ṁ OṀ namaḥ ūrdhvadantapaṅktau (salutation to the *mātṛkā OṀ* — on the upper teeth).

O'Ṁ AUṀ namaḥ adhodantapaṅktau (salutation to the *mātṛkā AUṀ* — on the lower teeth).

O'Ṁ AṀ (anusvāra) namaḥ mūrdhni (salutation to the *mātṛkā AṀ* — on the roof of the oral cavity).

O'Ṁ AḤ namaḥ jihvāgre (salutation to the *mātṛkā AḤ* — on the tip of the tongue).

O'Ṁ KAṀ namaḥ dakṣiṇabāhumūle (salutation to the *mātṛkā KAṀ* — on the right shoulder joint).

O'Ṁ KHAṀ namaḥ dakṣiṇakūrpare (salutation to the *mātṛkā KHAṀ* — on the right elbow).

O'Ṁ GAṀ namaḥ dakṣiṇamaṇibandhe (salutation to the *mātṛkā GAṀ* — on the right wrist).

O'Ṁ GHAṀ namaḥ dakṣiṇāṅgulimūle (salutation to the *mātṛkā GHAṀ* — on the roots of the right fingers).

O'Ṁ ṄAṀ namaḥ dakṣiṇāṅgulyagre (salutation to the *mātṛkā ṄAṀ* — on the right fingertips).

O'Ṁ CAṀ namaḥ vāmabāhumūle (salutation to the *mātṛkā CAṀ* — on the left shoulder joint).

O'Ṁ CHAṀ namaḥ vāmakūrpare (salutation to the *mātṛkā CHAṀ* — on the left elbow).

O'Ṁ JAṀ namaḥ vāmamaṇibandhe (salutation to the *mātṛkā JAṀ* — on the left wrist).

O'Ṁ JHAṀ namaḥ vāmāṅgulimūle (salutation to the *mātṛkā JHAṀ* — on the roots of the left fingers).

O'Ṁ ÑAṀ namaḥ vāmāṅgulyagre (salutation to the *mātṛkā ÑAṀ* — on the left fingertips).

O'Ṁ ṬAṀ namaḥ dakṣiṇapādamūle (salutation to the *mātṛkā ṬAṀ* — on the right hip joint).

O'Ṁ ṬHAṀ namaḥ dakṣiṇajānuni (salutation to the *mātṛkā ṬHAṀ* — on the right knee).

O'Ṁ ḌAṀ namaḥ dakṣiṇagulphe (salutation to the *mātṛkā ḌAṀ* — on the right ankle).

O'Ṁ ḌHAṀ namaḥ dakṣapādāṅgulimūle (salutation to the *mātṛkā ḌHAṀ* — on the roots of the right toes).

O'Ṁ ṆAṀ namaḥ dakṣapādāṅgulyagre (salutation to the *mātṛkā ṆAṀ* — on the right toetips).

O'Ṁ TAṀ namaḥ vāmapādamūle (salutation to the *mātṛkā TAṀ* — on the left hip joint).

O'Ṁ THAṀ namaḥ vāmajānuni (salutation to the *mātṛkā THAṀ* — on the left knee).

O'Ṁ DAṀ namaḥ vāmagulphe (salutation to the *mātṛkā DAṀ* — on the left ankle).

O'Ṁ DHAṀ namaḥ vāmapādāṅgulimūle (salutation to the *mātṛkā DHAṀ* — on the roots of the left toes).

O'Ṁ NAṀ namaḥ vāmapādāṅgulyagre (salutation to the *mātṛkā NAṀ* — on the left toetips).

O'Ṁ PAṀ namaḥ dakṣapārśve (salutation to the *mātṛkā PAṀ* — on the right side of the torso).

O'Ṁ PHAṀ namaḥ vāmapārśve (salutation to the *mātṛkā PHAṀ* — on the left side of the torso).

O'Ṁ BAṀ namaḥ pṛṣṭhe (salutation to the *mātṛkā BAṀ* — on the back side of the torso).

O'Ṁ BHAṀ namaḥ nābhau (salutation to the *mātṛkā BHAṀ* — on the umbilicus).

O'Ṁ MAṀ namaḥ udare (salutation to the *mātṛkā MAṀ* — on the abdomen).

O'Ṁ YAṀ tvagātmane namaḥ hṛdaye (salutation to the *mātṛkā YAṀ* who presides in the skin — on the heart).

O'Ṁ RAṀ asṛgātmane namaḥ dakṣāṁse (salutation to the *mātṛkā RAṀ* who presides in blood — on the right shoulder).

O'Ṁ LAṀ māṁsātmane namaḥ kakudi (salutation to the *mātṛkā LAṀ* who presides in the muscles — on the hump, the back of the base of the neck).

O'Ṁ VAṀ medātmane namaḥ vāmāṁse (salutation to the *mātṛkā VAṀ* who presides in the body fat — on the left shoulder).

O'Ṁ ŚAṀ asthyātmane namaḥ hṛdayādidakṣahastāntam (salutation to the *mātṛkā ŚAṀ* who presides in the bone — on the part of the body starting from the heart and ending in the right hand).

O'Ṁ ṢAṀ majjātmane namaḥ hṛdayādivāmahastāntam (salutation to the *mātṛkā ṢAṀ* who presides in the marrow — on the part of the body starting from the heart and ending in the left hand).

O'Ṁ SAṀ sukrātmane namaḥ hṛdayādidakṣapādāntam (salutation to the *mātṛkā SAṀ* who presides in the seed, sperm or ovum — on the part of the body starting from the heart and ending in the right foot).

O'Ṁ HAṀ prāṇātmane namaḥ hṛadayādivāmapādāntam (salutation to the *mātṛkā HAṀ* who presides in the *Prāṇa*, the vitalizing principle — on the part of the body starting from the heart and ending in the left foot).

O'Ṁ ḶAṀ jīvātmane namaḥ jaṭhare (salutation to the *mātṛkā ḶAṀ* who stays with the individual self — on the abdomen).

O'Ṁ KṢAṀ Paramātmane namaḥ mukhe (salutation to the *mātṛkā KṢAṀ* who stays with the Great Self — on the face).

ANTARMĀTṚKĀ NYĀSA

Ṛṣyādinyāsaḥ

It is the same as that given for the *bahirmātṛkānyāsa*.

Karanyāsaḥ

It is the same as that given for the *bahirmātṛkānyāsa*.

Hṛdayādiṣaḍaṅganyāsaḥ

It is the same as that given for the *bahirmātṛkānyāsa*.

Mātṛkānyāsaḥ

For the *nyāsa* of the inner divine mothers, the *yogī* must be acquainted with the Tantric anatomy of the *cakras*, their locations, the number of their petals and their colours. The pictures of the *cakras* have been given in chapter 1 of this book. The *nyāsa* starts with the *viśuddhi cakra* with 16 petals, located at the throat. Then it sequentially shifts to the *anāhata, maṇipūra, svādhiṣṭhāna* and *mūlādhāra,* with 12, 10, 6 and 4 petals, respectively. Finally, the process ends with the *nyāsa* on the two petals at the *ājñā* on the spot between the two eyebrows.

The arrangement of the *mātṛkās* on the petals is clockwie (*dakṣiṇāvarta*), starting with 1, and ending with 12 of the clock dial. All the *cakras* are placed horizontally. The *suṣumṇā,* traversing vertically in the core of the spinal cord, serves as the axis of all the *cakras*. (The *cakras* are not vertical and are not duplicated in the front and at the back.)

The details of the *antarmātṛkānyāsa* are given below :

I. At the *Viśuddhi Cakra*

1. *O'Ṁ AṀ namaḥ* (salutation to the *mātṛkā AṀ*).
2. *O'Ṁ ĀṀ namaḥ* (salutation to the *mātṛkā ĀṀ*).
3. *O'Ṁ IṀ namaḥ* (salutation to the *mātṛkā IṀ*).
4. *O'Ṁ ĪṀ namaḥ* (salutation to the *mātṛkā ĪṀ*).
5. *O'Ṁ UṀ namaḥ* (salutation to the *mātṛkā UṀ*).
6. *O'Ṁ ŪṀ namaḥ* (salutation to the *mātṛkā ŪṀ*).
7. *O'Ṁ ṚṀ namaḥ* (salutation to the *mātṛkā ṚṀ*).
8. *O'Ṁ ṜṀ namaḥ* (salutation to the *mātṛkā ṜṀ*).
9. *O'Ṁ LṚṀ namaḥ* (salutation to the *mātṛkā LṚṀ*).
10. *O'Ṁ LṜṀ namaḥ* (salutation to the *mātṛkā LṜṀ*).
11. *O'Ṁ EṀ namaḥ* (Salutation to the *mātṛkā EṀ).*
12. *O'Ṁ AIṀ namaḥ* (Salutation to the *mātṛkā AIṀ).*
13. *O'Ṁ OṀ namaḥ* (salutation to the *mātṛkā OṀ*).
14. *O'Ṁ AUṀ namaḥ* (salutation to the *mātṛkā AUṀ*).
15. *O'Ṁ Ṁ namaḥ* (Salutation to the *mātṛkā Ṁ).*
16. *O'Ṁ Ḥ namaḥ* (Salutation to *mātṛkā Ḥ).*

II. At the *Anāhata Cakra*

1. *O'Ṁ KAṀ namaḥ* (salutation to the *mātṛkā KAṀ*).
2. *O'Ṁ KHAṀ namaḥ* (salutation to the *mātṛkā KHAṀ*).
3. *O'Ṁ GAṀ namaḥ* (salutation to the *mātṛkā GAṀ*).
4. *O'Ṁ GHAṀ namaḥ* (salutation to the *mātṛkā GHAṀ*).
5. *O'Ṁ ṄAṀ namaḥ* (salutation to the *mātṛkā ṄAṀ*).
6. *O'Ṁ CAṀ namaḥ* (salutation to the *mātṛkā CAṀ*).
7. *O'Ṁ CHAṀ namaḥ* (salutation to the *mātṛkā CHAṀ*).
8. *O'Ṁ JAṀ namaḥ* (salutation to the *mātṛkā JAṀ*).
9. *O'Ṁ JHAṀ namaḥ* (salutation to the *mātṛkā JHAṀ*).

10. *O'Ṁ ÑAṀ namaḥ* (salutation to the *mātṛkā* ÑAṀ).
11. *O'Ṁ ṬAṀ namaḥ* (salutation to the *mātṛkā* ṬAṀ).
12. *O'Ṁ ṬHAṀ namaḥ* (salutation to the *mātṛkā* ṬHAṀ).

III. At the *Maṇipūra Cakra*

1. *O'Ṁ ḌAṀ namaḥ* (salutation to the *mātṛkā* ḌAṀ).
2. *O'Ṁ ḌHAṀ namaḥ* (salutation to the *mātṛkā* ḌHAṀ).
3. *O'Ṁ ṆAṀ namaḥ* (salutation to the *mātṛkā* ṆAṀ).
4. *O'Ṁ TAṀ namaḥ* (salutation to the *mātṛkā* TAṀ).
5. *O'Ṁ THAṀ namaḥ* (salutation to the *mātṛkā* THAṀ).
6. *O'Ṁ DAṀ namaḥ* (salutation to the *mātṛkā* DAṀ).
7. *O'Ṁ DHAṀ namaḥ* (salutation to the *mātṛkā* DHAṀ).
8. *O'Ṁ NAṀ namaḥ* (salutation to the *mātṛkā* NAṀ).
9. *O'Ṁ PAṀ namaḥ* (salutation to the *mātṛkā* PAṀ).
10. *O'Ṁ PHAṀ namaḥ* (salutation to the *mātṛkā* PHAṀ).

IV. At the *Svādhiṣṭhāna Cakra*

1. *O'Ṁ BAṀ namaḥ* (salutation to the *mātṛkā* BAṀ).
2. *O'Ṁ BHAṀ namaḥ* (salutation to the *mātṛkā* BHAṀ).
3. *O'Ṁ MAṀ namaḥ* (salutation to the *mātṛkā* MAṀ).
4. *O'Ṁ YAṀ namaḥ* (salutation to the *mātṛkā* YAṀ).
5. *O'Ṁ RAṀ namaḥ* (salutation to the *mātṛkā* RAṀ).
6. *O'Ṁ LAṀ namaḥ* (salutation to the *mātṛkā* LAṀ).

V. At the *Mūlādhāra Cakra*

1. *O'Ṁ VAṀ namaḥ* (salutation to the *mātṛkā* VAṀ).
2. *O'Ṁ ŚAṀ namaḥ* (salutation to the *mātṛkā* ŚAṀ).
3. *O'Ṁ ṢAṀ namaḥ* (salutation to the *mātṛkā* ṢAṀ).
4. *O'Ṁ SAṀ namaḥ* (salutation to the *mātṛkā* SAṀ)

VI. At the *Ājñā Cakra*

1. *O'Ṁ HAṀ namaḥ* (salutation to the *mātṛkā HAṀ*).
2. *O'Ṁ KṢAṀ namaḥ* (salutation to the *mātṛkā KṢAṀ*).

Glossary
(of Indic terms only)

abhiniveśa : 1. Fear of death. 2. Clinging to life. 3. *Saṁskāras* out of clinging to life or fear of death.

acetana : Unconscious.

adhaḥ : Lower.

adhara : Lower.

ādhāra : Base; foundation.

adharoṣṭha : The lower lip.

adhiṣṭhāna : Substratum; the underlying base.

adhodantapaṅkti : The lower line of teeth.

adhovasti : Lower abdomen.

Adhyakṣa : Chairperson.

adhyāsa : Something perceived or conceived as something else; B perceived or conceived as non-B.

ādi-mudrā : The primal gesture.

āgāmī karma : The *karmas* of the present life, cumulatively added to the *karma*-ledger, to bear fruit in the future lives.

agni : Literally means 'fire'. It symbolizes heat, heat and light, energy, energy produced from the oxidation of food.

agra : 1. Tip. 2. Front.

agra-bāhu : Forearm.

ahaṅkāra : Ego; the self-sense; the I-consciousness; the subtle mental apparatus that evolves from the *buddhi*.

ahiṁsā : Non-violence in thought, speech and action.

airāvata : The mythological heavenly elephant of Indra, the king of the heaven.

ajapā japa : The spontaneous repetition of the *mantra so'ham* (He is I), *so* (*saḥ*) while inhaling and *ham* (*aham*) while exhaling.

ājñā : The subtle psychic centre located behind the spot between the two eyebrows. It literally means 'command'.

akartā : Non-doer; one who is not an agent of actions.

ākāśa : Space, the subtlest state of matter.

akliṣṭa-vṛtti : Non-affective modes. These *vṛttis* are imprinted in the mental sheath of the subtle body.

akṛṣṇa : Non-black.

akuśala : Bad; not good.

ālamba : Prop; support.

ālambana : A support.

alambuṣā : One of the 14 major *nāḍī*s in the subtle body.

āmalaka : The tree *Emblica officinalis*; its fruit.

aṁsa : Shoulder.

anāhata : The subtle psychic centre located at the level of the heart, the fourth *cakra* from the bottom.

anāmikā : Ring finger.

ānanda-bhuk : One that experiences bliss.

ānandamaya : Blissful.

ananta : 1. Something without finitude; that which has no beginning, termination and limit to dimensions. 2. The name of the Divine Serpent, with a coiled body and a raised hood, a symbolic representation of Rudra, the God of annihilation.

ananta-nāga : The Divine Serpent whose name is Ananta.

ananta-śayana : The reclining of Lord Viṣṇu on the coiled body of the Divine Serpent, named Ananta, who also hoods over the Lord.

anāsakti : Detachment.

aṅguli : Finger.

aṅguṣṭha : Thumb.

annamaya : Material.

antaḥ (*antar*) : Internal.

antaḥkaraṇa : The internal subtle structure of the mind-complex.

antaḥ-prajña : One that cognises internal objects, stored in the form of concept in the subtle body.

antara kumbhaka : Internal breath retention.

anubhūti : Experience.

Āpaḥ : Cosmic Plasma; subtle cosmic fluid, evolved from *Virāḍ* or *Mahat*; the undifferentiated cosmic fluid that formed the cosmic egg.

āpaḥ : Symbolically means liquidity.

apāna : The name of the *Prāṇa* that resides in the *mūlādhāra*, acts in the area between the navel and the anus and functions in excretory activities.

aparājitā : The flower of a creeper, *Clitoria ternatia*.

aparigraha : The non-accumulation of property.

aparokṣa : Without the mediation of the senses; directly from the divine source.

aparokṣānubhūti : Directly perceived without any mediation; intuitive knowledge; revealed knowledge.

Ardhanārīśvara : God with a form — half female and half male; the presiding god of the *viśuddhi cakra*.

ārohaṇa : Ascent.

āsakti : Attachment.

āsana : The yogic posture.

āśaya : Reservoir.

asmitā : The *saṁskāra*s out of clining to the 'I'.

aṣṭāṅga namaskāra : Salute with eight limbs.

asteya : Non-stealing; non-acceptance of unearned cash or kind.

aśukla : Non-white.

āsura : Demoniac.

asūyā : Envy; jealousy.

aśva-sañcālanāsana : The equestrian pose.

aśvinī-mudrā : One type of yogic gesture in which the two anal sphincters make rhythmic movements, simulating what the horse does.

Ātman (*Ātmā*) : The Great Self; the Universal Self; *Brahman*.

ātman (*ātmā*) : The individual self; the embodied self.

AUṀ : A symbolic monosyllable or its sound that stands for *Brahman*. It comprises three components, namely, *A*, *U*, *Ṁ*. *A* stands for *sattva*; *U* for *rajas*; and *Ṁ* for *tamas*. The combined sound is devoid of the three attributes and it stands for *Brahman*.

avaccheda-vāda : The doctrine of limiting adjunct.

avacetana : The Subconscious.

āvaraṇa-śakti : Concealing power.

avarohaṇa : Descent.

avidyā : 1. Ignorance; the lack of knowledge. 2. The lack of knowledge on *Brahman*. 3. The Unconscious. 4. The *saṁskāra*s deposited in the Unconscious.

avyakta : Unmanifested; the Unmanifest.

baddha : Bound.

bahiḥ (*bahir*) : External.

bahiṣprajña : One who cognises external objects.

bāhu : Arm.

bāhu-mūla : The shoulder-joint; the arm-pit.

bāhya kumbhaka : External breath retention.

Bāla-Brahmā : Four-faced infant Brahmā, the presiding god of the *mūlādhāra*.

Bāṇa-liṅga : The name of the phallus symbol in the *anāhata cakra*.

bandha : Blocking; putting an obstruction to; locking;

holding.

bandhana : Binding; clenching.

bandha-traya : The triple lock — *mūla* + *uḍḍīyāna* + *jālandhara*.

bandhūka : The name of a tree with flowers deep red in colour.

bhairava-mudrā : The gesture of Bhairava, terrifying Lord Rudra.

bhairavī-mudrā : The gesture of Bhairavī, the terrifying consort of Lord Rudra.

bhakti-yoga : The *yoga* of devotion.

bhrūmadhya : The spot between the two eyebrows.

bhujaṅga : Snake.

bhujaṅga-śayana : Sleeping on a serpent; the reclining of Lord Viṣṇu on the coiled body of the divine serpent Ananta.

bhujaṅgāsana : The cobra pose.

bhūmi : Ground.

bhūrloka : The terrestrial plane of existence; the name of the world corresponding to the *mūlādhāra cakra*; the first division of the universe in the higher realm.

bhūtātmā : The self in a non-living entity.

bhuvarloka : The name of the world corresponding to the *svādhiṣṭhāna cakra*; the intermediate realm between the *bhūḥ* and the *svaḥ*; the astral plane of existence; the second division of the universe in the higher realm.

bīja : Seed.

bīja-mantra : The seed syllable.

bindu : 1. A point. 2. The singularity. 3. A minor psychic centre in the head between the *ājñā* and the *sahasrāra*, the same as the *bindu-visarga*.

bindu-visarga : See *bindu*.

Brahmā : One and only one God is known as Brahmā with reference to the creation of the universe.

brahmacarya : Non-indulgence in sexuality.

brahmadvāra : The opening gateway to the central *suṣumṇā nāḍī* in the *mūlādhāra cakra*.

brahmagranthi : The lowest knot at the *mūlādhāra*, formed by the *suṣumṇā*, *iḍā* and *piṅgalā*.

brahma-mudrā : The psychic gesture of all-pervading consciousness.

Brahman : The primary, fundamental, pure Consciousness; the non-dual being, without becoming, which is Existence, Consciousness and Bliss, and which is attributeless, actionless, formless, immutable, non-relational, homogeneous, unbroken whole; that which is great and big; the Supreme Being.

brāhmaṇa : A Hindu priest; a spiritual person with Brahma-realization.

brahmanāḍī : The central, vertical, hollow passage in the core of the *suṣumṇā*. It is without a wall and located inside the *citriṇī*. It is the core channel for the ascent and descent of Kuṇḍalinī.

brahmāṇḍa : Universe; cosmos; macrocosmos.

brahmanirvāṇa : The individual self becoming identified with the universal self (*Brahman*), consequent to the release from bondage.

Brahma-pariṇāma-vāda : The doctrine of the transformation of *Brahman* into the universe.

brahma-randhra : The terminal orifice of the *brahmanāḍī* at the *sahasrāra* in the head.

brahmopalabdhi : The realization of *Brahman*.

Buddhi : Synonymous with *Virāḍ* or *Mahat*; the first evolute from the *mūla-prakṛti*; the Cosmic Mind or the Cosmic Intelligence.

buddhi : 1. The Cosmic *Buddhi* encased in an individual entity that serves as a limiting adjunct. 2. Intellect that distinguishes good from bad and right from wrong.

cakra : 1. A discus; a wheel; a vortex. 2. A Major psychic centre in the subtle body. 3. Circling.

cakrāsana : The wheel pose.

cakrāyaṇa : Rotation.

caladdṛśya : Scenarios in motion.

calat : Moving.

candra : Moon.

candra-maṇḍala : Lunar circle.

candra-nāḍī : The lunar channel; the *iḍā*.

catuṣpāt : Four quarters.

cetana-manas : The conscious mind.

cetanā-sañcāraṇa : Rapid shifting of consciousness.

cetomukha : One that identifies oneself with true knowledge.

cinmaya-mudrā : The psychic gesture of pervading consciousness.

cin-mudrā : The psychic gesture of consciousness.

Cit : Pure Consciousness; Consciousness without any necessary relation to matter and energy; *Brahman*.

citrā : The subtle tubular structure for the *brahma-nāḍī*; the innermost tubular structure inside the *suṣumṇā*; the same as *citriṇī*.

citriṇī : See *citrā*.

citta : 1. The subtle, mental organ of conceptualization and creative activity. It is located in the intellectual sheath. 2. Mind-stuff.

citta-bhūmi : The ground of the mind.

civuka : Chin.

dāḍima : Pomegranate.

daiva : Divine.

Ḍākinī : The presiding goddess of the *mūlādhāra*.

dakṣiṇa : Right side.

dakṣiṇāvarta : Clockwise.

ḍamaru : A hand-drum.

darśana : 1. To see. 2. Philosophy.

darśanendriya : The supersensible, subtle, sensory organ of vision.

dhanurāsana : The bow-pose.

dhāraṇā : Concentration on a spot, a specific locality, or a specific organ.

dhruva : 1. Constant. 2. The *dhruva* of Yoga and the *bindu-visarga* of Tantra are identical.

dhvani : Sound; tone; tune.

dhyāna : Focusing the attention on a single idea that flows in the mind continuously without interruption.

dhyānaja citta : Mind generated by meditation.

dolana : Swinging.

dravya : Material; materiality.

dvandva : Contradictions and conflicts.

dveṣa : 1. Aversion due to painful experiences. 2. Aversion or anxiety to escape from pain. 3. *Saṁskāras* out of the painful experiences of life.

dveṣaja : Generated by painful experiences.

ekākṣara : A single syllable; monosyllable *mantra*.

ekībhuta prajñāna-ghana : Super-unified Consciousness in the blissful state.

gaṇanā : Counting.

gaṇḍa : Cheek.

gandha : Odour.

gāndhārī : One of the 14 major *nāḍīs* in the subtle body.

Gaurī : The Consort of Lord Śiva.

gāyatrī : 1. The name of a Vedic meter. 2. A celebrated Vedic *mantra*. 3. Mother Sarasvatī, the Consort of Lord Brahmā.

ghaṭa : A pot.

ghaṭākāśa : Space limited in a pot.

ghrāṇendriya : The supersensible, subtle, sensory organ of olfaction.

ghūrṇana : Crank; rotation.

granthi : Knot; joint; junction.

grīvā : Neck.

guda : Anus.

gulpha : Ankle.

guṇa : 1. Attribute; quality. 2. String or strand.

guru : A spiritual preceptor.

Hākinī : The presiding goddess in the *ājñā cakra*.

halāsana : The plough pose.

hasta-uttānāsana : The raised-arms pose.

hastendriya : The supersensible, subtle, motor organ of prehension.

hastijihvikā : One of 14 major *nāḍīs* in the subtle body.

Haṭha-Yoga : A system of Yoga specially dealing with rigorous practices for the invigoration and the purification of the body, and consequently of the mind.

hiṁsā : Violence.

hiṁsākṛta : Caused by violence.

hṛdaya : The heart lotus. It is the Yogic term for the *anāhata* of the Tantra.

iḍā : The *nāḍī* vertically traversing on the left side of the *suṣumṇā*; otherwise known as the *candra-nāḍī*.

Indra : One who subdues and conquers evil forces.

indriya : Supersensible sensory and motor organs in the subtle body.

Īśa : 1. The ruler and controller of the universe. 2. Lord Śiva. 3. The three-eyed presiding god of the *anāhata cakra*.

Īśvara : God; one who rules and controls the universe.

Īśvara-praṇidhāna : Complete surrender to God.

Itara-liṅga : The name of the phallus-symbol in the *ājñā cakra*.

jāgarita : Waking

jagat : Universe; the sum total of matter in motion.

jāgrata : Waking.

jālandhara bandha : The throat-lock or the chin-lock.

jala-tattva : Fluidity; liquidity.

janarloka : 1. The name of the world corresponding to the *viśuddhi cakra*. 2. The fifth division of the universe in the higher realm.

jaṅghā : Shank.

jānu : knee.

japa : The mental or verbal repetition of a *mantra*.

jatru : Clavicle; collar-bone.

jihvāgra : The tip of the tongue.

jīvana : Life.

jīvanmukta : Liberated although still living with a body.

jīvātmā : The individual self in a living entity.

jñānaja : Cognitive.

jñāna-mudrā : The psychic gesture of knowledge.

jñāna-yoga : The yoga of the knowledge on *Brahman*.

jñānendriya : Supersensible sensory organs in the subtle body.

kaivalya : The isolated state of the self in the Yoga concept of liberation; the state of the self completely separated and detached from the Primordial Nature or *Prakṛti*.

kāka : Crow.

Kākinī : The presiding goddess of the *anāhata cakra*.

kakut : The hump region in the back between the two shoulders.

kālpanika : Imaginary.

Kālī : The power or consort of God Rudra (Śiva); Mother Goddess pertaining to *Kāla* or Time.

kāma : Desire, lust; sexual desire.

kanda : Bulb; source.

kaniṣṭhikā : 1. The little finger. 2. Smallest, youngest, little.

kaṇṭha : The throat, the neck.

kaṇṭhakūpa : 1. The throat-pit. 2. The Yogic word for the *viśuddhi* of the Tantra.

kaṇṭha-mudrā : A special *mudrā* by which the front and sides of the neck get pressure.

kāraṇa : Cause; causal.

kāraṇa-śarīra : The causal body.

karapṛṣṭha : The back of the hand.

karatala : The palm.

karma : 1. Action or work. 2. The *vāsanā* prints in the causal body due to the five *kleśas* and the afflictive sub-type of conative (*kriyāja*) *saṁskāras*.

karmāśaya : The reservoir of *karmas*; repository of *karmas*; the Unconscious of the *antaḥkaraṇa* where *vāsanās* are stored.

karma-vāda : The doctrine of *karma*.

karma-vipāka : The fruition of a *karma*.

karma-yoga : The *yoga* of detached action.

karmendriya : The supersensible motor organs in the subtle body.

karṇa : The ear.

karṇikā : The pericarp.

kartrī : An executive agent (in the feminine gender).

kāśataṇḍī : *Sachharum spontaneum*.

kaṭi : The hip.

keśara : The filament.

khecarī-mudrā : The tongue-lock seal. The word *khecarī* literally means 'roaming through space'.

kleśa : A hindrance; an affliction; *avidyā*, *asmitā*, *rāga*, *dveṣa* and *abhiniveśa* are the five *kleśas*.

kleśaja : Affective. All *kleśaja*

saṁskāras are *vāsanās* that are stored in the causal body.

kośa : A sheath.

kriyā : 1. An action. 2. Any special yogic technique.

kriyāja : Conative. All conative *saṁskāras* are rooted in volitional activities — good or bad, non-afflictive or afflictive. The former are stored in the subtle body and the latter in the causal body.

krodha : Anger.

kṛpaṇa : Miserly.

kṛṣṇa : 1. Black. 2. Contextually in Yoga, it stands for actions of vices.

kṛṣṇasāra : A black antelope.

kṣaṇa : Moment.

kṣaṇika : Momentary.

kṣipra : Rapid, fast.

kuhū : One of the 14 major *nāḍī*s in the subtle body.

kumbhaka : The retention of breath.

Kuṇḍalinī : The Power of God, the Divine Mother, usually supine and dormant, like a coiled serpent in the *mūlādhāra*, with three and a half coils, with the tail-tip in the mouth. Her mouth closes the opening of the *suṣmṇā*.

kūrmanāḍī : A psychic centre in the chest between the *anāhata* and the *viśuddhi*, otherwise known as *hṛdaya-puṇḍarīkam*.

kūrpara : The elbow.

kuśala : Good.

kuśalākuśala : Good and bad.

Lākinī : The presiding goddess of the *maṇipūra cakra*.

Lakṣmī : The consort of Lord Viṣṇu.

lalana cakra : A small psychic centre, situated between the *bindu* and the *viśuddhi* in the back of the naso-pharynx.

lalāṭa : The forehead.

liṅga : 1. Subtle. 2. The phallus. 3. The symbol for the Father of the universe.

lobha : Greed.

lobhakṛta : Caused by greed.

loka : World.

mada : Pride with arrogance.

madhya : Middle.

madhyamā : 1. Middle (feminine). 2. The middle finger.

mahābandha : The great lock. The same as the triple lock.

mahākāśa : Great Space without any limiting adjunct.

Mahāmāyā : The Great *Māyā*; the same as *Māyā*, the Power of *Brahman* or *Īśvara*; the primordial, unmanifested Nature; the Mother of the universe.

mahāpralaya : Total dissolution.

maharloka : 1. The name of the world corresponding to the *anāhata cakra*. 2. The fourth division of the universe in the higher realm.

Mahat : A Sāṅkhya word for the first evolute from the *Mūla-Prakṛti*; the same as the Sāṅkhya *Buddhi* or the Vedic *Virāḍ*.

makara : An alligator.

makarāsana : The alligator pose.

manas : Mind; the subtle structure that coordinates the subtle organs of cognition and those of action.

mānasika : Mental.

maṇḍala : A kind of mystical diagram used in invoking a deity.

maṇibandha : The wrist.

maṇipūra : The third *cakra* in the subtle body in the ascending order; located at the level of the navel which corresponds to that of the solar plexus of nerves.

manomaya : Mental.

mantra : A mystical expression through which the mind's waves are transmitted for dissemination in all directions or for focusing on certain *locus*, person or object for specific activity.

mātṛkā : A letter of the *Devanāgarī* alphabet, representing a power of the Divine Mother.

mātsarya : Envy; jealousy.

matsyāsana : The fish pose.

Māyā : The power of *Brahman* and *Īśvara*; the feminine pole of the bipolar Reality; the executive agent under the chairpersonship of *Īśvara*.

Māyā-pariṇāma-vāda : The doctrine of the transformation of *Māyā* or *Prakṛti* into the universe.

meru : Spine.

meṣa : A ram.

mithyā-jñāna : Illusory knowledge; a rope (R) appearing as a snake (S); *Brahman* (B) appearing as the *jagat* (J).

moha : Delusion; infatuation.

moha-kṛta : Caused by infatuation.

mohinī śakti : Deluding power.

mokṣa : Liberation; freedom from bondage; the merging of the individual self with the universal Self, leading to the cessation of reincarnation.

mudrā : Seal; gesture.

mukta : Released.

mūla : Root.

mūla bandha : The perineum retraction lock.

mūlādhāra : 1. The base or root foundation. 2. The basal psychic centre located at the base of the spine in between the genital and the anus. Its level corresponds to that of the coccygeal plexus of nerves. Here dwells the *Kuṇḍalinī*.

Mūla-Prakṛti : The primordial Nature that is the mother of the manifested Nature; the Unmanifest Power of God.

mūrdhajyotis : The apex light; the Yogic term for the *sahasrāra* of the Tantra.

mūrdhan : 1. An apex point or summit. 2. The roof of the mouth.

muṣka : The scrotum.

muṣṭika : The fist.

nābhi : The navel.

nābhi-cakra : The umbilical psychic centre; the Yogic term for the *maṇipūra* of the Tantra.

nabho-mudrā : The tongue-lock seal. The word *nabhaḥ* means space or *ākāśa*.

nāda : Vibration.

nāḍī : The network of supersensible psychic channels in the subtle body, through which *Prāṇa* flows.

nāḍī-śodhana : The purification of the *nāḍī*s.

nāga : Snake.

namana : Bending.

nāsāgra : Nose-tip.

nāsāpuṭa : The nostril.

nāsikāgra-dṛṣṭi : Nose-tip-gazing.

nāsikāgra-mudrā : The nose-tip seal used in the process of *prāṇāyāma*.

naukāsana : The boat pose.

nāvāsana : The boat pose.

netra : The eyes.

nidrā : 1. Sleep. 2. Knowledge gained in dreams.

nirguṇa : Attributeless; devoid of qualities.

nirupādhikam : Devoid of limiting adjuncts.

niṣkriya : Functionless.

niṣpanda : A state free from mental pulsations; devoid of vibrations.

nistraiguṇya : Devoid of the three *guṇa*s — *sattva, rajas, tamas.*

nitamba : The buttocks.

nivṛtti-mārgī : A follower of the path of detachment and renuncia-tion.

niyama : 1. The performance of actions prescriptive in Yoga. 2. Rules.

nyāsa : The *Tāntrika* technique for the rapid shifting of awareness.

oṅkāra : The sacred sound of *O'Ṁ* (*AUṀ*).

pādacāra : Walking.

pādahastāsana : The hand to foot pose.

pāda-mūla : The root of the leg; the hip-joint.

pādāṅguli : Toes.

pādapṛṣṭha : The top of the foot.

pādatala : The sole.

pādendriya : The supersensible, subtle, motor organ of locomotion.

padmāsana : The lotus pose.

parama : Supreme.

pāramārthika : Absolute.

Paramaśiva : The supreme, auspicious Lord.

Paramātmā : The Supreme Self; *Īśvara* or God.

parārdha : One-half of a *para* (*para* = the cosmic period); the expanding or the contracting phase of one cosmic period.

parigraha : The accumulation of wealth.

pariṇāma-vāda : The doctrine of transformation.

pārṣṇi : The heel.

pārśva : Side; lateral.

parvatāsana : The mountain pose.

paśca-grīvā : The backside of the neck.

paśca-kapāla : The occipital head.

paścimottānāsana : The back-stretching pose.

Pātañjala : Pertaining to Patañjali.

pauruṣa : The will and effort to fight adversities and create opportunities.

pavana : 1. Wind. 2. *Prāṇa*.

pavana-muktāsana : The wind-releasing pose.

payasvanī : One of the 14 major *nāḍī*s in the subtle body.

pāyu : The excretory organs for faeces and urine (anus and urethra). The verb-root *pāy* means 'voiding excrement'.

pāyvindriya : The supersensible, subtle, motor organ of excretion.

phalaka : Blade.

Pinākī : The three-eyed presiding God of the *anāhata cakra*. *Pināka* is a three-pronged spear (a trident), the weapon of Rudra-Śiva.

piṇḍa : 1. Any round or roundish mass. 2. The human body. 3. The microcosm.

piṇḍa-brahmāṇḍa : The body as a microcosm. Whatever is present in the cosmos is present in the body in a miniature scale.

piṅgalā : The *nāḍī* vertically traversing on the right side of the *suṣumṇā*; otherwise known as the *sūrya-nāḍī*.

prājña : The self in the state of deep sleep.

Prakṛti : 1. The unmanifested primordial Nature, otherwise known as *Māyā*, the Power of God. She is the mother of the universe, the Father being

Īśvara. 2. The created Nature of matter and energy, born of the *Mūla-Prakṛti*.

pramāṇa : Knowledge obtained through sense-perception.

Prāṇa : The dynamic and acting principle; the evolute from *Āpaḥ* and the evolvent of heat, all forms of energy and the four fundamental forces.

prāṇa : 1. The five sub-*Prāṇas*, distributed in the body. 2. The *Prāṇa* that resides in the *anāhata cakra*, functions in absorptive processes and mainly acts in the area between the diaphragm and the collar-bone.

praṇāmāsana : The prayer pose.

prāṇamaya : Vital.

prāṇamuktāsana : The same as the *prāṇa-sañcālana-kriyā*.

prāṇa-sañcālana-kriyā: A series of yogic exercises that facilitate the removal of obstructions at joints and the free flow of *prāṇa* in the *nāḍīs*.

praṇava : The monosyllabic sacred sound *AUṀ*.

prāṇa-vāyu : The *prāṇa* in flowing motion that activates and vitalizes the body.

prāṇa-vāyu-mudrā : The vital gesture.

prāṇāyāma : The yogic process of breath-control through which *prāṇa* is collected, stored and restrained.

prapañcopaśamam : One (*Brahman*) into which the cosmos is resolved.

prārabdha : (*Karma*) already initiated (for the present life).

prārabdha karma : Part of the *sañcita karma* with which a person is born for fruition in the present life.

prastuti : Preparation.

prathama : First.

prātibha : Intuitional insight, through which a *yogī* gets direct knowledge on the past, present and future, and also on micro-objects, concealed objects and distant objects. The *prātibha* of Yoga and the *bindu-visarga* of Tantra are identical.

pratiprasava : Involution, the opposite process of evolution.

pravartaka : Inducer.

pravivikta-bhuk : One that experience things stored in the subtle body.

pravṛtti : Strong propensities for indulgence and sensual gratification.

pravṛtti-mārgī : A follower of the path of worldly attachment and sensual indulgence.

preya : Pleasurable.

pṛṣṭha : Back.

pṛthvī : 1. Earth. 2. A symbolic word for solidity.

pṛthvī-tattva : Solidity.

pūraka : Inhalation

Puruṣa : The Supreme Person; God. The Vedānta recognizes one and only one *Puruṣa*.

puruṣa : The sentient spirit of the Sāṅkhya school, according to which *puruṣa*s are multiple.

pūṣā : One of the 14 major *nāḍī*s in the subtle body.

rāga : 1. Attachment. 2. *Saṁskāra*s born out of craving for pleasure. 3. Passionate desire for pleasure, possession and power.

rāgaja : Generated by passionate attachment to sensual pleasure.

rahita : Without.

rajas : The string or strand of activity, motility and passion.

rājasika : 1. Pertaining to the *guṇa* of *rajas*. 2. The personality of restless activity, ambition and hankering.

Rākiṇī : The presiding goddess of the *svādhiṣṭhāna cakra*.

rasa : 1. Fluid. 2. Taste.

rasanendriya : The supersensible, subtle, sensory organ of gustation.

recaka : Exhalation.

ṛṣi : Seer, saint, monk.

Rudra : 1. Roaring and terrifying. 2. The Hindu God of annihilation and dissolution. 3. The three-eyed presiding god of the *maṇipūra cakra*.

rudra-granthi : The highest knot at the *ājñā*, formed by the *suṣumṇā*, *iḍā* and *piṅgalā*.

rūpa : Form.

śabda : Sound.

saccidānanda : Existence, Consciousness and Bliss; *Brahman*.

Sadāśiva : 1. Always benevolent, 2. The presiding god of the *viśuddhi cakra*.

sahasrāra : The thousand-petalled lotus at the level of the cerebrum; the seat of Lord Śiva in the body.

sahita : With.

Śaiva : 1. Pertaining to Śiva. The philosophy centring around Lord Śiva.

Śākinī : The presiding goddess of the *viśuddhi cakra*.

Śakti : 1. Power, 2. Consort.

Śaktimān : The possessor of Power.

śalabhāsana : The locust pose.

samādhi : The supreme yogic state devoid of thoughts, forms, attributes, functions and material existence in the mind; complete union or complete identification with

Brahman; the yogic state in which the *buddhi* is completely absorbed in the self or Self.

samāna : The name of the *Prāṇa* that resides in the *maṇipūra*, acts in the area between the navel and the diaphragm and functions in the digestion and metabolism of food.

samāpti : Finish; end.

Śambhu : 1. Lord Śiva, the auspicious and benevolent. 2. The presiding god of the *ājñā cakra*.

saṁśaya : Doubt; doubt with vacillation.

saṁskāra : Karmic impressions stored in the Subconscious and the Unconscious. *Vāsanā saṁskāra*s are stored in the Unconscious whereas non-*vāsanā saṁskāra*s (cognitive and non-afflictive conative) are stored in the mental sheath of the Subconscious.

saṁskāra-piṇḍa : The accumulated mass of karmic impressions.

saṁskārāśaya : The reservoir of *saṁskāra*s.

saṁyama : *Dhāraṇā*, *dhyāna* and *samādhi* done together.

sāmyāvasthā : Equipoise.

sañcālana : Movement.

sañcita karma : All *karma*s of past lives, cumulatively stored in the *karmāśaya*.

saṅkalpa : Resolve.

śaṅkhinī : One of the 14 major *nāḍī*s in the subtle body.

Sāṅkhya : An Indian school of philosophy, founded by Kapila before 1,000 BC; atheistic and dualistic; the insentient primordial Nature (*Pradhāna* or *Prakṛti*) is one category of existence, and the innumerable, sentient selves (*puruṣa*s) belong to the second category; it is the first philosophical school in the world to advocate the doctrine of evolution.

santoṣa : Contentment.

Sarasvatī : The consort of Brahmā; the Divine Mother who created the universe by playing her string instrument, *vīṇā*, and generating the primal vibration *AUṀ*.

sarasvatī : One of the 14 major *nāḍī*s in the subtle body.

śarīra : Body.

sarvāṅgāsana : The shoulder-stand pose.

sattva : The string or strand of goodness, purity and serenity.

sāttvika : 1. Pertaining to the *guṇa* of *sattva*. 2. The personality of goodness, calmness, serenity and benevolence.

satya : 1. Truthfulness. 2. That which exists.

satya-loka : One of the seven worlds, finer and subtler than the *taparloka;* the uppermost of the seven *lokas* or worlds; the abode of Brahmā.

śauca : Cleanliness of mind, speech and body.

śavāsana : The corpse pose.

saviloma : Reverse.

śayana : Sleep.

siddha : Accomplished.

siddhāsana : The accomplished pose.

siddhi : Miraculous power; supernormal power.

śikhā : The top of the head.

śīrṣāsana : The head-stand pose.

śithilīkaraṇa : Relaxation.

sīvana : 1. The perineum. 2. Sewing, stitching. 3. A suture.

skandha : 1. The shoulder, 2. The shoulder-socket.

smṛti : 1. Memory. 2. Knowledge from memory.

śodhana : Purification.

so'ham : He is I.

spanda : Vibration.

sparśa : Touch.

sparśanendriya : The supersensible subtle, sensory organ of touch and other cutaneous sensations.

śravaṇendriya : The supersensible, subtle, sensory organ of audition.

śreya : Good and beneficial.

śroṇī/śroṇi : The hip.

sthūla : Gross.

sthūla-bhuk : One who experiences the gross universe.

śuddhi : Purification.

sukhāsana : The easy pose.

śukla : 1. White. 2. Symbolic expression for virtues.

sūkṣma : Subtle.

supta-vajrāsana : The sleeping thunderbolt pose.

sūrya : The sun.

sūrya-nāḍī : The solar channel; the same as *piṅgalā.*

sūrya-namaskāra : Salutation to the sun. It comprises a series of 12 postures.

suṣumṇā : The central vertical psychic channel, starting from the *mūlādhāra* and ending in the *sahasrāra*. Its base orifice is the *brahmadvāra* and terminal orifice is the *brahmarandhra*.

suṣupti : Deep sleep; dreamless sleep.

svabhāvataḥ : Naturally; by one's own nature; spontaneously.

svādhiṣṭhāna : The second *cakra* (psychic centre) in the subtle body in the ascending order, located at the point where the spinal cord terminates; its level corresponds to that of the sacral plexus of nerves.

svādhyāya : The study of books on *Brahman* and liberation; the study of sacred scriptures; the repetition of the mystic syllable *o'ṁ*.

svapna : Dream; sleeping state.

svarloka : 1. The third division of the universe in the upper realm. 2. The world corresponding to the *maṇipūra cakra*.

svastika : A kind of mystical mark denoting good luck; a *maṇḍala* of the Hindus and Jainas; a symbol of creativity and auspiciousness.

svastikāsana : The auspicious pose.

svayambhū liṅga : The name of the *liṅga* in the *mūlādhāra*.

tāḍa : The palm-tree.

tāḍāsana : The palm-tree pose.

taijasa : The self in the sleeping or the dreaming state.

tamas : The strand or string of inertia, inactivity and darkness.

tāmasika : 1. Pertaining to the *guṇa* of *tamas*. 2. The personality of inertia, lethargy, inactivity and angry temperament.

tāṇḍava : The vigorous dance of Lord Śiva; the cosmic dance.

tanhā : Buddha's use of the Pālī word for the Sanskrit *tṛṣṇā*.

tanmātra : It literally means 'only that'. The field state of matter.

Tantra : An Indian system of philosophical theory and ritual practices, in which Mother Goddess is worshipped.

tapaḥ : 1. Heat. 2. Readiness for undertaking any suffering for a noble cause. 3. Spiritual austerity.

tapoloka : 1. The sixth division of the universe in the upper realm. 2. The name of the world corresponding to the *ājñā cakra*.

tarjanī : The index finger.

tattva : The subtle essence.

tejaḥ : Energy; fire; heat; light; the subtle essence of fire.

trikoṇāsana : The triangle pose.

triśūla : The trident.

triveṇī : 1. A confluence of three streams. 2. The confluence of the *suṣumṇā*, *iḍā* and *piṅgalā* at the *ājñā cakra*.

tṛṣṇā : Thirst.

turīya : Fourth; the fourth and the final states in meditation, in which the self is identified with *Brahman*.

udāna : The name of the *Prāṇa* that resides in the *viśuddhi*, acts in the area above the collar-bone and functions in the upward motion.

udara : The abdomen.

uḍḍīyāna bandha : The abdominal retraction lock.

udgītha : The primal sound *AUṀ*.

ujjayī : Victorious.

ujjayī prāṇāyāma : A type of *prāṇāyāma* in which inhalations and exhalations are done through both nostrils without retention of breath.

unmocana : Opening.

upādhi : A limiting adjunct; something, X, confining or limiting some other thing, Y.

upastha : The generative organs; the private parts of the body; the genitals.

upasthendriya : The supersensible, subtle, motor organ for reproduction.

upekṣā : Ignoring the other person's faults.

uraḥ : Chest.

ūrdhva : Upper; higher.

ūrdhva bāhu : The upper arm.

ūrdhva-danta-paṅkti : The upper line of teeth.

ūrdhva-mukhī : With face upwards.

ūrdhvoṣṭha : The upper lip.

ūrjā : Energy; the manifested material energy of the universe.

ūru : The thigh.

ūrusandhi : The groin.

vācaka : Verbal representation.

vāgindriya : The supersensible, subtle, motor vocal organ.

vāhana : Vehicle.

Vaiśvānara : The self in the waking state.

vajrā : A *nāḍī*, orginating from the *kanda* of the *mūlādhāra* and flowing inside the *suṣumṇā* and outside the *citrā*. It is the same as the *vajriṇī*.

vajra-nāḍī : The same as the *vajrā*.

vajrāsana : The thunderbolt pose.

vajriṇī : The same as the *vajrā*. It is a subtle tubular structure outside the *citriṇī* and inside the *suṣumṇā*.

vakra : A curve; a twist; a bend.

vakṣas : The chest.

vāma : The left side.

vāmāvarta : Anticlockwise.

varṇa : Any letter of the alphabet.

Varuṇa : The Sanskrit verb-root *vṛ* means 'to envelop', 'to cover', 'to veil', 'to conceal'. Varuṇa is God who pervades the subtle Cosmic Plasma (*Āpaḥ*) as the presiding Deity and conceals himself. He is with a noose (*pāśa*). He safeguards the moral structure of the universe.

vāruṇī : One of the 14 major *nāḍīs*

in the subtle body.

vāsanā : *Saṁskāras* printed and stored in the causal body; they form the Unconscious. All the affective (*kleśaja*) *saṁskāras* and the afflictive sub-type of the conative (*kriyāja*) *saṁskāras* use the causal body as their reservoir. They are the *vāsanās*.

vāsanāśaya : The reservoir of *vāsanās*.

vāyu : 1. Air, 2. A symbolic word for gaseousness. 3. *Prāṇa*; that which energises.

vāyu-tattva : The essence of gaseousness.

Vedānta : Literally the end-product (*anta*) of knowledge (*Veda*). One of the six philosophical systems of India, arising after the period of the Vedas, in response to the heterodox system. Its central theme is *Brahman*, through which the empirical universe is explained.

vidyā : Knowledge; consciousness.

vijñānamaya : Intellectual.

vikalpa : Hullucinatory knowledge; something really non-existent (but existent as traces in *smṛti* or as *saṁskāras*) appearing as existent due to projectory perception.

vikṣepa-śakti : Projecting power.

vīṇā : A classical, musical string instrument; the musical instrument of Mother Sarasvatī.

viniyoga : The preamble in a *pūjā* (worship), introducing the purpose.

vipāka : Fruition.

viparyaya : Illusory knowledge; something X appearing as Y.

Virāḍ : The first evolute from the *Mūla-Prakṛti* or *Māyā*; the Cosmic Mind or Supermind. It is the same as the Sāṅkhya *Mahat* or *Buddhi*.

Viṣṇu : 1. Derived from the verb-root *viś* which means to pervade. The all-pervading Lord who sustains and protects the universe. 2. The four-handed presiding god of the *svādhiṣṭhāna cakra*.

viṣṇu-granthi : The middle knot at the *anāhata*, formed by the *suṣumṇā*, *iḍā* and *piṅgalā*.

viśuddha : Pure.

viśuddhi : The fifth psychic centre (*cakra*) in the subtle body in the ascending order; located at the level of the throat-pit; this level corresponds to that of the cervical plexus of nerves.

viśvodarī : One of the 14 major *nāḍīs* in the subtle body.

vivarta-vāda : The doctrine of

empirical appearance, according to which B (*Brahman*), being the substratum (*adhiṣṭhāna*), appears as J (*jagat* or the universe) in multiple forms.

vṛtti : Waves emanated from the mind-stuff; mental modes.

vyāna : The name of the *Prāṇa* that resides in the *svādhiṣṭhāna*, acts in the whole body and pervasively functions in physiological activities such as the circulation of blood and lymph and nerve conduction.

vyāvahārika : Empirical.

yama : Abstentions; yogic proscriptions; they are five in number, namely, non-violence, truthfulness, non-stealing, continence and non-accumulation.

yantra : A geometrical diagram inside a *cakra* or a worshipping site; a kind of mystical diagram used for invoking a deity; synonymous with the *maṇḍala* for this purpose.

yaśasvinī : One of the 14 major *nāḍī*s in the subtle body.

Yoga : An Indian school of philosophy founded by Patañjali in the pre-Christian era. It specifically prescribes physical and mental practices for the well-being of the body and the mind and for spiritual attainment.

yoga : Derived from the Sanskrit verb-root *yuj*, meaning 'to unite', 'to yoke'. The Yoga-Vedānta holds that, through yogic practices, one can bring about a union between the *ātmā* (self) and the *Paramātmā* (God). The yogic means are special techniques for physical restraints and exercises, and mental concentration.

yoga-nidrā : Literally means 'yogic sleep'. It is really a yogic trance, intermediate between sleeping and waking states. It prescribes a yogic method for inducing the trance and for the subsequent recording of a resolve in the Subconscious and/or the Unconscious.

yogī : One adept in *yoga*; one who can link up his self with the Great Self.

yoni : 1. The female sex organ. 2. The symbol for the mother of the universe. 3. The source.

Bibliography

Adams, D.D., Kennedy, T.H. and Purves, H.D., 1969, "Comparison of the thyroid stimulating hormone . . . of serum from thyrotoxic and euthyroid people", *J. Clin. Endocrinol.*, *29*; 900.

Allen, R.J., 1983, *Human Stress: Its Nature and Control*, Minneapolis, MN: Burgess Publishing Company.

Atharvaveda Saṁhitā, The, with *Sāyaṇa-Bhāṣyam*, Varanasi: Chaukhamba Vidyabhavan, 1997.

Avalon, Arthur (ed.), 1996 (1st publ. 1933), *Śāradā-Tilaka-Tantram*, Delhi: Motilal Banarsidass.

———, and Sarasvatī Aṭalānanda (eds.), 1989 (1st publ. 1935), *Prapañcasāra-Tantram* of Śaṅkarācārya, Delhi: Motilal Banarsidass.

Baggaley, Ann (ed.), 2001, *Human Body*, New York: Dorling Kinderley Publishing.

Bammer, K. and Newberry, B.H., 1983, *Stress and Cancer*, Toronto : C. J. Hogrefe.

Barber, T.X., 1969, *Hypnosis: A Scientific Approach*, New York: Van Nostrand Reinhold.

Benson, H., 1975, *The Relaxation Response*, New York: Morrow.

———, Greenwood, M.M. and Klemchuk, H., 1977, "The relaxation response: Psychophysiologic aspects and clinical applications." In: Lipowski, Z. J., *et al.*, *Psychosomatic Medicine*, New York: Oxford University Press.

———, and Klipper, M.Z., 1975, *The Relaxation Response*, New York: Avon Publishers.

Best, C.H. and Taylor, N.B., 1966 (1st publ. 1937), *The Physiological Basis of Medical Practice*, 8th edn., Baltimore: The Williams and Wilkins.

Bhagavadgītā, The, with *Śāṅkara-Bhāṣyam*, Gorakhpur (U.P., India): Gita Press.

Bhattacharya, V. (ed. & trans.), 1989 (1st publ. 1943), *The Āgamaśāstra of Gauḍapāda*, Delhi: Motilal Banarsidass.

Brahma-Sūtraṁ Śāṅkara-Bhāṣyam (Vol. I & II), 1982 (1st publ. 1981), Delhi: Parimal Publications.

Braunwald, Fauci, Kasper, Hauser, Longo and Janeson, 2001, *Harrson's Principle of Internal Medicine*, 15th edn., New Delhi : Milan Montreal.

Breaux, Charles, 1998 (1st publ. 1989 by Nicolas-Hays, USA), *Journey into Consciousness: The Chakras, Tantra and Jungian Psychology*, Delhi : Motilal Banarsidass.

Cozort, Daniel, 1986, *Highest Yoga Tantra: An Introduction to the Esoteric Buddhism of Tibet*, Ithaca, N.Y. : Snow Lion Publications.

Danielou, Alain, 1973 (1st publ. 1949), *Yoga*, London: Johnson Publications.

Dhiravamsa, 1982, *The Dynamic Way of Meditation : The Release and Cure of Pain and Suffering*, Wellingborough, Northamptonshire : Turnstone Press.

Diemer, Deedre, 2000 (1st publ. 1998 by Samuel Weiser, USA), *The ABC's of Chakra Therapy*, Delhi : Motilal Banarsidass.

Eccles, J.C., 1953, *The Neuro-Physiological Basis of Mind*, Oxford : Oxford University Press.

———, (ed.), 1966, *Brain and Conscious Experience*, Berlin/New York : Springer International.

———, 1973, *The Understanding of the Brain*, New York : McGraw-Hill.

Gorakṣanātha, Yogī, *Gorakṣa-Saṁhitā*.

Goyandka, Sriharikrishnadas, *Śrīmad-Bhagavad-Gītā Śāṅkara-Bhāṣyam*, Gorakhpur (U.P., India) : Gita Press.

Guinness, A.E. (ed.), 1990, *ABC's of the Human Mind*, New York : Reader's Digest.

Guyton, A.C., 1966, *Textbook of Medical Physiology*, Philadelphia : W.B. Saunders.

Hilgard, E.R., 1973a, "A neodissociation interpretation of pain reduction in hypnosis", *Psychological Review, 80*; 396-411.

———, 1977, *Divided Consciousness : Multiple Controls in Human Thought and Action*, New York : Wiley Interscience.

———, Atkinson, R.L. and Atkinson, R.C., 1979 (1st publ. 1953), *Introduction to Psychology*, 7th edn., New York: Harcourt Brace Jovanovich.

Iyengar, B.K.S., 1997 (1st publ. 1966 by George Allen & Unwin), *Light on Yoga*, New Delhi : HarperCollins Publishers India.

———, 1981, *Light on Prāṇāyāma (Prāṇāyāma Dīpikā)*, London: George Allen & Unwin.

———, 1993, *Light on the Yoga-Sūtras of Patañjali*, New Delhi: Indus, HarperCollins Publishers India.

Joshi, K.S., 1983, *Yogic Pranayama : Breathing for Long Life and Good Health*, Delhi: Vision Books.

Lansdowne, Z.F., 1996 (1st publ. 1986 by Samuel Weiser, USA), *The Chakras and Esoteric Healing*, Delhi : Motilal Banarsidass.

LeShan, Lawrence, 1974, *How to Meditate : A Guide to Self-Discovery*, Wellingborough, Northamptonshire : Turnstone Press.

Lidell, Lucy, Narayani and Rabinovitch, Giris, 1983, *The Book of Yoga*, London : Ebury Press.

Lipowski, Z.J. *et al.*, 1977, *Psychosomatic Medicine*, New York : Oxford University Press.

Lysebeth, André van, 1988 (1st publ. 1979), *Pranayama: The Yoga of Breathing*, London: Unwin Hyman.

Mahāyogīndra, Śrīnivāsabhaṭṭa, *Haṭharatnāvalī*.

Malaviya, Sudhakar (ed. & trans.), 1999, *Rudrạyāmalam*, Part I & II, Delhi : Chaukhamba Pratishthan.

Manu-Smṛti, The, ed. Pt. Rameshwar Bhaṭṭ, Delhi : Chaukhamba Sanskrit Pratishthan, 1998.

Mckenzie, J. M., 1968, "Humoral factors in the pathogenesis of Graves' disease", *Physiological Review*, *48*: 252.

Morgan, C.T., King, R.A., Weisz, J.R. and Schopler, J., 1986 (1st publ. 1956), *Introduction to Psychology*, 7th edn., New York: McGraw-Hill.

Motoyama, Hiroshi, 2001 (1st publ. 1981 by The Theosophical Publishing House), *Theories of the Chakras : Bridge to Higher Consciousness*, New Dehi : New Age Books.

Ostrander, S. and Schroeder, L., 1973, *Psi — Psychic Discoveries Behind the Iron Curtain*, UK: Abacus.

Panda, N.C., 1999 (1st publ. 1991), *Māyā in Physics*, Delhi : Motilal Banarsidass.

———, 2000 (1st publ, 1995), *The Vibrating Universe*, Delhi : Motilal Banarsidass.

———, 1996, *Mind and Supermind*, Vol. 1 & 2, New Delhi: D.K. Printworld.

———, 2002, *Cyclic Universe*, Vol. 1 & 2, New Delhi: D.K. Printworld.

Pandit, Shambhu Nath, 1992, *Stress Management Through Yoga and Meditation*, New Delhi: Sterling Publishers.

Pātañjala Yoga-Darśana with Vyāsa-Bhaṣya, Varanasi: Chaukhamba Surabharati Prakashan, 1998.

Popper, K.R. and Eccles, J.C., 1977, *The Self and Its Brain*, Part I & II, Berlin/New York: Springer International.

Pūrṇānanda's *Śrītattvacintāmaṇi*, ed. Bhuvanmohan Sankhyatirtha and Chintamani Bhattacharya, Delhi: Motilal Banarsidass, 1994 (1st publ. 1936 in Kolkata).

Radhakrishnan, S., 1967 (1st publ. 1948), *The Bhagavadgītā*, London: George Allen & Unwin.

———, 1969 (1st publ. 1953), *The Principal Upaniṣads*, London: George Allen & Unwin.

———, 1960, *The Brahma Sūtra*, London: George Allen & Unwin.

Ṛgveda Saṁhitā, The, with *Sāyaṇa-Bhāṣyam*, Varanasi: Chaukhamba Vidyabhavan, 1991.

Rodriguez, T. and Ram, K. (ed. & trans.), 1992, *Pure Yoga*: *The Gheraṇḍa Saṁhitā*, Delhi: Motilal Banarsidass.

Russell, B., 1945, *History of Western Philosophy*, New York: Simon & Schuster/ London: George Allen & Unwin, 1975.

Sachdeva, I.P., 1978, *Yoga and Depth Psychology*, Delhi : Motilal Banarsidass.

Śaṅkarācārya, *The Saundaryalaharī*, ed. V.K. Subramaniyam, Delhi : Motilal Banarsidass, 1990 (1st publ. 1977).

Sankaranarayanan, P. (ed.), 1988 (1st publ. 1973), *Vivekacūḍāmaṇi*, 3rd edn., Mumbai: Bharatiya Vidya Bhavan.

Saraswati, Swami Karmananda (ed. & trans.) 1985, *Haṭha Yoga Pradīpikā* (by Yogīndra Svātmārāma), Munger (Bihar, India) : Bihar School of Yoga.

Saraswati, Swami Niranjanananda, 1998 (1st publ. 1994), *Prāṇa Prāṇāyāma Prāṇa Vidyā*, Munger (Bihar, India): Bihar School of Yoga.

Saraswati, Swami Satyananda, 1983 (1st publ. 1969), *Asana Pranayama Mudra Bandha*, 6th edn., Munger (Bihar, India): Bihar School of Yoga.

———, 2000 (1st publ. 1974), *Meditations from the Tantras*, 2nd edn., Munger (Bihar, India): Bihar School of Yoga.

———, 1998 (1st publ. 1976), *Yoga-Nidrā*, 6th edn., Munger (Bihar, India): Bihar School of Yoga.

———, 1993 (1st publ. 1977), *Yogic Management of Asthma and Diabetes*, 5th edn., Munger (Bihar, India): Bihar School of Yoga.

———, 1984, *Kundalini Tantra*, Munger (Bihar, India): Bihar School of Yoga.

Sarbin, T.R., 1950, "Contributions to role-taking theory: 1. Hypnotic behaviour", *Psychological Review*, *57*, 255-70.

———, and Coe, W.C., 1972, *Hypnosis : A Social Psychological Analysis of Influence Communication*, New York : Holt, Rinehart and Winston.

Sastri, G.D. (ed.), 1990 reprint, *Sāṅkhya-Yoga-Darśanam* (*Yoga-Darśanam of Patañjali with Bhāṣyas*), Varanasi : Chaukhamba Sanskrit Samsthan.

Śatapatha Brāhmaṇa, The, vols. 1-5, Reprinted in 1990 by Nag Publishers, Delhi.

Schwarz, M.S. and Associates, 1995, *Biofeedback: A Practitioner's Guide*, 2nd edn., New York: The Guilford Press.

Selye, H., 1976 (1st publ. 1956), *The Stress of Life* (rev. edn.), New York: McGraw-Hill.

———, 1974, *Stress Without Distress*, New York: J.B. Lippincott.

Shankardevananda, Swami, 1998 (1st publ. 1978), *The Effects of Yoga on Hypertension*, 2nd edn., Munger (Bihar, India): Bihar School of Yoga.

Sharamon, Shalila and Baginski, Bodo J., 2000 (1st publ. 1991 by Lotus Press, USA), *Chakra Handbook: From Basic Understanding to Practical Application*, Delhi: Motilal Banarsidass.

Shrivastava, S.C. (ed.), 1988, *Pātañjala-Yoga-Darśana with Vyāsa-Bhāṣya*, 2nd edn., Varanasi: Chaukhamba Surbharati Prakashan.

Sinha, Nandalal, 1979 (1st publ. 1915 by Panini Office, Allahabad), *The Sāṅkhya Philosophy* (containing the *Sāṅkhya Pravacana Sūtram*, the *Sāṅkhya Kārikā* and others), 2nd edn., New Delhi : Oriental Books Reprint Corpn.

Sivananda, Sri Swami, 1971 (1st publ. 1935), *Kundalini Yoga*, 6th edn., Sivanandanagar (Uttaranchal, India): The Divine Life Society.

Śrīmad-Bhagavad-Gītā Śāṅkara-Bhāṣyam, Gorakhpur (U.P., India): Gita Press.

Śukla-Yajurveda Saṁhitā, The, with *Bhāṣya of Ubaṭācārya and of Mahīndra*, Varanasi: Chaukhamba Vidyabhavan, 1996.

Swami Madhavananda (ed. & trans.), 1972, *Vedānta Paribhāṣā of Dharmarāja Adhvarīndra*, 4th impr., Kolkata: The Ramakrishna Mission Saradapitha.

Swami Nikhilananda (ed. & trans), 1974, *Vedāntasāra of Sadānanda*, 6th edn., Kolkata: Advaita Ashram.

Tagare, G.V. (ed. & trans.), 1987-88, *Ancient Indian Tradition & Mythology: The Vāyu Purāṇa*, Vol. 1 & 2, Gen. ed. G.P. Bhatt, Delhi: Motilal Banarsidass.

Udupa, K.N. (M.D.), 1985 (1st publ. 1978), *Stress and Its Management by Yoga*, 2nd edn., Delhi: Motilal Banarsidass.

Upaniṣads, Ten Principal, with Śāṅkara-Bhāṣyam, Delhi: Motilal Bnarsidass, 1992.

Upaniṣatsaṅgrahaḥ, ed., J. Shastri, Delhi : Motilal Banarsidass, 1984 (1st print 1970).

Vasu, R.B.S.C., 1990 (1st publ. 1914-15 by Panini Office, Allahabad), *The Śiva Saṁhitā*, 4th edn., New Delhi : Munshiraṃ Manoharlal Publishers.

Vidyaratna, T., 1987 (1st publ. 1941), *Ṣaṭcakra-Nirūpaṇa* and *Pādukā-Prapañca*, New Delhi : Aditya Prakashan.

Vinekar, Kuvalayananda, 1963, *Yogic Therapy: Its Basic Principles and Methods*, New Delhi : Ministry of Health, Govt. of India.

Walters, J. Donald, 2000, *Awaken to Superconsciousness*, Delhi : Motilal Banarsidass.

Warrier, A.G. Krishna (trans.), 1983, *Śrīmad Bhagavad Gītā Bhāṣya of Śrī Śaṅkarācārya*, Chennai : Sri Ramakrishna Math.

Waugh, Anne and Grant, Allison, 2001, *Ross and Wilson Anatomy and Physiology in Health and Illness*, 9th edn., London: Churchill Livingstone, Harcourt Publishers.

Woodroffe, Sir John, 1975, *Śakti and Śākta*, 8th edn., Chennai: Ganesh.

———, 1981 (1st publ. 1918), *The Serpent Power*, 12th edn., Chennai: Ganesh.

Woods, J.H., 1983 (1st publ. 1914 by Harvad University Press), *The Yoga-System of Patañjali*, Delhi : Motilal Banarsidass.

Yogi, Maharishi Mahesh, 1975 (1st publ. 1963 by George Allen & Unwin, London), *Transcendental Meditation*, New York: New American Library (Plume Book).

Index